THAILAND

A Global Studies Handbook

Other Titles in
ABC-CLIO's
GLOBAL STUDIES: ASIA
Series

China, Robert LaFleur

India, Fritz Blackwell

Indonesia, Florence Lamoureux

Japan, Lucien Ellington

The Koreas, Mary E. Connor

Nepal and Bangladesh, Nanda R. Shrestha

Vietnam, L. Shelton Woods

DS
563.5
.H63

#3387733 0

GLOBAL STUDIES: ASIA

THAILAND

A Global Studies Handbook

Timothy D. Hoare

LIBRARY
WAUKESHA COUNTY TECHNICAL COLLEGE
800 MAIN STREET
PEWAUKEE, WI 53072

A B C ❧ C L I O

Santa Barbara, California • Denver, Colorado • Oxford, England

Copyright © 2004 by Timothy D. Hoare

All rights reserved. No part of this publication may be reproduced, stored in a retrieval system, or transmitted, in any form or by any means, electronic, mechanical, photocopying, recording, or otherwise, except for the inclusion of brief quotations in a review, without prior permission in writing from the publishers.

Library of Congress Cataloging-in-Publication Data

Hoare, Timothy D.
    Thailand : a global studies handbook / Timothy D. Hoare.
        p. cm.—(Global studies, Asia)
    Includes bibliographical references and index.
    ISBN 1-85109-685-X (hardcover : alk. paper)
    ISBN 1-85109-690-6 (e-Book)

    1. Thailand — Handbooks, manuals, etc. I. Title. II. Series.
DS563.5.H63 2003
959.3—dc22

                                                    2004009631

8   7   6   5   4   3   2   1

This book is also available on the World Wide Web as an e-book.
Visit http://www.abc-clio.com for details.

ABC-CLIO, Inc.
130 Cremona Drive, P.O. Box 1911
Santa Barbara, California 93116–1911

This book is printed on acid-free paper.
Manufactured in the United States of America

Contents

Series Editor's Foreword

It is imperative that as many Americans as possible develop a basic understanding of Asia. In an increasingly interconnected world, the fact that Asia contains almost 60 percent of all the planet's population is argument enough for increased knowledge of the continent on our parts. In addition, there are at least four other reasons why it is critical that Americans become more familiar with Asia:

First, Americans of all ages, creeds, and colors are extensively involved economically with Asian countries. U.S.-Pacific two-way trade surpassed U.S. trade with Europe in the 1970s. American companies constitute the leading foreign investors in Japan. With the world's second-largest economy, Japan is also the second-largest foreign investor in the United States.

The recent Asian economic crisis notwithstanding, since World War II, East Asia has experienced the fastest rate of economic growth of all the world's regions. Recently, newly industrialized Southeast Asian countries such as Indonesia, Malaysia, and Thailand have joined the so-called Four Tigers—Hong Kong, the Republic of Korea, Singapore, and Taiwan—as leading areas for economic growth. In the past decade China has begun to realize its potential to be a world-influencing economic actor. Many Americans now depend upon Asians for their economic livelihoods, and all of us consume products made in or by Asian companies.

Second, it is impossible to be an informed American citizen without knowledge of Asia, a continent that directly impacts our national security. America's war on terrorism is, as this foreword is composed, being conducted in an Asian country—Afghanistan. (What many Americans think of as the "Mideast" is, in actuality, Southwest Asia.) Both India and Pakistan now have nuclear weapons. The eventual reunification of the Korean Peninsula is fraught with the possibility of great promise or equally great peril. The question of U.S.-China relations is considered one of the world's major global geopolitical issues. Americans everywhere are affected by Asian political and military developments.

Third, Asia and Asians have also become an important part of American culture. Asian restaurants dot the American urban landscape. Buddhism is rapidly growing in the United States, and Asian movies are becoming increasingly popular. Asian Americans, though still a small percentage of the overall U.S. population, are one of the fastest-growing ethnic groups in the United States. Many Asian Americans exert considerable economic and political influence in this country. Asian sports, pop music, and cinema stars are becoming household names in America. Even Chinese-language characters are becoming visible in the United States on everything from baseball caps to T-shirts to license plates. Followers of the ongoing debate on American educational reform will constantly encounter references to Asian student achievement.

Fourth, Asian civilizations are some of the world's oldest, and their arts and literature rank as some of humankind's most impressive achievements. Anyone who is considered an educated person needs a basic understanding of Asia. The continent has a long, complex, and rich history. Asia is the birthplace of all the world's major religions, including Christianity and Judaism.

Our objectives in developing the Global Studies: Asia series are to assist a wide variety of citizens in gaining a basic understanding of Asian countries and to enable readers to be better positioned for more in-depth work. We envision the series being appropriate for libraries, educators, high school, introductory college and university students, businesspeople, would-be tourists, and anyone who is curious about an Asian country or countries. Although there is some variation in the handbooks—the diversity of the countries requires slight variations in treatment—each volume includes narrative chapters on history and geography, economics, institutions, and society and contemporary issues. Readers should obtain a sound general understanding of the particular Asian country about which they read.

Each handbook also contains an extensive reference section. Because our guess is that many of the readers of this series will actually be traveling to Asia or interacting with Asians in the United States, introductions to language, food, and etiquette are included. The reference section of each handbook also contains extensive information—including Web sites when relevant—about business and economic, cultural, educational, exchange, government, and tourist organizations. The reference sections also include capsule descriptions of famous people, places, and events and a comprehensive annotated bibliography for further study.

—*Lucien Ellington*
Series Editor

Preface

As a professor of humanities and world religions, and the spouse of a Thai who just recently became a U.S. citizen, I am both excited and humbled to have been given the opportunity to author a text about a subject that is so close to my heart: the Kingdom of Thailand.

This book is neither a popular travel guide nor an arcane reference work. It has been written for the nonspecialist who wishes to supplement his/her academic research or enhance his/her overall interest in Thai history, culture, and society. But not to dismiss the serious and inquiring traveler, it can most certainly serve as an informative reference for those who want to know considerably more about Thailand than merely where to stay and what to see.

Academic specialization—the quest to know almost everything about one thing—can sometimes be constraining. One of the curious ironies of the Ph.D experience is that if one successfully converts and transcribes years of intense research into a coherent dissertation that is restricted to a narrowly focused subject (in my case, the classical masked dance and theater of Thailand), one is subsequently given the freedom to talk and to write about all of the other interrelated facets encountered along the way that had to be put on the shelf until the degree was conferred. In other words, although I enjoyed my years of research and specialization, the experience of being able to write as a generalist author for a generalist reader has been just as satisfying, if not more so.

I therefore have tried to keep my methodology as user-friendly as possible. My students often tell me that they like my teaching style because I illuminate my points by telling them stories about the things I have done and the places I have been. This is no less apparent in my approach to this book. Though such topics as history, politics, and economics will necessarily be presented in the form of objective and descriptive narrative, other topics—for example, fine arts, food, religion, language, social relationships, and popular culture—will utilize illustrative examples from my own subjective experience as well (some experiences more ennobling than others!).

As I reflect back upon the adventures and the misadventures of the past seventeen years—the several visits I have made to Thailand, my doctoral program and formal Thai language studies at the University of California–Berkeley, the dissertation field research in Bangkok, my Thai friends and relatives, as well as my intercultural marriage of more than fifteen years—such a text seems like an exceedingly appropriate way to celebrate such an odyssey. Indeed, my exposure to the Thai has utterly transformed my consciousness of the world around me. But these events and experiences have also served as both a gentle and sometimes not-so-gentle reminder that I have chosen to live in the midst of an irresolvable, multilayered paradox.

In short, the Kingdom of Thailand is a glorious mystery, and, if I am truly lucky, I will never get to the bottom of it.

Among the myriad fields of human cultural experience and expression, the most fascinating subjects are those whose quintessential cores are impenetrable. Regardless of how much I may know about Thai history, culture, fine arts, and language, they remain the expressions of a time, a place, and a consciousness that are ultimately not my own. To be sure, in the midst of my accumulated knowledge, I have uncovered precious kernels of insight, some commonly shared perspectives, an archetypal parallel or two; but at some point, sooner or later, I encounter a wall that cannot be breached, a glass through which I cannot see clearly. And that is the way that it should be. I can never fully know that which I am not; yet it is Thailand's unknowable and elusive mystery that continually compels me to court her.

In Thailand, all Westerners (and particularly those of European descent) are called *farahng* (like more than a few things in Thailand, a word of Muslim/Arabic origin). Farahng is by no means a derogatory term but simply a reference to a non-Asian who is obviously not from "around here." Regarding their experience with westerners—and especially Western tourists—Thais usually have good reason to employ the expression *Farahng mai roo reuang,* which means, "the westerner doesn't know about it," or "the foreigner doesn't get it." Though I am pleased to say that I don't hear that remark as often as I used to, the simple fact remains: I will always be a farahng because, as a westerner, I can never truly "know" the Thai identity (a fact to which my wife, Baikaew, with all of her Thai mystery, grace, and charm, can readily attest!). But this is not a problem as long as one recognizes it. For this reason, I have engaged the assistance of the Thais who once have and currently do populate both my personal and professional life. Through interviews, letters, and conversations, I have sought their opinions and reflections on the various topics about which I have written. In this way, the "Thai-ness" of the Thai has served as the sounding board and reality check for the farahng.

At this point the reader may well ask, "If what you say is so, then why should you, a farahng, be entrusted with the authorship of this book? Wouldn't a Thai author be more appropriate?" Indeed, I cannot deny that a Thai certainly knows more about this elusive "Thai-ness" than I do. But herein dwells another facet of the paradox with which we began: the closer one is to something, the harder it is to see it clearly. Or, as the Thais put it, *Sehn pohm bahng pookao,* which means, "A strand of hair (in your face) covers a mountain." And there is yet another paradox buried within that one: as I tell the students in my world religions courses, the best way to gain some insight into your own tradition is to go out and learn all you can about someone else's; the best way to understand the workings of your own native language is to go out and learn to speak someone else's. One can develop a much broader and deeper understanding of another culture when one has the capacity to describe and interpret it not only from within, but from without. In turn, when my consciousness as a farahng is placed in direct juxtaposition to my experience of the Thai, I find myself learning ever so much more about them both. In a world that is currently suffering under the weight of so much alienation, distrust, and unilateralism, it seems to me that this is a noble and worthwhile endeavor to pursue. It is my sincere hope that this book, in concert with the other volumes in the Global Studies Series, will inspire you to do the same. At the end of the day, we've fewer choices and less time than we might imagine.

Thai school children. (Courtesy of Anuchit and Khanittha Chaiarsa)

Acknowledgments

Creative projects such as this are never brought to fruition in a vacuum. It is therefore most important to take this opportunity to express my appreciation to those individuals who contributed their time, support, and encouragement. To Stephen and Panchat Hoare and Michael Smail: thank you for graciously allowing me to use your photographs to fill some omissions in my own collection. To Anuchit and Khanittha Chaiarsa: my heartfelt thanks to you for giving up so much of your free time to drive all over downtown and suburban Bangkok to make the photographs that no one else had (Khun Eed, my dear sister-in-law, I promise the next time I travel *anywhere,* I will take pictures of *everything!*). To Barbara Gliddon and Arun Liberda: my sincere appreciation for your memories, encouragement, and inspiration. To Lucien Ellington, editor of the Global Studies Series: thank you for your keen editorial eye and your tireless devotion to your authors. To Alicia Merritt, Laura Stine, and Giulia Rossi of ABC-CLIO: thank you for "being there"; you have been my guardian angels in cyberspace. And finally to my wife, Baikaew, and my niece, Gebdao Kaiwalweroj: thank you both for your abiding love, your faithful encouragement, and your endless patience with a farahng who has tried his best to create a text that will do justice to your remarkable culture and to this ongoing odyssey on which we embarked together so many years ago.

Author's Note

The reader who is familiar with the conventional English transliterations of Thai words and/or proper names may notice that I have chosen in some cases to utilize alternate spellings in my transliterations. I have done so in order to present a more accurate rendering of the pronunciation of the Thai words. Direct literal transliteration from Thai to English can be very misleading, as certain Thai letters have multiple sounds, depending on where they happen to appear in the structure of a word. For example, if a Thai letter that is by definition equivalent to an "S" sound should appear at the end of a syllable, it is pronounced as a "T"; similarly, if a Thai letter that is equivalent to an "L" sound appears at the end of a syllable, it is pronounced as an "N." As conventional English transliteration has never taken these variations into account (except in reputable Thai-English lexicons), this book has provided me with an ideal opportunity to do so.

Following my introductions of both historical and contemporary Thai persons, the reader will notice that in my subsequent references, I identify them by their first names only. As written in Chapter Two of my text, " . . .the identification of Thais by surnames (last names) is a relatively new development, having been instituted in 1913 by King Vajiravudh (Rama VI). But as Thai surnames are very long and difficult to pronounce (even for Thais!), they are reserved for only the most formal of circumstances." Therefore, Prime Minister Thaksin Shinawatra, for example, will be initially introduced as such, but subsequently referred to as simply "Thaksin." Be assured that this is not an act of undue familiarity or disrespect, but a convention of Thai culture.

It should also be noted that the listing of Thai names in the index follows the same practice, with the exception of those who are listed in Significant People, Places, and Events who are listed under both first names and surnames.

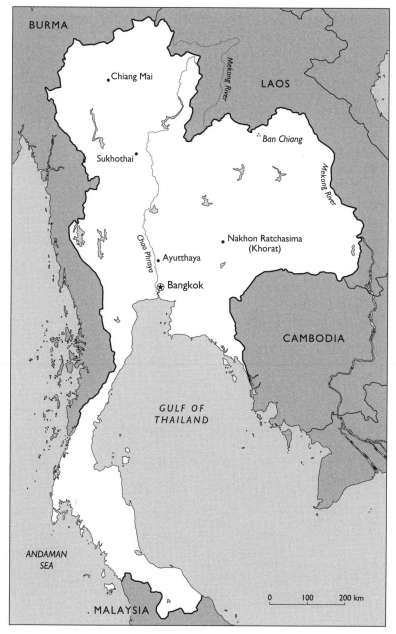

BURMA

• Chiang Mai

LAOS

Mekong River

∴ Ban Chiang

Sukhothai •

Mekong River

• Nakhon Ratchasima
(Khorat)

Chao Phraya

• Ayutthaya

⊛ Bangkok

CAMBODIA

GULF OF
THAILAND

ANDAMAN
SEA

0   100   200 km

• MALAYSIA

Map of Thailand and surrounding regions.

PART ONE
NARRATIVE SECTION

CHAPTER ONE

Thailand's Geography, Demographics, and History

THE GEOGRAPHY OF THAILAND: GENERAL AND REGIONAL

A single white elephant against a field of red comprised the national flag of "Siam" (present-day Thailand) from 1855 until 1917. Oddly enough, Thailand's physical shape seems almost preordained, in that it visually suggests this most revered symbol: the elephant. If one looks at Thailand on a map, it is not difficult to imagine the southern peninsula as the elephant's trunk, and the northern and the northeastern regions as the flapping ears, with Bangkok and the delta of the Chao Praya River forming the elephant's mouth.

Although relatively small in land area, the Kingdom of Thailand presents a wide array of geographic features: rugged mountains, dense (but ever-dwindling) forests, an arid plateau, fertile river valleys, tropical rain forests, and sand-covered coastlines. Nestled into the center of Southeast Asia, Thailand is bordered on the west by Myanmar (Burma) and the Andaman Sea, on the east by Cambodia, on the north by Laos, and on the south by Malaysia and the Gulf of Thailand. Thailand's total land mass is 513,120 square kilometers (198,270 square miles). It extends 2,500 kilometers (1,550 miles) from north to south, and 1,250 kilometers (775 miles) from east to west, with a coastline of approximately 1,840 kilometers (1,140 miles) on the Gulf of Thailand and 865 kilometers (536 miles) on the Andaman Sea. In the visual context of the United States, Thailand is closest in size to the states of California and

Texas. Thailand's land mass is 20 percent larger than California, and about 25 percent smaller than Texas.

As of this writing, the population of Thailand stands at about 64 million. Of that number, almost 10 million people live in and around the capital city of Bangkok. Compared to other Southeast Asian countries, Thailand's population is on the high end, along with Vietnam, whose population is even greater—75 million. Myanmar comes in third with 47 million, followed by Malaysia, Cambodia, and Laos, with 20 million, 10 million, and 5 million, respectively.

Thailand has twenty-five major river systems, the most important being the mighty Chao Praya River, which runs southward through the fertile plains of Central Thailand, and the fabled Mekong River, which marks the north/northeastern boundary between Thailand and Laos. The Thai word for river is *maanahm,* which literally means "mother water." From an economic standpoint, this meaning is quite appropriate, for Thailand's rivers play an essential role in the life of the nation. They are, in a word, its bloodstream. For centuries, the rivers have generated fertile soil for Central Thailand's vast agricultural output. And although Thailand has a well-developed network of paved highways, the rivers continue to serve as the primary channels through which Thailand's produce and natural resources are transported. They are also essential in the continuing development of hydroelectric power throughout the kingdom.

Thailand is one of Asia's most prosperous nations, with a gross domestic product (GDP) of US$143 billion (based upon 2003 figures, Bank of Thailand). Thailand's per capita income averages just over $2,000 (2002 figures, U.S. Embassy in Thailand)—the overwhelming majority of that income concentrated in urban centers like Bangkok. In a global region where the rate of unemployment has averaged as high as 11 percent in the twenty-first century, Thailand's unemployment in 2003 was just over 2 percent (CIA World Factbook, 2004).

In its simplest terms, the Thai economy is built upon "four

pillars": agriculture (farming), natural resources (fishing, minerals, rubber, timber), manufacturing (electronics, machinery, textiles), and, of course, tourism. Thailand's crops, resources, and manufactured goods are exported throughout the world. Though it should come as no surprise that rice is the most important crop, it is nevertheless astonishing to learn that Thailand is the world's leading exporter of rice. Other important export crops include tapioca, rubber, cotton, tobacco, and sugarcane. Thailand exports numerous natural resources. Mined resources include tin (its most valuable mineral export), as well as tungsten, lead, and zinc. Although timber is no longer a major export, fine hardwoods, such as teak, continue to be valuable and sought-after commodities for home and furniture construction. But as a result of decades of radical deforestation practices, the timber industry in Northern and Northeastern Thailand has been at the center of intense environmental controversies that have gained global attention (this problem will be addressed in greater detail in Chapter Two). Thailand also has a very active fishing industry. Next to rice, seafood serves as a fundamental component of the Thai diet. In addition to fresh seafood, Thailand is a major exporter of canned tuna and "farmed" shrimp, that is, shrimp that are raised in a human-made environment. But in the 1990s, manufactured goods became the foremost export commodities. Agricultural produce still accounts for about 22 percent of Thailand's exports (and two-thirds of the population's employment), manufactured goods such as electronics, machinery parts, and textiles make up almost 70 percent. This shift has resulted in a variety of economic challenges that will be addressed in the next chapter.

Thailand has four distinctive regions, each with unique geographic and cultural characteristics. These regions are Northern Thailand (Pahk Neuah), Northeastern Thailand (Pahk Eesahn), Central Thailand (Pahk Glahng), and Southern Thailand (Pahk Dai). These regions are not defined in any strict or formal sense. They may be compared to the various regions of the United States ("the Southwest," "the Midwest," or "the Northeast") in that each of these embodies significant differences in regional ambience and geographic terrain. But by far the most striking features are the ethnic/cultural differences among the people of the four Thai regions, differences that are made all the more impressive by the fact that they exist together in such a small country (see Demographics, page 16).

Northern Thailand

Virtually unknown to anyone except the boldest of travelers only twenty-five years ago, Northern Thailand is now regarded worldwide as the most geographically impressive region in the country. Although a limited amount of rice and other crops are grown here, Northern Thailand is essentially an idyllic, mountainous area, marked by forested peaks, deep valleys, hidden caves, cascading waterfalls, and winding rivers that are bordered by high cliffs. Four major rivers flow southward across Northern Thailand: the Ping, the Wahng, the Yom, and the Nahn. Alternating with deep valleys across the landscape, these rivers eventually join to form the Chao Praya River in Central Thailand. Another important waterway in this northern region is the famous Mekong River. The Mekong does not flow through Thailand; rather, it marks Thailand's north/northeastern border with Laos. The American consciousness usually associates the Mekong River with Vietnam, as its delta is located near Ho Chi Minh City (formerly Saigon). But the river's association with Northern Thailand is much more storied, in that it is the waterway that runs through the legendary "Golden Triangle"—the northern crossroads of Thailand, Myanmar, and Laos—through which drug smugglers and mercenary armies have passed or sought sanctuary, and where opium warlords have fought one another for control of the drug traffic throughout Southeast Asia.

Thailand's highest point is found in the mountains of the

northern region. Doi Inthanon (*doi* means "mountain"), located in Chiang Mai Province, is 2,565 meters (8,417 feet) tall. Northern Thailand's largest city is Chiang Mai, the cultural center of this region. With a population of some 250,000, and surrounded by a substantially populated province of the same name, Chiang Mai is regarded as Thailand's "second city," even though it ranks third in population. The "discovery" of Chiang Mai late in the twentieth century, first by adventurous travelers and then by the tourist industry, has been a mixed blessing. Although Chiang Mai has wonderful shopping and dining, a multitude of attractions, beautiful Buddhist temples, an internationally known university, and northern charm, it is also beginning to suffer under the weight of industrial pollution, ongoing commercial development, and unending traffic gridlock—problems that were previously found only in Bangkok, Thailand's capital city.

Northeastern Thailand

Known by the Thai people as Eesahn, Northeastern Thailand is essentially a broad, sandy, and arid plateau region that is bordered on the north and east by the great Mekong River, and on the south and west by small mountain ranges. The three principal rivers in this region are the Moon, the Chi, and the Po, the latter of which feeds and empties into two freshwater lakes. These rivers flow east/southeast, eventually emptying into the Mekong River as it flows into Southern Laos. Encompassing approximately 170,000 square kilometers, Eesahn constitutes one-third of Thailand's land area, most of it located on the Khorat Plateau, approximately 300 meters (990 feet) above sea level. Due to its sheer size and comparatively limited development, Eesahn is not a common tourist destination. On the plus side of this equation, Eesahn is a region where genuine Thai traditions and customs continue to survive relatively untouched by Western commercial incursion. It should be noted, however, that Western developmental and environmental organizations such as the U.S. Peace Corps have maintained a long tradition of cultural involvement and developmental assistance with the people of Eesahn; in fact, they are likely to be more familiar with this region and its people than are most Thais who live in other parts of the country. Despite its predominantly rural ambience, Eesahn is home to Thailand's second-largest city, Nakhon Ratchasima (also known as Khorat), which in 2001 recorded a population of almost 440,000 (Report of the National Economic and Social Development Board of Thailand 2001). Westerners were familiar with Khorat primarily in the 1960s and 1970s because it served as a major military airbase for U.S. forces during the Vietnam War. In fact, a number of American Vietnam War veterans have retired there.

Tragically, Eesahn is also the most impoverished region of Thailand, and, more so than other regions of Thailand, even the seasonal patterns themselves seem to curse it with either one of two extremes. During the rainy season (*radu fohn dohk*), Eesahn's precipitation is minimal, although it can be deluged by brief torrents of rain. For this reason, virtually every rural house in Eesahn has a huge five-foot-tall ceramic or concrete *ohng gep nahm* ("water reservoir") in which precious rainfall is collected and stored, both from the direct downfall and through downspouts connected to the roof's guttering system. In the hot season (*radu rawn*), water is extremely scarce, and famine conditions are not unknown. Due to these conditions, rice farmers in Eesahn are limited to one crop per year. There is a paradox to this, for the soil and climate are such that the finest jasmine rice in Thailand is produced in Eesahn. If a rice farmer has only one opportunity, he learns to do it well the first time!

Central Thailand

The primary geographical features of Central Thailand are the Chao Praya River and the fertile plain that it renews and sustains on a regular seasonal basis. As noted earlier, four major rivers in Northern Thailand flow into the Chao Praya. During the rainy season, the inundated waters of the Chao Praya River carry rich alluvial soil downstream and deposit it along the river basin's vast rice-growing areas before emptying into the Gulf of Thailand. Central Thailand is composed essentially of sedimentary soil; subsequently, the central plain is only a little higher than sea level. This condition presents something of a problem for the region's largest city, Bangkok, as will be discussed in Chapter Four.

Americans often refer to the Midwestern United States as the "bread basket" of the country, because its fertile soil is the source of the majority of the nation's agricultural production. In the same manner, many Thais refer to Central Thailand as the country's "rice bowl." If one looks down from an airliner cruising over the Midwestern United States during the spring or summer months, one will see a "patchwork quilt" of fields with various crops, such as corn and wheat. But look down from an airliner flying over Central Thailand, and one will see a web-like network of irrigation canals that feed and support its countless rice fields, which at the outset of the growing season resemble a vast geometric patchwork of ponds. The water will slowly be absorbed, transforming the ponds into rich, green fields as the rice grows, and eventually turning golden brown when the rice is ready for harvest. Each plot is surrounded by a thin perimeter of earth, no wider than a footpath, so that farmers can make their way around these "floating fields."

If any city in the world deserves the appellation "cosmopolitan" in its entire spectrum of meaning, both positive and not-so-positive, it is Central Thailand's largest city—and Thailand's capital city—Bangkok. A city of some ten million people, Bangkok could serve as a good example of what Charles Dickens was trying to express when, in his introduction to *A Tale of Two Cities,* he wrote, "It was the best of times, it was the worst of times." Bangkok presents a similar paradox.

*A barge travels along Bangkok's Chao Praya River heading toward the
Silom Road District. (James Marshall/Corbis)*

Bangkok is the best: the home of the national government and
monarchy, the Old Royal City and Grand Palace, breathtak-
ing temple complexes, world-renowned museums and universities, incredible shopping, and truly friendly people. But
Bangkok is also the worst: never-ending traffic jams, overpopulation, uncontrolled commercial development, environmental pollution, profound poverty juxtaposed against opulent
affluence, and gaudy commercialism geared toward an unending onslaught of Western tourism. In short, Bangkok is at once
the most fascinating and the most unnerving city this author
has ever visited.

Located at the mouth of the Chao Praya River at the Gulf of
Thailand, Bangkok has been Thailand's capital since 1782. The
name *"Bangkok"* is actually a Western pronunciation of *Bang
Makok,* or "place of hog plums," a small trading/fishing village
that originally occupied the site. The Thai name—and the
name that Thais will use—is *Grungtayp,* or sometimes *Grungtayp Mahanakawn.* But take a deep breath—the real Thai

name is *Grungtayp Mahanakawn Amawn Rattanakosindra Mahindrayutthaya Mahadeelohkpohp Noparatana Rajadhani Burirohm Udom Rajanivayt Mahasatawn Amawn Pimawn Awatawn Satit Sakatatutiya Wisanukawm Prasit.* This world-record–length name translates as "The City of Gods, the Great City, the Residence of the Emerald Buddha, the Impregnable City (of Ayutthaya) of God Indra, the Grand Capital of the World, Endowed with Nine Precious Gems, the Happy City, Abounding in Enormous Palaces which Resemble the Heavenly Abode Where Reigns the Reincarnated God, a City Given by Indra and Built by Vishnu." Mercifully, no one actually uses this formal name in everyday conversation. But it is nevertheless acknowledged in written Thai script: one will often see a small y-shaped symbol following the shorter name Grungtayp. Appropriately, that symbol means "and so on and so forth," or "et cetera." Perhaps the exhaustive length of the name was predestined to reflect the fact that Bangkok is at once an ongoing wonder to behold and an unrelenting issue to endure. We will take a closer look at some of the social and environmental issues faced by this highly populated capital city in Chapter Four.

Southern Thailand

Sometimes called Peninsular Thailand, Southern Thailand comprises a substantial portion of the Malay Peninsula and the vast majority of Thailand's coastal land area. This "trunk of the elephant" is essentially a long, slender mountain range covered in tropical rain forest, with narrow strips of flat land facing the Gulf of Thailand on the east and the Andaman Sea on the west. Southern Thailand's coastline and island beaches—dozens of them—rank among the most beautiful in the world, and are major tourist attractions for Thais and foreigners alike.

Southern Thailand's principal cities include Petchaburi (known for its Buddhist temples), the beach communities of Songkhla, Hua Hin, and Narathiwat (almost at the Malaysian border, and therefore steeped in Muslim tradition), as well as the resort islands of Puket off the west coast of the peninsula and Ko Samui off the east coast. In addition, the vast majority of Thailand's major commercial seaports are located on the coasts of the southern peninsula, on either the Andaman Sea or the Gulf of Thailand.

Due to its proximity to Malaysia, there is a significant Muslim population in Southern Thailand. As one travels southward, the Islamic influence becomes ever more apparent—in dress, in architecture, in behavior, and in politics. Unfortunately, there are some long-standing tensions between Thai Muslims and the Thai Buddhist majority. Some of these issues will be addressed in greater detail in Chapter Three.

The preceding regional descriptions provide but a brief geographic introduction to the diversity of the Kingdom of Thailand. As suggested at various points above, each of Thailand's four regions faces its own set of social, political, and economic issues. Many of these will be discussed in greater depth in the chapters that follow.

THE CLIMATE OF THAILAND

Thais enjoy a good joke. If a westerner asks a Thai to give a brief explanation for Thailand's climate, he/she might grin, pause, and then, with an authoritative air, reply that Thailand's climate is composed of three basic seasons: *rawn, rawn mahg gwah, laa rawn teesoot*, which means "hot, hotter, and hottest." To the Western visitor who is accustomed to a temperate climate, this may sound like an accurate meteorological assessment! But like all of Southeast Asia, Thailand is tropical, and even a tropical climate has seasonal variations. To the Thai, those variations are quite evident and, depending on the region in which he/she lives, quite vital to one's way of life. There are essentially three seasonal variations: the dry/cool season (December–February), the hot season (March–June), and the rainy season (June–November).

The patterns of the Southeast Asian monsoons determine the three seasons of Thailand. Those in temperate zones who are not familiar with tropical climates and seasons tend to equate the word *monsoon* with *typhoon*. *Typhoon*, from the Chinese/Cantonese term *tai fung*, refers to a severe hurricane-like storm. But *monsoon*, from the Arabic word *mausim*, refers to the overall wind patterns that determine the seasons of a tropical region.

In Southeast Asia, there are two monsoon patterns: the northeast monsoon and the southwest monsoon (the words *northeast* and *southwest* refer to the directions from which the winds blow). The dry season in Thailand (December–February) occurs because the land cools faster than the sea, thereby creating a high-pressure zone over Southeast Asia. This high pressure generates the northeast monsoon, blowing from the land to the sea, resulting in drier and relatively cooler weather; in Northern Thailand, for example, night temperatures have been known to drop to the freezing level. For obvious reasons, this has become the most popular time to visit Thailand.

But all good things must come to an end—once the northeastern monsoon has run its course, there is an interim period that one must endure prior to the arrival of the next monsoon. This interim is the hot season (March–June), when temperatures in Bangkok, for example, will hold steady in the upper nineties (Fahrenheit), dropping minimally during the evening hours. Humidity stays high as well.

The rainy season (June–November) commences when the winds finally change direction. The southwestern monsoon brings warm, humid air up from the Indian Ocean. When this airflow from the relatively cooler sea encounters the much warmer low-pressure area that has held sway over the mainland, the result is rain, usually during the late afternoon and evening hours. The amount of rain varies, however, depending on the region. The streets of Bangkok may be flooded while those in the extreme northeast receive very little rainfall. The rainy season is a blessing to the farmers throughout Thailand, but a headache to those who end up bailing water out of their street-level homes and businesses.

The only exception to this seasonal pattern is the peninsular region of Southern Thailand, as it is directly in the paths of both the northeastern and the southwestern monsoons. By the time the northeastern monsoon has reached Southern Thailand, it has already accumulated significant humidity on its southwesterly journey. Southern Thailand, therefore, has only two seasons: rainy and dry, although rain can fall during both seasonal periods.

THAILAND'S TRANSPORTATION AND TELECOMMUNICATIONS INFRASTRUCTURE

Thailand's infrastructure covers the developmental spectrum, in that it is state-of-the-art in some areas and in dire need of improvement in others. Thailand has 158,425 kilometers (almost 100,000 miles) of roads. Of that number, paved national highways in 2001 accounted for 51,775 kilometers (32,100 miles), distribution roads (connecting roads) covered 59,200 kilometers (36,700 miles), and rural roads (most likely both paved and unpaved) covered 47,450 kilometers (29,420 miles). Ongoing master plans call for a thirteen-route motorway (expressway) network totaling 4,150 kilometers (2,753 miles). Some of these routes already serve as convenient express loops that encircle major urban areas such as Bangkok and Chiang Mai (Report of the National Economic and Social Development Board of Thailand 2001).

Thailand has 4,119 kilometers (2,554 miles) of conventional rail service, but it does not yet extend throughout the country. The most impressive rail-related development thus far has been the Bangkok Transit System (BTS), the elevated mass-transit railway designed to ease Bangkok's chronic traffic gridlock. Ten years in the making, the BTS opened on

The BTS has eased some of Bangkok's nightmarish traffic gridlock.
(Courtesy of Michael Smail)

December 5, 1999 (appropriately, the birthday of the current king of Thailand). The BTS consists of two major routes totaling 23.5 kilometers (14.5 miles). They run through Bangkok's business district and shopping venues. More important, they connect with other major transportation hubs, such as Bangkok's major bus stations. Although the BTS does not yet have a route to the Dawn Mueahng International Airport, there are currently plans to construct a route that will pass within 2–3 kilometers (1–2 miles) of the airport. Construction is scheduled to begin in 2004. There is also an underground mass transit system currently under construction in Bangkok that is scheduled to begin service by the end of 2004.

Air travel service in Thailand is well-developed. Thailand currently has thirty commercial airports, consisting of Dawn Mueahng International Airport in Bangkok, six regional airports, twenty-one provincial airports, and two private airports. A new and larger international airport is currently under construction in Bangkok and is scheduled to open in 2005. Started in 1956, Thai International Airlines is one of the finest in the world. It has approximately eighty aircraft that serve domestic, regional, and international routes. For efficiency and service, Thai International is consistently ranked among the top three airlines in the world.

Thailand's telecommunications system is quite advanced, but still running behind in its providing of basic services to the Thai public. Employing fiber-optic cable, microwave, and satellite technologies, Thailand's basic telephone services have a carrying capacity of 7.55 million lines, which averages nationwide to approximately 12 per 100 persons. But the ratio of urban to rural service is still quite unbalanced: in urban/municipal areas in 2001, there were 4.38 million lines, or 53.77 per 100 persons, whereas in rural areas there were 3.17 million lines, or just 5.9 per 100 persons. The ever-increasing demand for cell phone and Internet service is very competitive and proven to be something of a distraction from the needed improvement of basic telephone services. As of 2001, there were still some 43,000 rural villages without public telephone service (Report of the National Economic and Social Development Board of Thailand 2001).

THE DEMOGRAPHICS OF THAILAND

From a demographic standpoint, approximately 80 percent of Thailand's population is of pure "Thai" descent (for an explanation of what "Thai" means in terms of ethnicity, see the overview of Thailand's historical origins, below). The remaining 20 percent is composed primarily of Chinese, Malay, Lao, Mon, and Cambodian, both as immigrants and as ethnic mixes with the Thai. There is also a significant South Asian/Indian population, primarily in Bangkok. But there are also some distinctive tribal groups, particularly in the northern mountains, to which we will give closer attention. Of the 80 percent of the population that is "pure Thai" (as noted above), the majority of that percentage live in Central Thai-

land; that is, the Chinese, Malay, Lao, and Cambodian ethnicities and tribal groups that characterize the other three
"border regions" are generally not present in Central Thailand, with the exception of Bangkok.

The mountains and valleys of Northern Thailand are home
to a diverse array of ethnicities, cultures, beliefs, and languages. More than simply "Thai," these storied hill-tribe
groups migrated to Thailand over the course of the nineteenth
and twentieth centuries from as nearby as Myanmar and
China and from as far away as Tibet and Mongolia. Over the
years, they have been persecuted by the Thai majority (due
to supposed communist sympathies during the 1970s),
exploited by tourism, and coerced to forsake their traditional
ways by the pressures of a market-based economy. But
throughout it all, they have maintained their distinctive cultural identities and independence. The hill tribes are known
for their exquisite handicraft work, particularly in textiles and
silver, as well as for their friendly natures. The economic reality being what it is, however, some of them are also traditionally known for being among the foremost cultivators of poppies and producers of opium (which grows well in mountain
altitudes), the raw source of heroin to both Asia and the West.
But in recent years, royal-sponsored cooperatives have been
created to enable Thailand's hill tribes to manufacture and
market their handicraft goods throughout Thailand and the
world. And in an effort to lessen their economic dependence
on the production of opium, many are being encouraged to
cultivate alternative cash crops.

The Thai government officially recognizes six major hill
tribes (although each one can be further divided into various
subgroups with distinct dialects and customs). These tribes
are as follows:

- The Karen: this is the largest tribal group, with a population
  of about 300,000. Although they live in the mountains, the
  Karen are the only tribe known to grow paddy rice in the

valleys. Coming originally from Burma, they live primarily in the area of the Thai-Myanmar border.

- The Lisu: from a visual perspective, the Lisu's traditional costuming is probably the most visually stunning of all the hill tribes. As they came originally from Tibet in the early twentieth century, one can see a resemblance between their respective styles of dress. The Lisu now live primarily in the high altitudes of the extreme northwest where, once again, opium poppies grow well.
- The Ahka: also from Tibet, the Ahka live in the high altitudes of the far north. They are noted for, of all things, their ornate ceremonial gates, which are decorated with an array of explicit sexual imagery that ensures fertility and frightens away malevolent spirits.
- The Lahu: originally a hunting and gathering society, the Lahu migrated from northern Burma. A lack of game eventually forced them to take up agriculture. Although all of the hill tribes are essentially animistic in their religious beliefs, the Lahu are the only group to have a central temple for worship and ritual.
- The Mien: originally from southern China, the Mien are scattered throughout upper Northeast Thailand. Though they, too, are animists, much of their belief system is grounded in a form of Chinese Taoism as well.
- The Hmong: probably the most familiar tribal group to westerners, the Hmong originally came to Thailand from China, or perhaps even Mongolia. They are found throughout Northern Thailand and Laos, but primarily in the Chiang Mai region. During the Vietnam War era, Hmong volunteers from Laos fought side-by-side with U.S. soldiers against the communist forces in Laos. About 70,000 Hmong refugees came to the United States in the 1970s.

Due to their proximity to the nations of Laos and Cambodia, the people of Eesahn (Northeastern Thailand) comprise a uniquely diverse ethnicity as well. Most of the Thais in this region migrated west across the Mekong River from Laos, or north from Cambodia. Especially significant is the Laotian influence. Were it not for the Mekong River, one would find it extremely difficult to determine where Thailand ends and Laos begins. *Pahsah Eesahn,* the form of Thai language that is spoken in this region, is a mixture of Thai, Lao, and other regional dialects. To the urban Thai from Bangkok, pahsah Eesahn can sometimes sound like a foreign tongue. The people of Eesahn are also known for their expertise in traditional textile weaving, especially silk. We will take a closer look at Eesahn and the Thai silk industry in Chapter Two.

As we have seen, the Kingdom of Thailand is marked by a wide array of geographic and demographic dimensions. Each region has its own particular character, but together they comprise a singular Thai identity that has been shaped and nurtured by a remarkable cultural history. It is to that history that we will now turn our attention.

THE HISTORY OF THAILAND

Mueang Thai or *Brahtayt Thai*, the Thai names for the Kingdom of Thailand, both translate as "Land of the Free." More than a remote reference to a vague sense of patriotism, this name proclaims the fact that among all Southeast Asian nations, Thailand alone has never been the colony of a foreign power—particularly a Western power. While cultures throughout the Asian continent fell prey to the colonial oppression of European nations such as Spain, Great Britain, France, the Netherlands, and Portugal over the past five hundred years, Thailand preserved its independent sovereignty while yet developing and maintaining profitable trade relations and cultural exchanges with the West. For this reason, the Thai people exude a profound sense of national pride and cultural identity.

Thailand's Prehistory: The Archaeological Evidence

Archaeological discoveries from many locations throughout Thailand have revealed compelling evidence of organized human cultures from the early Paleolithic period. Simple stone tools, weapons, and utensils, dating back to circa 500,000 BCE (BCE means "before common era," the more inclusive equivalent of the traditional "BC") have been found at numerous sites in the central plains, the northeast plateau, and the northern mountains. It has been suggested that the Thai/Malay peninsula may have even served as a kind of land bridge between Asia and Australia, over which a variety of interrelated racial/ethnic groups may have migrated from China. Such a migration may be responsible for some of the tribal groups that we find in Malaysia, Indonesia, and the Philippines. But probably the most remarkable archaeological discovery in Thailand is the civilization that developed at a tiny village called Ban Chiang, located on the Khorat Plateau in Northeastern Thailand near the Laotian border. It is believed that early farmers began to settle in this area around 4000 BCE. In the early to mid-1970s, Dr. Chester Gorman, the prominent figure in twentieth-century Thai archaeology, uncovered a remarkable collection of artifacts at Ban Chiang, including a variety of tools and utensils made of both bronze and iron, well-executed ceramic vessels incised with intricate designs, evidence of sericulture (silk making), as well as stone and glass ornamental beads. The people of Ban Chiang also printed their own textiles, as evidenced by the discovery of clay rollers with line patterns incised on them. Notable also was the apparent scarcity of offensive weapons, which indicates a peaceful and stable society with a knowledge of metallurgy, ceramics, and agriculture that would have required a long period of prior development. All of this is quite significant because many of these bronze and iron tools have been dated to about 3500–3000 BCE, a date that challenges the long-held assumption that the advent of metallurgy (i.e., the "Bronze Age") took place solely in Mesopotamia and/or China and then gradually spread throughout the world.

What became of the Ban Chiang civilization? Some archaeological authorities believe that the land was eventually "used up," succumbing to deforestation and soil exhaustion, which in turn led to a migration into the central plains of the Chao Praya River Valley. This hypothesis is supported by the fact that bronze implements have been found in the central plains that have been dated to about 2000 BCE. Was the bronze technology brought to this region by the Ban Chiang culture, or was it the indigenous product of a civilization that was already in place? Regardless of the answer, both Ban Chiang and subsequent Chao Praya River Valley bronzes provide solid evidence of a developed "Bronze Age" culture that is at least concurrent with the bronze technology of China's Shang Dynasty (ca. 1760–1100 BCE).

The Early Kingdoms

The genesis of every great ancient civilization is a river valley: the Tigris/Euphrates of Mesopotamia, the Nile of Egypt, the Indus of the Pakistani/Indian subcontinent, the Yangtze of China. In Southeast Asia we find the great rivers called the Mekong and the Chao Praya. As noted earlier, the Thai word for river is *maanahm,* or "mother water," the source of all that is. In other words, the life-giving water that ebbs and flows with the seasons is like a nurturing goddess. The Chao Praya River Valley served as both the physical and the spiritual "mother" of the historically documented civilizations of what is now Thailand.

The Chao Praya River basin of Central Thailand is bordered by mountains on the west and north, and by a plateau on the east/northeast. It is readily accessible only from the coast, that is, from the Gulf of Thailand. As such, the Chao Praya river basin was well protected from excessive incursions of new populations and settlements. This area, therefore, would come to serve as the center of the sustained and flourishing cultures that shaped and defined Thai cultures to come.

Some of the most significant "pre-Thai" civilizations of Southeast Asia were strongly influenced by Indian culture. The multifaceted religious tradition of Hinduism, the belief in the divine status of rulers, sculptural/architectural styles, and eventually both Theravada and Mahayana Buddhism were introduced to Southeast Asia through Indian traders on their eastward land and sea routes to China. Politically, theologically, and artistically, Indian culture took a firm hold and remains evident in Thailand to this day.

We shall briefly examine four of the most significant kingdoms that existed both prior to and concurrent with the first Thai kingdoms. These are the Dvaravati, the Srivijaya, the Khmer, and the Lanna.

The Dvaravati (ca. 1st century BCE–11th century CE)

After migrating from India through Myanmar, a people known as the Mons settled in an area stretching from Northern Thailand to the western half of the Chao Praya River Valley, where they established the kingdom of Dvaravati in the first century BCE. Although there is minimal historical documentation about the Davaravati and the Mons, it is known that Buddhism, the primary religion of Thailand, was introduced into the region during the Dvaravati period. This concurs with the fact that King Ashoka (273–232 BCE), the first Indian ruler to embrace Buddhism during its short-lived official presence in India, sent Buddhist missionaries into Asia in the third century BCE. It is therefore quite possible that some of these missionaries came into Thailand with the Mons.

Additional migrations into the region took place during the Dvaravati period. There was a Tibetan-Burmese migration from the northwest that formed the basis of the hill tribes found in Northern Thailand today. But most important for our purposes, it was during the Dvaravati period that the Southern Chinese civilization known as the Tai would gradually migrate into Northern and Central Thailand to form the basis of the first independent Thai kingdom in the thirteenth century.

The Dvaravati were a loosely organized confederacy of villages with no substantial military power base. Due to the increasing expansion and military conquests of the more centralized Khmer Empire, the Dvaravati civilization of the Mons disappeared in the eleventh century. Today, Mon communities can still be found in Thailand, but they remain particularly prevalent in Myanmar (Burma).

The Srivijaya (ca. 7th–13th centuries CE)

Very little is known about the Srivijaya Empire, except that it was initially a very powerful Hindu (and eventually Buddhist) civilization that was centered in the Malay Peninsula and the southernmost provinces of Thailand. Due to its strategic location, it had significant control over sea routes and maritime trade between India, Southeast Asia, and China. Although physical evidence of this culture is limited, what does exist is exquisite, such as a superbly crafted bronze statue of Avalokitesvara, an Indian Buddhist bodhisattva (in the Mahayana Buddhist tradition, a bodhisattva is a celestial being who embodies the compassion of the Buddha). This now-famous bronze sculpture was found in Surat Thani Province in Southern Thailand and is now at the National Museum in Bangkok (see Rawson 1995, 138).

The Khmer (802–1431)

In approximately the first century BCE, the population that established the Khmer civilization settled in a region just south of the Khorat Plateau, in what is now northern Cambodia. In 802, King Jayavarman II (802–834) established his magnificent capital of Angkor, approximately 100 kilometers (62 miles) south of the current Thai border. Over the next several hundred years, Angkor developed into the seat of a powerful empire that controlled most of Southeast Asia.

Whereas the Dvaravati civilization introduced Buddhism to the region, the Khmer civilization embraced Hinduism as the state religion. Jayavarman II proclaimed himself as the divine incarnation of the Hindu god Shiva. He was called *devaraja*, or "the god-king," a role that most likely necessitated the development of a complex priestly cult to uphold and maintain that divine identity.

The Khmer civilization is remembered primarily for the magnificent architectural complex called Angkor Wat. Composed of more than one hundred temples, immense courtyards, and long sculpture-lined causeways, Angkor Wat was built and expanded over a period of some three hundred years (879–1191) when the Khmer civilization was at the height of its power. The largest temple structure in Angkor Wat was built by King Suryavarman II (1112–1152), in honor of the Hindu god Vishnu, with whom the devaraja identified himself. Overall, Angkor Wat served as something of an *axis mundi* ("center of the world"): an earthly representation of the mythical Mount Meru, the home of the Hindu pantheon and, according to ancient Hindu mythology, the source of all creation (see "Religion" in Chapter Three).

The Khmer capital of Angkor was sacked by the Thai kingdom of Ayutthaya (discussed below) in 1431, and the Khmers abandoned the capital a year later. Even so, the Khmer civilization had a profound influence, both artistically and politically, on the development of modern Thai culture.

The Lanna (1259–1558)

Also known as Lannatai, the Kingdom of Lanna encompassed the majority of Northern Thailand for three centuries. The founder and first king of Lanna was Mengrai. He came from a Chinese Tai family that controlled a large portion of the Mekong River Valley in the Chiang Saen region. While growing up, Mengrai despaired over the continual infighting that took place among the various Tai factions and warlords throughout the northern region. Finally, in 1259, after having succeeded his father's rule, Mengrai set out to conquer these neighboring factions one by one, with the purpose of uniting them under one rule. In 1262 he moved his capital to Chiang Rai, and in 1281 he moved it again, this time to Chiang Mai. In the space of twenty-two years, Mengrai had succeeded in uniting all of Northern Thailand into a kingdom called Lanna, which translates as "the land of a million rice fields."

Mengrai was gifted not only with keen military skills but also with shrewd diplomatic sense. In 1282, for example, he formed a significant alliance with the coexisting Thai kingdom of Sukhothai to the south. It was a pact that came to serve both parties at pivotal times. Mengrai's most formidable and constant threat had been from the Chinese Mongols, who continually attacked Lanna from the north. But Mengrai's alliance with Sukhothai resulted in their shared victory over the Mongols in 1301. And conversely, when an ambitious king from Ayutthaya attempted to conquer Sukhothai in 1372—fifty-five years after Mengrai's death—an army from Chiang Mai moved south to assist Sukhothai. The Ayutthayan army was turned back.

Other notable kings of Lanna include Ku Na (1355–1385), whose continued alliance with Sukhothai allowed for the spread of Theravada Buddhism to Northern Thailand; and Tilok (1441–1487), who was responsible for vast and numerous building projects in and around Chiang Mai. The Kingdom of Lanna subsequently fell to the Burmese in 1558.

The First Thai Kingdoms

In the eleventh through the thirteenth centuries, the people who would eventually form the first definitively Thai kingdom migrated into Northern Thailand from southern China. But was this an initial migration, or was it a return? The early history of the Mon/Dvaravati and Khmer civilizations, juxtaposed against archaeological evidence found at Ban Chiang, has generated a controversy that presents two conflicting theories about the origins of the Thai people. Because the history of the Kingdom of Lanna is more or less contemporary with that of the first Thai kingdom of Sukhothai, it does not play a role in these hypothetical equations.

The traditional theory is that a people known as the "Tai" established the Nanchao Empire in the southern Chinese province of Yunnan in 651 BCE, a date supported by ancient Chinese chronicles. A spirited, proud, and militant culture, the Tai were in a constant state of conflict with neighboring Chinese warlords. This state of affairs resulted in a gradual migration of the Tai into Northern and Central Thailand during the Dvaravati period, as noted above. Ultimately, however, it was the thirteenth-century Mongol expansion of Kublai Khan that pushed the Tai southward once and for all.

However, the archaeological findings at Ban Chiang support a countertheory, which suggests that there was an indigenous population in "Thai land" that may have been driven northward into the Yunnan Province by the superior numbers of the Mon/Dvaravati and Khmer cultures. There they established the Tai empire of Nanchao before being forced southward once again by the aforementioned thirteenth-century Mongol expansion. In any case, these early cultures helped to set the stage for—and, indeed, would continue to play a seemingly destined role in—the development of the first kingdoms of "Siam" (from an ancient Malay word for the region: *sayahm*, meaning "a brown race").

The Sukhothai Period (1238–1350)

"This Sukhothai is good. In the water there is fish, in the field there is rice . . ." (from the 1292 stone inscription of Sukhothai's greatest king, Ramkhamheng, who developed the first written Thai script).

In the early thirteenth century, Northern/Central Siamese kingdoms were modest city-states with minimal human, economic, or military resources. Separated from one another by dense forests or mountains, they were individually powerless to present any significant challenge to the suzerainty of the powerful Khmer Empire based at Angkor. But in 1238, two Thai princes, Khun Bang Klang Hao and Khun Pha Muahng, combined their resources and, after attacking and defeating a local Khmer military commander, established the first truly independent Siamese kingdom at Sukhothai. The name Sukhothai comes from an ancient Pali language word *sukho-*

daya, which means "dawn of happiness" (in modern Thai, the word *kwahmsukh* means "happiness").

Khun Bang Klang Hao became Sukhothai's first king (under the name of Sri Indraditya). As other minor Siamese states became aware of what had taken place, they, too, realized that their independence and survival required a united front against outside aggression. Accordingly, they merged with Sukhothai, thereby increasing the size and power of this first independent Siamese kingdom.

Their first challenge came soon. In 1278, Sukhothai was attacked by Maa Sawt, a city-state near the Burmese border. But the kingdom was saved through the heroic efforts of the nineteen-year-old son of Indraditya. According to legend, he defeated the king of Maa Sawt in combat as they fought one another on elephant back (in ancient Southeast Asia, mounted elephants were the traditional vehicles of battle). For his bravery, he was given the title *Ramkhamheng,* which means "Ram the bold." Following the brief reign of Bahn Muang (his older brother), Ramkhamheng ascended the throne and, as the most famous and prolific of Sukhothai's eight kings, reigned from 1275–1317.

King Ramkhamheng is responsible for numerous achievements during his long reign. Even though he was revered and respected as an accomplished warrior, Ramkhamheng was a wise and thoughtful administrator who knew when and when not to fight. He acknowledged and respected the sovereignty of other powerful Thai kingdoms in the region, such as Chiang Mai and Chiang Saen, with whom he concluded pacts of non-aggression. He established diplomatic relations with China, Burma, India, and Ceylon (contemporary Sri Lanka). Because Ceylon was a very strong center of Theravada Buddhism, Ramkhamheng, who was a devout Buddhist, invited Sinhalese ("Ceylon-ese") monks to "purify" the Khmer-influenced Buddhism that was being practiced in Sukhothai. In turn, delegations of Sukhothai monks traveled to Ceylon to study the newly revised Buddhist scriptures of the Theravada tradition.

As Theravada Buddhism became firmly established, monks in Sukhothai began to practice a more meditative, disciplined, and monastic lifestyle. Numerous temples were built, and new large-scale metal casting techniques produced exquisite images of the Buddha that reflected the meditative emphasis of the Theravada sect. In contrast to the Mahayana Buddhist traditions of most East Asian cultures, Theravada Buddhism serves as the spiritual base of every Southeast Asian nation except Vietnam. (The particular character of the Theravada sect—and its difference from the Mahayana tradition—will be discussed in a later chapter.) The Sukhothai Buddha image is unique: its smooth, elongated and continuous contours place it among the most beautiful forms of Buddhist art in the world. It is the prime example of what we have come to recognize as "classicaal Thai style." (For a definitive image of this style, see Rawson 1995, 147). When the Sinhalese Buddhist monks came to Sukhothai, we are told they brought a Buddha image with them as a gift for Ramkhamheng. Because early Sinhalese Buddha images embody some of these same stylistic elements, it is believed that the Sukhothai Buddha evolved out of its precursor from Ceylon.

As intrinsic as Buddhist visual arts are to the Sukhothai period, Ramkhamheng's greatest achievement was the creation of the written Thai alphabet in 1283. Whereas spoken Thai evolved from the languages of Sankrit and Pali, the written language was based on previously existing Mon and Khmer scripts. A shared written language became the cultural glue that joined the scattered city-states into one Thai nation with an identity of its own. The modern Thai alphabet of forty-four consonants, over thirty vowels, and five tones has changed minimally since its inception (see "The Thai Language," later in this text).

Ramkhamheng was a very paternal and just ruler. By all reports, he maintained a remarkably close proximity to his subjects and embodied a spirit of accessibility that in modern times has come to define the ideal Thai monarch. Sukhothai kings were referred to as *dhammaraja,* which loosely translates as "the ideal Buddhist kingship," one whose reign embodies the virtues of the Buddhist *dhamma,* or *dharma*— the Buddha's wisdom and teachings: compassion, forbearance, and justice (in direct contrast to the previously mentioned *devaraja,* or "god-king," practiced by the Khmer). In fact, so accessible was Ramkhamheng that, according to the 1292 stone inscription cited above, if any person had a grievance or concern, he could simply walk up to the palace, ring a bell that was mounted next to the front door, and be granted an audience with the king.

When Ramkhamheng died in 1317, the Kingdom of Sukhothai entered into a period of decline from which it never truly recovered. A series of less-than-visionary kings reigned and, by 1350, Sukhothai's influence had begun to wane under the shadow of a new and powerful star rising to the south: the Kingdom of Ayutthaya.

The Ayutthaya Period (1350–1767)

Located some four hundred kilometers (248 miles) south of Sukhothai on a large island in the Chao Praya River, the powerful Kingdom of Ayutthaya brought about a radical change in the manner in which monarchical identity was expressed and perceived. As noted earlier, the Sukhothai monarchy is remembered for practicing dhammaraja, the embodying of a paternal spirit and a close proximity to its subjects. In stark contrast, the Siamese kings of Ayutthaya were influenced by that Hindu concept of devaraja—"the god-king"—that shaped the Khmer monarchical style at Angkor. Such an influence was perhaps inevitable, considering the fact that the Siamese and the Khmers had been living side by side, albeit not amiably, for at least a century.

From his initial coronation to the execution of his daily routine, the Ayutthayan monarch's reign was infused with the trappings of Hindu/Brahmanic ritual and divine association, all of which served to distance the king from the temporality of the mundane world. Indeed, his very identity was surrounded with an aura of the supernatural. He was without equal, above the law, the exclusive "owner" of every material and human resource in his kingdom. The royal Siamese court was literally enveloped in a rigid system of court etiquette, elaborate protocol, and byzantine hierarchy. For example, no common person could touch the king's person or look upon the face of the king, nor could he utter the king's personal name. No one's head could be higher than that of the king. In short, the Ayutthayan Siamese king was wholly transcendent and remote from his subjects.

The Kingdom of Ayutthaya was founded by U Thong, better known by the name given to him at his crowning, Ramathibodi I. As yet another example of the concept of devaraja, note the prefix "rama" in his royal name: in Hindu mythology, Rama is the earthly incarnation of Vishnu, the god of preservation. So also, the king was regarded as nothing less than the incarnate preserver and maintainer of his realm.

As a ruler, Ramathobodi did not embody the same gifts as Ramkhamheng, but he was nevertheless responsible for some innovative accomplishments. He created a formal political bureaucracy for the administration of his kingdom that included a minister of local government (*khun meuang*), who was responsible for the maintenance of peace and order, as well as the punishment of criminals; a minister of finance (*khun klahng*), who was the manager of state properties and the collector of taxes; a minister of agriculture (*khun nah*), who managed the production and storage of the kingdom's food supply; and a minister of the royal household (*khun wahng*), who, among other things, acted as a judge in legal disputes among the people of the kingdom.

Related to the resolution of public disputes, Ramathibodi was also responsible for the enactment of a wide variety of casuistic (i.e., conditional, based on the principle of "if this,

Ruins of ancient Ayutthaya today. (Courtesy of Timothy Hoare)

then that") laws that formally defined the parameters of punishment and recompense—in essence, what could and could not be required from or imposed upon an offender in various relational situations. The point, therefore, is not uncontrolled revenge but warranted justice.

Throughout his reign, Ramathibodi followed an expansionist policy. Ever wary of the Khmer to the east, Ramathibodi launched a pre-emptive strike against the Kingdom of Angkor in 1352. He placed his son, Prince Ramesuan, at the head of the army. But due to Ramesuan's inexperience and tactical errors, his army was routed. The king was forced to send his brother, Prince Boromaraja, with another army to retrieve Ramesuan and what remained of his soldiers. Not only did the king's brother rescue Ramesuan, but he also went on to defeat the Khmer forces at Angkor. Boromaraja returned to Ayutthaya as a hero.

Ramathibodi I died in 1369, and Ramesuan ascended the throne. But Ramesuan was simply not equipped to deal with the heroic reputation and political ambition of his uncle who had swooped in to pick up the pieces of his failed expedition against the Khmer; so Ramesuan stepped aside willingly and surrendered the throne to Boromaraja. Ramesuan then quietly withdrew northward, to the region of Lopburi, where he ruled as governor.

Boromaraja continued Ramathibodi's aggressive expansionist policy throughout his eighteen-year reign (1370–1388). In this respect, his character could be aptly described as "determined to a fault." In 1372 and twice thereafter, Boromaraja attempted to force the final submission of the still-existing Kingdom of Sukhothai, but forces from Chiang Mai moved south to offer assistance and repelled his army. Boromaraja finally conquered Sukhothai in 1378, on his fourth expedition.

As soon as matters in Sukhothai were under control, Boromaraja set his sights on Chiang Mai, for he had neither forgiven nor forgotten how its previous assistance had undermined his multiple attempts to conquer Sukhothai. In 1380 he marched with an army against the Chiang Mai forces but was repelled. Not to be deterred, Boromaraja led yet another army against Chiang Mai in 1388. He was defeated yet again; this time, however, it was not at the hands of the opposing army but his own natural mortality. Boromaraja fell ill and died during the expedition, and his army returned to Ayutthaya.

The power vacuum was not devoid of struggle and intrigue for long. The throne was initially given to Boromaraja's son, Tonglun, who was all of fifteen years old. But after reigning as the King of Ayutthaya for a mere seven days, he was confronted by the ex-king, Ramesuan. Claiming his right to the throne of Ayutthaya, Ramesuan seized the boy-king and had him put to death according to the traditional royal protocol: Tonglun was placed in a soft velvet sack and slowly beaten to death with a sandalwood stick.

Ramesuan thus became King of Ayutthaya for a second time. During his short reign (1388–1395), he conquered Chiang Mai, and, perhaps in atonement for the youthful inexperience that led to his embarrassing defeat at the hands of the Khmer in 1352, dealt the Khmer a major defeat in 1393. This was the beginning of the end for the Khmer Empire; it no longer posed a significant threat to Ayutthaya. Finally, in 1431, the forces of Ayutthaya overran the Khmer capital of Angkor and, by 1432, the Khmer were forced to abandon the once incomparable city for good.

In 1512 a Portuguese diplomatic mission made the first Western contact with the Siamese at Ayutthaya. Having already established trade relationships with Malacca (Malaysia) just to the south, the Portuguese saw the Kingdom of Ayutthaya as an opportunity to further their commercial relationship with Southeast Asia overall. By 1517, Ayutthaya had established a formal trade agreement with Portugal in exchange for arms, munitions, and Western military training. In due course, Western trade agreements were established with the Netherlands (1605), Great Britain (1612), Denmark (1621), and France (1662). But as we shall see, Ayutthaya's increasing willingness to open itself to the commercial incursion of Western powers was not without consequences.

Throughout the sixteenth to the eighteenth centuries, the Burmese replaced the Khmer as the new Siamese nemesis. In

1538, a border dispute initiated Ayutthaya's first war with Burma. Other wars followed in 1549, 1563, and 1569. Two of these conflicts warrant closer attention.

In 1549, Maha Chakraphat became king of Ayutthaya. When Chakraphat was only six months into his twenty-year reign, Burma attacked Ayutthaya once again. Led by King Tabengshweti, the Burmese invaders greatly outnumbered the Siamese defenders. Mounted on elephants, the two opposing kings came face to face in combat. Unknown to Chakraphat, his consort, Queen Suryothai, having donned the clothing and armor of a soldier, mounted an elephant and joined her husband on the battlefield. Seeing that Tabengshweti was gaining the upper hand over Chakraphat, Suryothai drove her elephant between them and was herself slain by Tabengshweti. According to legend, this selfless act of devotion so moved and ashamed the Burmese king that he ceased fighting and withdrew his army. Today, Suryothai is revered as one of Thailand's greatest heroines. Her ashes are enshrined in a *chedi,* or reliquary, at Suan Luang Sob-sawan Temple, located in the modern province of Ayut-thaya. Maha Chakraphat died of natural causes in 1569, and Prince Mahin, a considerably weaker ruler, ascended the throne.

The war of 1569 was the result of petty jealousy within the Siamese court that ultimately led to treachery. Two Ayut-thayan princes, Praya Chakri and Maha Thammaracha, nego-tiated with King Burengnong of Burma, and through an elab-orate ruse essentially handed Ayutthaya over to him. Ayutthaya was overrun and fell under the control of Burma for the next fifteen years. The Burmese placed Thammaracha on the Ayutthayan throne as little more than a puppet king. His nine-year-old son, Naresuan, was taken to Burma, more or less as a hostage, in order to insure that Thammaracha would continue to comply with Burmese policies. Thinking that Naresuan was well-indoctrinated and controllable, the Burmese king allowed Naresuan to return to Ayutthaya when he was sixteen years old. But to the surprise of everyone, Naresuan organized his own army, maintained a low profile, and waited for the right moment to proclaim Siamese independence. In 1584, Naresuan led his army against the Burmese and drove them out of Ayutthaya. "Naresuan the Great" reigned as King of Ayutthaya from 1590 to 1605.

As noted earlier, commercial trade pacts between Ayutthaya and the West multiplied during the seventeenth century. By the reign of King Narai (1656–1688), Ayutthaya was the shining star of Southeast Asia. There had been nothing like it since the days of the Khmer kingdom of Angkor, except that Ayutthaya had become a truly cosmopolitan city. But by 1675, Ayutthaya naively began its way down a road that led to disaster.

Most every educated Thai is familiar with the story of "Phaulkon the Greek." Phaulkon was an opportunistic European adventurer whose travels brought him to Ayutthaya in 1675, where he more or less ingratiated himself into the very heart of the royal Siamese court. In a short period of time, Phaulkon became fluent in the Thai language and conversant in Ayutthaya's political and economic network. Starting out as an official translator, Phaulkon worked his way up to become the favorite adviser and confidant of King Narai himself. In order to boost Ayutthaya's trading position and advantage, Phaulkon began to orchestrate circumstances that would pit one Western power against another. In some cases he would grant special favor to "interlopers," freelance Western traders who operated outside the jurisdiction of the officially recognized trading companies. In time, Phaulkon's unofficial maneuverings made him a very wealthy man, and the extravagance of his personal lifestyle began to rival that of the king. Nevertheless, his shrewdness and insight into Ayutthaya's diplomatic and economic affairs lifted him up to an advisory position in the Siamese government that to this day has never been equaled by any foreigner.

Phaulkon's demise was brought about when he attempted

to convert the Siamese king to Christianity. But even this was a mere façade that he played out for the benefit of the French Jesuit mission in Ayutthaya. Not a particularly spiritual man himself, Phaulkon feigned his theological allegiance in order to marry a Japanese-Portuguese Roman Catholic. With the Jesuits behind him, Phaulkon began to initiate philosophical/theological discussions with the royal court on the merits of the Christian faith versus those of Buddhism. As one would expect, the scene scandalized the royal court. This incident, combined with the ever-imposing presence of Western trade in all shapes and forms, culminated in revolt from the military sector of the Ayutthayan government. When Narai fell mysteriously ill and died in 1688, rumors of Western conspiracy emerged that pointed particularly toward Phaulkon, as well as the French mission. In the power struggle that resulted, a military leader named Phra Petraya assumed control and expelled both the French mission and the French trading company from Ayutthaya. He then turned his wrath on Phaulkon, who was imprisoned and executed later that same year. Though a minimal Western trade presence was allowed to remain in Ayutthaya, Phra Petraya's reign as king initiated a period of virtual isolation from the West that lasted until the mid-nineteenth century.

The period that followed Narai's reign is considered to be Ayutthaya's golden age; but it may be more accurate to refer to it as a swan song. During the reign of Boromakot (1733–1758), the cultural focus turned inward. Royal patronage was concentrated on artistic and architectural projects, as opposed to territorial expansion and further trade development. But this inwardly directed agenda blinded Ayutthaya to the threat that was building to the northwest, not from any Western power, but from Burma. After almost two hundred years, Burma's 1584 defeat at the hands of Naresuan the Great was perhaps regarded by the Siamese as a mere footnote from another time. But the Burmese memory was not so remote. The invasion began in 1763, and the Burmese forces swept across Northwestern Thailand. They reached the walls of Ayutthaya in 1766, and in April 1767, after a fifteen-month-long siege, the Burmese overran Ayutthaya, destroying virtually everything in sight. Thousands were killed, soldiers and civilians alike, and the city was burned to the ground. Buddhist temples were torn down and stripped of their gold, and even images of the Buddha were melted down. Along with the immense human toll, an incalculable repository of literary and artistic work was lost forever.

As a concluding comment on the Ayutthaya period, it should be noted that though Sukhothai is most certainly embraced as the classical standard by which "Thai style" is evaluated even today, Ayutthaya is nevertheless regarded as the "golden age" of Siamese cultural expansion and international exposure. Due to its expansion over a period of control that lasted for over four centuries, much of Ayutthaya's cultural character was "imported"—assimilated through the annexation of other kingdoms, and then more or less reshaped in a Siamese mold. Thus, in the same manner that earlier Southeast Asian culture was "Indianized," perhaps it can be said that under Ayutthayan control, certain cultural characteristics that were originally Khmer, Burmese, Mon, or even Chinese became "Siam-ized" (recall how the classic Sukhothai Buddha image had its beginnings as a gift from the monks of Ceylon); but the ever-volatile Ayutthaya-Khmer connection provides us with an example that has a rather interesting twist to it. When Ayutthaya conquered Angkor in 1431, much of the Khmer population—some ninety thousand—were carried off into slavery. This number included poets, musicians, dancers, and actors. The classical Thai dance-drama begins with this importation. In the eighteenth and nineteenth centuries, Siamese performers moved back to Cambodia and revived the Khmer theater and dance traditions that existed there some six hundred years before. Thus the Thai theater and dance tradition began with an importation of Khmer origin, and the renewed Cambodian tradition was resurrected through a re-importation of what was originally theirs to begin with, but shaped, evolved, and modified by Siamese artists during its six hundred-year residency at Ayutthaya. It can therefore be said today that the National Theater of Thailand and the Royal Cambodian Ballet, both world-famous performing arts traditions, are inextricably linked to one another.

It is worth noting that the relationship between Thailand and Cambodia continues to have its moments of tension, and in some cases, it borders on the absurd. In January 2003, a Thai television actress who was visiting Cambodia's capital city of Phnom Penh reportedly commented during an interview that the famous Khmer ruins of Angkor Wat rightfully belong to Thailand, apparently because of Ayutthaya's victory over the Khmer Empire in 1431. The alleged comments were heavily embellished by a local radio talk show host. As a result, riots broke out in Phnom Penh, and the Thai Embassy and other Thai-related offices were burned and looted. Thai embassy staff and businesspersons fled to the airport and had to be evacuated back to Thailand. Amid much anger and finger-pointing on both sides, diplomatic ties were temporarily severed. But by the end of the first week of February, tensions eased as apologies and financial remunerations were exchanged.

The Thonburi Interval (1767–1782)

As devastating as it was, the destruction of Ayutthaya was not a permanent setback for the Siamese. Just before Ayutthaya's fall, Taksin, a provincial governor from Western Siam, fled to the southeast with five hundred soldiers. Within a period of seven months, they regrouped and returned to face the Burmese garrison at Ayutthaya. Taksin's army defeated the Burmese, and they reclaimed the capital. There was, of course, little there to reclaim. Ayutthaya lay in ruins, and its location was determined to be dangerously open to future

Burmese aggression. Taksin therefore took a conservative stance and moved his capital southward to Thonburi, a small town on the west side of the Chao Praya River, just opposite present-day Bangkok (which at that time was little more than a small trading village).

As his new agenda of rebuilding the Siamese kingdom proved to be more administrative than military, Taksin turned his army over to his brothers, Chao Praya Chakri and Chao Praya Sarasih. Under their command, the Siamese recovered much of their former territory and more. Not only did they reclaim Chiang Mai from the Burmese in the north, they also conducted campaigns that brought much of Cambodia and Laos under Siamese control. Chao Praya Chakri is particularly remembered for his Laotian campaign of 1779, during which he took possession of the celebrated Emerald Buddha, which was eventually enshrined in Bangkok's famous Wat Pra Gaow, where it remains today as Thailand's most venerated Buddhist relic (for a more in-depth account of the origins of the Emerald Buddha, see "Wat Pra Gaow" in the Significant People, Places, and Events section of this book).

Meanwhile, the weight of kingship seemed to be taking its toll on Taksin. His mental capacity began to deteriorate. Taksin believed himself to be the earthly reincarnation of the Buddha. He demanded that monks and government officials acknowledge his divinity; if they refused, he had them imprisoned. As is usually the case in these situations, a military coup ensued, and Taksin was taken into custody. And in accordance with the unique Siamese convention of supreme justice that we noted earlier, Taksin was "given the velvet sack" in 1782. The crown was offered to his brother, Chao Praya Chakri, who ascended the throne under the name of Ramathibodi, later known as Rama I. (The name Chao Praya is a royal title that refers to the highest rank of conferred nobility; the Chao Praya River was named after him.) "Rama's" reign (1782–1809) initiated the current Chakri Dynasty of the Rattanakosin (or Bangkok) period.

The Rattanakosin (Bangkok) Period (1782–present)

Still wary of the possibility of future Burmese aggression, King Rama I moved his capital to the eastern side of the Chao Praya River. There he began the transformation of the little trading village of Bang Makok into Grungtayp Mahanakawn (etc.), or Bangkok. The king's wariness proved prophetic, for in 1785, the Burmese once again attempted to invade the Siamese capital. But the Burmese army—one hundred thousand strong—was repelled by the Siamese forces. Never again would Burma pose any significant threat to Siam's sovereignty.

In an attempt to emulate the magnificent architecture of Ayutthaya, Rama I began construction of Bangkok's famous Grand Palace. He also created innovative new laws, such as *Tra Sahm Duang,* or "The Law of the Three Seals," that dealt with the interrelationship of military, administrative, and economic affairs. And, as yet another example of the assimilation of Indian and Siamese culture, Rama I is also credited with translating the ancient Indian literary epic the *Ramayana* ("the Glory of Ram") into Thai verse. Known in Thailand as the *Ramakien,* the Thai version is in essence the same as its Indian predecessor, but it has a distinctly Thai flavor to it. The *Ramayana* is so famous that virtually every nation in Southeast Asia has a literary and/or dramatic version of this story, each version reflecting its unique cultural perspective. For more about the *Ramakien,* see Chapter Three.

Chakri's son, Pra Puttalaytia, reigned as Rama II from 1809 to 1824. Favored with an era of relative peace and stability, Rama II was able to concentrate much of his attention on aesthetic and literary endeavors. For example, he funded the construction of one of Bangkok's most famous temple complexes, Wat Arun ("Temple of the Dawn"). And, following his father's literary lead, Rama II created the first dramatic version of the Ramakien. Originally restricted to royal court audiences, excerpts from the Ramakien are performed today by the National Theater of Thailand for audiences throughout the kingdom and abroad.

Pra Nahngklao, the son of one of Rama II's consorts, reigned as Rama III from 1824 to 1851, because the actual crown prince, Mongkut, had just entered the Buddhist priesthood, an endeavor that took precedence over such secular matters as political rule. Pra Nangklao was a devout Buddhist who supported Mongkut's monastic endeavors. With the Khmer and the Burmese empires no longer in the picture, Pra Nahngklao saw Western economic and colonial expansion as the major threat to Siam's sovereignty. But even though he resisted commercial advances from both Britain and the United States, Pra Nahngklao allowed for the establishment of a Baptist mission post in Bangkok in 1833. In addition to promoting a Buddhist openness to other religious traditions, this move had certain technological advantages as well: the Baptist mission introduced smallpox vaccinations to the Siamese population, as well as the printing press.

Pra Nahngklao's successor was the aforementioned Crown Prince Mongkut, who reigned as Rama IV (1851–1868). Having spent twenty-seven years as a Buddhist monk in temples throughout Bangkok, Mongkut was an exceptional scholar. He had mastered Latin, English, geography, Western history, and astronomy. While his research and study had opened a huge window to the outside world, his monastic life gifted him with a profound humility. Mongkut regarded himself not as a devaraja but as an ordinary human being whose lifelong appetite for learning would lead Siam into the modern age.

Unlike his half-brother who reigned before him, Mongkut recognized the fact that Siam's only hope for continued growth—and independence—was to be found in developing friendly diplomatic and trade relationships with numerous Western powers. He actively pursued relations with several European nations as well as the United States. But he favored no single nation over another; by shrewdly playing them off of each other, Mongkut succeeded in preserving Siam's neutrality and independence in a world in which virtually every other Southeast Asian nation—for example, Indochina (France), Burma and Malaya (Britain), and Indonesia (Holland)—had become a colonial subject of the West.

In direct relationship to the establishment of international diplomatic and trade relationships, a particularly important event for the reign of King Mongkut and for Thai history overall was the signing of the Bowring Treaty in 1855. It was named after Sir John Bowring, the British envoy who traveled from Hong Kong to Siam to negotiate the opening of Siam's formal trade relationships with the West. In this treaty, Mongkut conceded a certain degree of sovereignty by allowing Britain to have extraterritoriality rights over its citizens living in Siam, as well as the removal of all restrictions on trade, such as fixed duties and taxes from which the kingdom had derived considerable income. But as noted earlier, he was very careful to preserve and ensure Siam's independence so as not to fall prey to Western colonization. And over time, the loss of such restrictions was more than covered by the increase in trade volume. For example, the number of ships coming to Siam from Singapore (the primary conduit for Siam's trade with the West) increased from 146 vessels in 1855 to 302 vessels in 1862, and the total value of annual trade rose from 5.6 million baht in 1850 to 10 million baht in 1868. This formal opening of Siam to international trade relationships with the West can be regarded as Siam's first step in the process of becoming a modern nation-state.

Mongkut also introduced a variety of social and political reforms. Though not abolishing slavery altogether, he did much to improve slave conditions. He created Siam's first mint for the standardization of Siamese coinage. He studied and promoted scientific approaches to technical problem-solving. Mongkut also supported Christian missions and hired Western tutors to teach English to his children.

Of course, one cannot broach the subject of King Mongkut and Western tutors without acknowledging the famous Anna

H.R.H. King Mongkut (Rama IV), 1851–1868. (Library of Congress)

Leonowens (1834–1914), who worked as a governess and a tutor for the royal family from 1862–1867. The traditional Western account of Anna and the nineteenth-century Siamese court of Rama IV is, by most contemporary assessments, a curious blend of fact and fiction in all its literary, theatrical, and cinematic dimensions. Although not everyone is acquainted with Leonowens's autobiographical account (1870), or with Margaret Landon's novelized adaptation (1944) that brought Anna into the public eye, most westerners are quite familiar with one or more of the stage and screen versions of her story (e.g., *Anna and the King of Siam*, a 1946 film; *The King and I*, a Broadway play in 1951 and a film in 1956; and *Anna and the King*, a 1999 film). From the Thai perspective, most of the events as written and presented simply never took place; they are regarded as the fanciful products of romantic delusion, literary imagination, and, of course, creative stage and screen writing. Whereas Leonowens wrote that she openly took issue with the king on slavery and other human rights abuses that she encountered in Siam, we are told that Siamese royal records give no indication that she functioned in any advisory capacity to Mongkut, or that she had access to the workings of the inner court. But in deference to Leonowens, one must at least consider the possibility that, given the patriarchal nature of Siamese culture at this time, it is very unlikely that such a thing would be acknowledged in "official" records even if she did have such access. And out of a profound respect for the monarchy, most Thais (but not all) categorically dismiss the suggestion that there was any familiar relationship between them. At the same time, one must also understand that Anna Leonowens regarded her world through nineteenth-century Eurocentric eyes: she saw what she was predisposed to see, and no more. But because they present what is regarded as a disrespectful image of the revered King Rama IV, these books and films are banned in Thailand today. As one Thai historian put it, "Whatever have been the impressions of Western people about the play and the film, they should be definitely looked upon as nothing more than a kind of entertainment cleverly arranged to draw money from those who wish to be amused" (Syamananda 1988, 124). But placing theatrical presentations aside, Leonowens's and Landon's literary works are still worth reading, for they do serve as interesting expressions of Western Orientalism, which has taken its toll even on the most culturally sensitive westerner. Coined by author Edward Said, *Orientalism* is a term that refers to a kind of cultural mindset that the colonizing West has traditionally held toward Asian cultures. In the seventeenth through nineteenth centuries, "the Orient" was regarded as separate, backward, and eccentric, as well as sensual, exotic, and dangerous. But Asian cultures were also believed to be rather passive, as though they were simply waiting for westerners to come over and enlighten them. Oriental rulers were regarded as little more than brutal despots—but at the same time treated as petulant "little boys" who needed an authority figure to civilize them. In a strange way, Anna Leonowens is portrayed not only as the bearer of the light of empirical reason (she is "scientific" and therefore called "Sir") but also as the mother figure whose task it is to lovingly but firmly transform the king of Siam into "a gentleman." Despite the fact that Siam never fell victim to the oppression of Western colonialism, Anna nevertheless served as a metaphor for the colonial consciousness that presumed that Western enlightenment—technology, religion, and so on—was the only hope of salvation for the Orient (as long as the Western parent figure was always nearby to keep an authoritative eye on them). The following excerpt from Leonowens's account is indicative of this patronizing attitude. Upon being asked by the collective voice of the wives of the Siamese prime minister "if I should not like to be the wife of the prince, their lord, rather than that of the terrible Chow-che-witt ['the Lord of Life,' i.e., King Mongkut]," Leonowens writes:

Seeing it impossible to rid myself of them, I promised to answer their question, on condition that they would leave me for that day. Immediately all eyes were fixed upon me. "The prince, your lord, and the king, your Chow-che-witt, are pagans," I said. "An English, that is a Christian, woman would rather be put to the torture, chained and dungeoned for life, or suffer a death the slowest and most painful you Siamese know, than to be the wife of either." (Leonowens 1870, 21)

Even so, along with her oft-expressed outrage with slavery, patriarchalism, and absolute monarchy, Leonowens could also articulate considerable awe and at least a modicum of cultural sensitivity as she beheld the wonder of Wat Pra Gaow, or the Temple of the Emerald Buddha:

As often as my thought reverts to this inspiring shrine, reposing in its lonely loveliness amid the shadows and the silence of its consecrated groves, I cannot find it in my heart to condemn, however illusive the object, but rather I rejoice to admire and applaud the bent of that devotion which could erect so proud and beautiful a fane (temple or church) in the midst of moral surroundings so ignoble and unlovely, a spiritual remembrance perhaps older and truer than paganism, ennobling the pagan mind with the idea of an architectural Sabbath, so to speak, such as a heathen may purely enjoy and a Christian may not wisely despise. (Leonowens 1870, 53)

As far as Margaret Landon's 1944 literary interpretation of Anna Leonowens's experience is concerned, she herself remarked, "If I were asked to give the fabric content of the book I should say that it is 'seventy-five per cent fact and twenty-five per cent fiction based on fact'" (Landon 1944, 391).

Finally, many of us recall the late actor Yul Brynner's famous stage and screen portrayals of King Mongkut. In the final scene, he is shown on his deathbed, due to a self-imposed starvation brought on by a violent confrontation with Anna (again, the king portrayed as "the pouting little boy" even unto death!). Surrounded by a well-arranged tableau made up of Anna and the royal children, he peacefully slips away into death. This scene is pure fiction created for the stage and screen. The truth is that Mongkut succumbed to a bout with malaria, contracted while he was on a scientific expedition to view a solar eclipse in 1868. Astronomy having been one of his favorite subjects, it is also worth noting that it was an eclipse that he himself successfully mapped and predicted. And furthermore, Leonowens departed Siam in 1867, a year before Mongkut's death (as she herself reports in her account).

It was noted earlier that official Siamese royal records give no indication that Leonowens functioned in any advisory capacity to Mongkut, or that she had access to the workings of the inner court. But is this, in fact, the case? In a recent article published in *Silapawatanatahm* (Kreuatawng, January 1, 2004), it was revealed that in 2003, eight letters written by King Mongkut were uncovered in a royal library. Addressed to Anna Leonowens, these letters openly discuss a variety of social and political issues. One letter in particular, dated May 12, 1864, deals with the moral question of slavery and, more specifically, the welfare of two female slaves whose freedom Anna was seeking to secure. The language style in which the letters are written is not the formal style of a superior to a subordinate, but rather the familiar style of one who is on an equal social footing with his/her correspondent (in the Thai language, style and word usage indicate the social status of the person with whom one is corresponding). What is even more interesting is that these letters are stamped with official file numbers, which would indicate that they had already been seen in any one of three separate years—1919, 1921, and 1922—during which Mongkut's records were organized. Furthermore, the letters were found in the archival records of Mongkut's son, Chulalongkawn, who became the next king (see photo on page 49). Were these letters simply lost, or were they intentionally removed from the official files and hidden in Chulalongkawn's archives, for fear of placing Mongkut in a bad light? In either case, their very existence would seem to support Leonowens's account of her discussions and/or confrontations with Mongkut regarding slavery and human rights. Pending royal approval from H. R. H. King Pumipohn Adunyadayt, Thailand's current reigning monarch, these letters will hopefully be published at some time in the near future.

Mongkut was succeeded by his oldest son, Chulalongkawn, who reigned as Rama V from 1868 to 1910. Of all past kings, Chulalongkawn is the most celebrated and revered. In Thai homes or businesses today, one will almost assuredly find a portrait of Chulalongkawn alongside those of the current king and queen of Thailand. Building on the foundations laid by his father, it was Chulalongkawn who once and for all transformed Siam from a medieval kingdom into a modern nation-state. Like his father before him, he successfully maintained equilibrium among foreign trade interests, whereby he was able to avoid the colonialist threat that had befallen so many of Siam's neighbors. Chulalongkawn was also the first Thai monarch to travel to Europe. In turn, he sent Thai students to study in Western nations, including his own son who attended Oxford University in England. It is worth noting that while Chulalongkawn was a young crown prince, he was a student of the previously mentioned Anna Leonowens. It is known that he maintained contact with her in England following his father's death in 1868, and even came to visit her some thirty years later, in 1897.

Chulalongkawn did much to develop Siam from within as well. He established the first postal and telegraph systems. He created government ministries of health and education, which included the building of many new hospitals and schools. But most important, Chulalongkawn worked for the elimination of human slavery. So as not to create a major social upheaval all at once, he decreed at his initial coronation that all persons born into his reign would be free. By 1905, the institution of slavery in Siam had been abolished altogether (he was apparently a good student of Anna Leonowens; could this be why the aforementioned letters of

H.R.H. King Chulalongkawn (Rama V), 1868–1910. (Hulton Archive/Getty)

his father Mongkut were mysteriously found among his archival records?). Chulalongkawn died on October 23, 1910. Chulalongkawn Day, one of modern Thailand's most important national holidays, is celebrated each year on this date.

Chulalongkawn's Oxford-educated son, Vajiravudh, reigned

as Rama VI from 1910 to 1925. Highlights of his tenure include the founding in 1917 of Chulalongkawn University as a memorial to his father. Originally a civil service college, it grew to become Thailand's most prestigious institution of higher learning. In that same year, Siam adopted a new national flag, which continues to fly over Thailand today. It consists of five horizontal stripes, of red, white, blue, white, and red. Red, white, and blue represent the nation, Buddhism, and the monarchy, respectively. In 1918 the king sent an expeditionary force to Europe to assist the Allies in the final battles of World War I. This gesture of support helped to solidify Siam's ongoing relationships with its European trade partners. Vajiravudh was also instrumental in founding the Boy Scouts Organization of Siam in 1911, and in 1913 he decreed that all citizens of Siam would adopt surnames (as was the case in many traditional cultures, persons until then were identified by a first name, coupled with the father's name or the name of the village in which one resided).

But Vajiravudh's reign was the context for significant political metamorphosis as well. In 1911 he uncovered a plot to overthrow his government. Instigated by a small group of military officers and civil servants, the attempted coup was one of the first signs that, no matter how paternal a king's reign might be, absolute monarchy was simply not compatible with the democratic spirit of a twentieth-century nation-state. And so, despite the fact that Vajiravudh was most magnanimous about the entire affair (the plotters were sentenced only to minimal prison terms), the seeds of change had been sown.

The Beginning of the Constitutional Monarchy

Vajiravudh died in 1925, but he left no male heir to the throne. His younger brother, Prajadhipok, was chosen to ascend the throne as Rama VII and reigned from 1925 to 1935. Trained primarily as a military officer, Prajadhipok never had the opportunity—nor did he foresee the need—to develop the administrative knowledge necessary for such a responsibility. His reign, therefore, was not a smooth one. Like the rest of the world, Siam was suffering from the economic effects of the Great Depression of the 1930s; Prajadhipok was forced to cut salaries and raise taxes, thereby alienating many within both civilian and military circles. And so, on June 24, 1932, seven hundred years of absolute monarchy came to an end in a bloodless coup, which had, in effect, begun two decades before.

The year 1932 saw the appointment of Siam's first prime minister, Manopakawn Nitithada, while Prajadhipok remained on the throne as Siam's first constitutional monarch. But when his disputes with the government over royal prerogatives versus constitutional limitations reached a stalemate, Prajadhipok was forced to abdicate in March 1935. But he did so graciously, keeping the welfare and interests of the Siamese people at the forefront.

The National Assembly in Bangkok subsequently offered the throne to Prajadhipok's nephew, Ananda Mahidohn. Not only was Mahidohn studying overseas in Switzerland at the time, but he was also only ten years old. Therefore, a council of regents was assigned to rule in his stead until he completed his studies and came of age.

After 1932, the king was no longer a major component in decision making or government policy, although he continued to be a very strong symbol of moral authority and national identity among the people. In light of this, as well as the fact that the young Mahidohn was still in Switzerland, the 1930s proved to be an extremely volatile period in Siamese politics. Civilian bureaucrats led by left-wing intellectual Pridi Panomyong, and a military alliance headed by Phibul Songkram, competed for political control of Siam. Prime Minister Manopakawn more or less mediated the tension between them. Power balances shifted until 1938, when, following Manopakawn's retirement, Phibul's military-based alliance took control of Siam. Being a very strong nationalist, Phibul announced in 1939 that the nation's name—Siam—was now Thailand: *Brahtayt Thai,* or "Land of the Free."

On December 8, 1941, the day following Japan's attack on Pearl Harbor in Hawaii, Japanese forces invaded Thailand at nine different points along the southern peninsula. On the official level, the Thai government under Phibul was forced into collaboration with the Japanese, even to the point of drafting a formal declaration of war against the Allies. Thailand more or less retained its sovereignty by allowing the Japanese to have unfettered northward access to Myanmar (Burma), setting the stage for the construction of the infamous "Death Railway" and the River Kwaa Bridge in Kanchanaburi Province in Western Thailand. As slave laborers, untold thousands of Allied (primarily British and Australian) POWs and Southeast Asians lost their lives—as the British put it, "a life for every 'sleeper'" (a slang term for a railroad tie).

In the face of British and French objections following the Japanese surrender, the United States dismissed the Thai declaration of war, as it was never formally delivered and was quite obviously a result of Japanese coercion. Also, the United States had maintained an ongoing relationship with a Thai underground resistance movement throughout the war, a movement that was led by Phibol Songkram's political rival, Pridi Panomyong.

Within a few months of the Japanese surrender in 1945, the then twenty-year-old Ananda Mahidohn returned to Thailand to take his seat on the throne. For the first time in some ten years, Thailand held its first democratic election, and a new civilian government was put into place; for although Phibol Songkram was never arrested or punished for his collaboration with the Japanese, he nevertheless was forced to resign following the Japanese surrender in 1945. The new prime minister was none other than Pridi Panomyong, the underground resistance leader. But this renewed stability was short-lived: on June 9, 1946, King Ananda Mahidohn, Rama VIII, was found dead in his bedroom with a gunshot wound to his head. Though conjectures and suspicions abounded—accident, suicide, and even murder—no truly definitive explanation for his death has ever been determined. Due to the unique nature of the situation and its victim, the six-year investigation was hampered and inefficient from the start. Certain bodyguards were taken into custody; they were tried, acquitted, retried, convicted, and eventually executed in 1954. Known for his antiroyalist positions, Prime Minister Pridi Panomyong was believed by many to be, at the very least, morally responsible. Within three months of Mahidohn's death in 1946, he quietly resigned and went into a self-imposed exile. It is generally held today that Mahidohn had been examining or cleaning a .45-caliber automatic pistol that discharged accidentally. But out of a profound respect for the institution of the Thai monarchy, his death remains a mystery about which few if any Thais will offer comment.

Following Mahidohn's death, the kingship of Thailand was offered to his younger brother, nineteen-year-old Pumipohn Adunyadayt, who ascended the throne as Rama IX, the present king of the Chakri dynasty, and Thailand's longest-reigning monarch (1946–present). Throughout a reign of almost sixty years, His Royal Highness King Pumipohn and his family have worked for the welfare of Thailand and its people in innumerable ways. We will take a closer look at the current royal family and their vital role in Thai society in Chapter Three.

The Constitutional Monarchy since 1946

Since the coup of 1932 that transformed it from an absolute to a constitutional monarchy, Thailand has been governed by a long succession of prime ministers whose appointments have most often been the products of military-based coalitions, with one or two brief periods of civilian-based rule. These governments have been built by bloodless coups, shattered once or twice by bloody revolts, and, not unlike most any modern nation-state, tainted now and again with internal corruption. They have been influenced by regional events of profound proportions, such as China's fall to Mao Tse Tung in 1949, France's loss of Indochina to Ho Chi Minh in 1954, and the ensuing tragedy of the U.S. presence in Vietnam that lasted until 1975, as well as the horror of the Khmer Rouge in Cambodia throughout the late 1970s. Combined with a deeply instilled sense of Thai identity and the moral strength of the monarchy, the successive Thai governments through-out the mid-to-late twentieth century have traditionally main-tained a radically anticommunist stance in response to these changes. At the same time, however, Thailand's geographic proximity to these unstable regions led to the development of numerous procommunist insurgency groups over the years, particularly in rural border areas where poorer economic con-ditions were conducive to their growth. We will now take a closer look at some highlights of these late-twentieth-century governments and the events that shaped them.

Following Pridi's resignation in 1946, Phibul Songkram, who had been in internal exile since the end of World War II, reemerged to take the reins of power as prime minister once again. His eleven-year tenure was a tumultuous one, as it saw the advent of communist rule in both China (1949) and Indochina (1954), and the communist invasion of South Korea (1950). The fear of communist insurgency spread throughout the middle and upper classes of the Thai popula-tion, reaching a level of paranoia not unlike the early Cold War era in the West. Chinese residents in Thailand were tar-geted and monitored, and the activities of Chinese businesses, schools, and social organizations were either curtailed or closed down altogether. Recognized as a bulwark of anticom-munism in the region, Thailand became the recipient of sub-stantial financial aid from the United States, which feared that all of Southeast Asia would fall to communism like "a snake of dominoes" if a stand were not made. Once Ho Chi Minh drove the French from Indochina in 1954, the relationship between Thailand and the United States grew exponentially, particularly during the Vietnam War era (1960–1975).

By the mid-1950s, Phibul attempted to introduce some democratic reforms that were intended to ease fears and reestablish a broad constituency of support for himself. He allowed resident Chinese businesses, schools, and organizations to operate unrestricted once again; granted greater freedom to the news media; and paved the way for democratic elections in 1957. By its very nature, a free election opens the door to contenders. Enter General Sarit Thanarat, a rising favorite among the military elite. Even though Phibul eked out a questionable victory in the 1957 election, he was forced to flee after a bloodless military coup placed Sarit in power. Still maintaining a strong anticommunist stance, Sarit undid any reforms that Phibul had attempted to initiate. The news media were controlled and monitored, constitutional process was suspended, and political parties were outlawed. But even under this condition of virtual martial law, Thailand did recover some political and economic stability in the face of the regional upheavals that surrounded them. And for good or for ill, adding to this sense of stability was the growing presence of the U.S. military, whom Sarit had invited and encouraged to establish bases.

During the Vietnam War era, the American presence in Thailand was massive. Throughout the 1960s and early 1970s, Thailand received millions of dollars in financial aid from the United States in order to support the tens of thousands of U.S. military personnel that were stationed there. Thailand's economy blossomed—new jobs, new construction projects, new highways, and increased industrial output. In Northeastern Thailand, Khorat served as a major U.S. airbase, whose bomber groups conducted daily missions over North Vietnam, and Bangkok became flooded with American servicepersons and U.S. dollars. But along with those dollars came American culture, fashion, music, and morality. Many Thais saw their own culture being turned on its head, their identities lost amid a growing economic dependency on the American presence. The pros and cons of this state of affairs led to a rise in political sentiments on both the left and the right. Normally avoiding such "worldly" issues, even Buddhist monks began to take political stances against the cooperative war effort, and young Thais—particularly students—became attracted to the grassroots ideologies of communist and socialist organizations.

General Sarit died in 1963. He was replaced by his deputy commander, Thanom Kittikachorn. Though Thanom maintained martial law, he also encouraged democratic reforms and even approved a new constitution in 1968. General elections were held in 1969. But change is never instantaneous; due to internal conflicts within Thanom's government and an overextended optimism on the part of a public that was perhaps expecting too much too soon, the project failed. In addition to this, a growing number of university students were being exposed to the communist teachings of internal grassroots insurgency movements that, although originating in the border regions of the north and northeast, had made themselves known among the university populations of Bangkok. By 1973, Thanom had forsaken his reforms and returned his own government to the military-based rule with which he had begun.

The public outcry against Thanom's return to military rule was largely ignored until mid-1973, when government authorities overreacted to a relatively minor incident that sparked massive student-led demonstrations numbering in the tens of thousands. In June 1973, government authorities discovered an underground student-run newspaper at Ramkahmheng University. Highly critical of the government, it was shut down. But the government overreacted and went on to force the university to expel those responsible. This action resulted in massive student demonstrations throughout Bangkok. As is often the case in such tenuous circumstances, miscommunications and misunderstandings abounded among military forces, police, and students alike. Demonstrations erupted into riots over the next few months, and on October 14, 1973, more than four hundred people—mostly students—lost their lives in the ensuing chaos. October 14 is still commemorated each year as *Wan Maha Wippasok* ("the most tragic day").

Following that terrible day, King Pumipohn himself entered into the arena as a mediator and advised Thanom and his staff to resign and leave the country. After they wisely took his advice, the king went on television and announced that he had appointed Sanya Dharmasakti, the rector of Thammasat University, as head of a new civilian-based interim government.

A new constitution was ratified in 1974. In that January's general election, no less than twenty-two separate political parties vied for mandates. In February, Seni Pramoj (pronounced "pramoht") was elected prime minister by a three-party coalition. But within two weeks, his younger brother, Kukrit, replaced Seni when the majority of party representatives refused to support his agenda. Although primarily a politician, Kukrit Pramoj (1911–1995) also gained notoriety as a prolific novelist, poet, and screenwriter. Some older westerners may be familiar with him as well, for he played a supporting role in the 1963 film *The Ugly American*, starring Marlon Brando as a U.S. ambassador caught up in the political struggles of a fictitious Southeast Asian country. Strangely enough, Kukrit's role is that of prime minister of the portrayed nation.

However, in light of the 1975 communist victories in Vietnam, Cambodia, and Laos, Kukrit's strong leftist policies were soon deemed unacceptable by the more conservative parliamentary majority. In March 1975, for example, Kukrit not only met with Mao Tse Tung of China but also gave diplomatic recognition to the Khmer Rouge in Cambodia. By April 1976, the more politically moderate Seni was once again elected prime minister. But just as Kukrit had faced strong pressure from the moderates, Seni was challenged by intense pressure from the left, in the form of student radicalism and procommunist insurgency groups.

In late 1976, elements of the Thai military staged yet another coup and regained control of the government. When it was discovered that former prime minister Thanom had been smuggled back into the country disguised as a Buddhist monk, the resulting outrage and protests led to more university invasions and crackdowns, this time not only by police but by several independent right-wing paramilitary organizations whose members reportedly attacked and killed hundreds of university students. After suffering through the combined chaos of 1973 and 1976, a violence-weary Thai public was more than ready to accept any form of rule that would bring stability and order, no matter how authoritarian it might be. Soon thereafter, Thanin Kraivichien was appointed prime minister. In response to the recent events, his rule was highly repressive: martial law was reinstated, newspaper censorship was renewed and dissident elements were identified and purged from university campuses. Many students and professors fled Bangkok for the countryside, where they aligned themselves with armed communist insurgency groups. But in 1977 Thanin was replaced by a more moderate prime minister, Kriangsak Chomanand, who allowed for the safe return of political dissidents.

After a year of armed border conflicts, Vietnamese forces invaded Cambodia in 1979 and toppled the Khmer Rouge government at Phnom Penh. As the genocidal horrors of the Khmer Rouge regime were revealed to the world, Thailand saw this new territorial expansion of the Communist Vietnamese as a distinct threat. In spite of global outrage toward the Khmer Rouge, Thailand nevertheless supported remnants of the Khmer Rouge forces that had fled across the Cambodian-Thai border. At the time, they were regarded as something of a counter balance against the Vietnam-sponsored communist government in Cambodia.

In 1980, General Prem Tinsulanonda was appointed prime

minister when his predecessor, Kriangsak, was unable to resolve the crisis brought about by the situation in Cambodia, which also included thousands of Cambodian refugees who had fled into Thailand. To the surprise of many, Prem retired from the military as soon as he took on his ministerial responsibilities, thereby symbolically severing himself from the influence and favoritism of the military elite that had shaped so many previous administrations. "Papa Prem," as he was sometimes known, due to his refreshingly paternal manner, accomplished many things during his eight-year rule. With strong support from the royal monarchy, he relaxed censorship of the news media, kept a lid on military spending, and revitalized Thailand's economy. Moreover, Prem succeeded in dismantling the Communist Party in Thailand once and for all, a result of the surrender of the largest of the Communist insurgency forces in Northeastern Thailand. The surrender took place on December 1, 1982, exactly forty years to the day of the Communist Party's formal creation in 1942. Due to his popularity and support among the Thai people, Prem survived two coup attempts. And finally, in stark contrast to the tumultuous political tone of Thailand's twentieth-century history, Prem's most impressive act was his refusal of re-nomination, followed by his voluntary retirement in 1988. Prem Tinsulanonda, the head of Thailand's longest civilian administration, will be remembered as a prime minister with integrity, foresight, and genuine concern for the welfare of his country.

The 1990s saw five more political administrations in Thailand. Following Prem's retirement, Chatichai Choonhavan became prime minister and vowed to continue to work for democratic reform and economic growth. But many within the military ranks became distrustful of Chatichai when he reduced their political role by turning over a significant portion of their traditional responsibilities to civilian government officials. In fact, Thai public sentiment was leaning toward the consensus that the very concept of a military coup d'état was archaic, and that the desire of generals to "play soldier" by treating the government as a battlefield was outdated and even childish. In addition, it was coming to light that many of these military officers had been amassing immense wealth through their political influence for quite some time, even to the point of assuming the CEO positions of major Thai corporations.

In an attempt to regain some of their power losses, elements of the military staged yet another bloodless coup in 1991 that in the following year led to student protests, authoritarian repression, and a loss of life that rivaled the turmoil of the 1970s. Once again, King Pumipohn's intervention was required in order to bring about an end to the violence. The king appointed Anand Panyarachun as an interim prime minister. He was followed by Chuan Leekpai (1992–1995), whose administration was marked by the 1992 ratification of a new constitution which radically limited the military influence and coercion to which Thailand had become accustomed. The elections of July 1995 were the first truly legitimate parliamentary elections in which the military had no power to veto the democratic election of successful candidates.

From an economic standpoint as well, the 1990s were tumultuous years for the Kingdom of Thailand. When I was there in 1991, I was rather struck by the fact that major construction projects seemed to be taking place everywhere I went—office buildings, apartment complexes, and shopping malls. What I did not know is that I was witnessing the early steps down an optimistic but ill-fated road that would lead to disastrous economic consequences for Thailand by 1997. In the 1980s and 1990s, many nations of East and Southeast Asia were gaining international notoriety as "tiger economies," e.g., Pacific Rim/Asian economies that were very aggressive in their pursuit of foreign investment opportunities, real estate/property development, and loan opportunities, both commercial and private. These tiger economies included Japan, Hong Kong, South Korea, Singapore, Thailand, Taiwan, Indonesia, the Philippines, and Malaysia. The interrelationship of Thailand and Japan provides a very illustrative example. In the 1980s, the United States experienced a trade deficit with Japan (the United States was importing much more from Japan than it was exporting to Japan). As a result of this imbalance, the United States was forced to place rigid limits and tariffs on the amount of Japanese imports they would accept. In response to these restrictions, the Japanese began to seek out more profitable investment opportunities elsewhere. One of the nations that caught their attention was Thailand, a nation with desirable natural resources, historically productive agricultural output, an ever-increasing tourist industry, high interest rates, and low labor costs. The rapid influx of foreign currency into the Thai economy produced a collective rise in spending and high-interest loans. In short, Thailand took off on a spending spree, but one that was grounded in foreign currencies—not only Japanese yen but U.S. dollars as well. And, as it is a traditional rule of thumb that real estate investment is a relatively safe and stable sanctuary for one's money, many of these foreign-supported loans went into the massive development projects I described above. But because of this dependence on foreign currency (combined with a sharp drop in export profits), the value of the Thai currency (the baht) fell sharply and was unable to keep up with the necessary rate of repayment. In turn, the majority of these very costly properties were never occupied by tenants. Then, in January 1997, it was revealed that a mid-level property development firm had defaulted on a U.S.$80 million loan. In something of a domino effect, it became rapidly apparent that overextended bank loans and unregulated property development were not simply isolated missteps of a single property firm but the widespread components of a national economic crisis.

When Prime Minister Bonharn Silpaarcha (1995–1997) was unable to manage the crisis, he was forced to resign. Another interim prime minister was hastily appointed, but he lasted a mere eleven months. By August 1997, the International Monetary Fund (IMF) approved a $17.2 billion bailout package for Thailand. A new coalition government was created, and former prime minister Chuan Leekpai was asked to return to office to put the kingdom on the road to recovery. In order for the IMF bailout package to be maintained, the Thai government would have to demonstrate in its annual economic report that revenues had exceeded expenditures by approximately sixty billion baht, an equation made all the more challenging because, by December 1997, the value of the Thai baht had fallen to a record low of forty-five per U.S. dollar (from a pre-crisis norm of approximately twenty-five). Leekpai was forced to make drastic cuts in government spending and to increase public taxes. By January 1998, the recovery process had begun, but not before the Thai baht dropped to an all-time low of fifty-six per U.S. dollar. As of this writing, the value of the baht to the U.S. dollar stands at about forty. Chapter Two will present a more comprehensive and contextual picture of what led to the crisis, how it played out, and the current state of Thailand's economic recovery.

The economic crisis of 1997–1998 also resulted in the adoption of a new (and current) constitution in October 1997. Among its sweeping changes were various reforms in voting practices. In order to discourage "vote-buying," i.e., the practice of special interest groups simply paying Thai citizens for their votes, voting became compulsory. In the senate elections of 2000 and the general elections of 2001, 70 percent of the eligible Thais exercised their right to vote (for more on voting and political structure, see Chapter Three). In addition to reforming election practices, the new constitution also created a "checks and balances" system of independent commissions and organizations to regulate and inspect the affairs of the Thai parliament, human rights issues, and internal political corruption.

Thailand's current prime minister is Thaksin Shinawatra (pronounced "Chinowaht"). Born in 1949, his initial career path was in law enforcement. Thaksin received his masters and doctoral degrees in criminal justice in 1975 and 1978, respectively. He served on the Royal Thai Police Force from 1973 to 1987, when he founded the Shinawatra Computer and Communications Group. As his company grew, he recognized that satellite and wireless communication technologies were the wave of the future. Instead of "renting space" from the existing satellites of other nations, Shinawatra negotiated a twenty-year contract with the Telephone Organization of Thailand (TOT, "the telephone company," the equivalent of what Bell Telephone once was in the United States). This contract enabled him to launch Thailand's first independent communications satellite. Because of his foresight, Thailand's international communications capabilities are now on a par with any in the world. A call to or from Thailand is now cheaper, more rapid, and more efficient than ever before. In 1994, Shinawatra reentered public service as minister of foreign affairs; by 1995 he was deputy prime minister. In 1998 he established his own political party, the *Thai Rahk Thai*, which means "Thais love Thais" (for an overview of the function and nature of Thai political parties, see Chapter Three). Under this banner, Shinawatra became Thailand's prime minister in 2001, the twenty-third since the constitutional monarchy was created in 1932. We will examine his ongoing economic recovery plans more closely in the following chapter.

References

Bangkok Fine Arts Department. *The World Heritage Sukhothai, Sri Satchananalai, and Khampaeng Phet Historical Parks*. Bangkok: Fine Arts Department, n.d.

Chadchaidee, Thanapol. *Essays on Thailand*, 2d ed. Bangkok: D. K. Today, 1994.

CIA World Factbook. 2002. http://www.cia.gov/cia/publications/factbook (accessed May 29, 2003).

Keyes, Charles F. *Thailand: Buddhist Kingdom as Modern Nation State*. Boulder, CO: Westview Press, 1987.

Kreuatawng, Bramin. "Anna Leonowens: Kraiwahlawndawlaa? (Who Says She's Lying?)." *Silapawatanatahm (Art and Culture)*. http://www.matichon.co.th (accessed January 1, 2004).

"A Lady of Substance." *The Nation.* http://www.nationmultimedia.com (accessed January 25, 2004).

Landon, Margaret. *Anna and the King of Siam.* New York: Harper and Row, 1944.

Leonowens, Anna. 1870. *The English Governess at the Siamese Court: Being Recollections of Six Years in the Royal Palace at Bangkok.* Reprint, New York: Oxford University Press, 1988.

Library of Congress. *Thailand: A Country Study.* Washington, DC: Federal Research Division, Library of Congress, 1989.

National Identity Office. *Thailand in the 80s.* Bangkok: National Identity Office, Office of the Prime Minister, 1984.

National Statistical Office of Thailand. "2002 Statistics." http://www.nso.go.th.

Parkes, Carl. *Thailand Handbook,* 3rd ed. Emeryville, CA: Moon Travel Handbooks, 2000.

Publicity Committee for the Ninth Pacific Congress. *Thailand: Past and Present.* Bangkok: Publicity Committee for the Ninth Pacific Science Congress, 1957.

Rawson, Philip. 1967. *The Art of Southeast Asia.* Reprint, London: Thames and Hudson, 1995.

Report of the National Economic and Social Development Board of Thailand. March 2001. http://www.unescap.org/tctd/gt/files/thailand2001.pdf (access requires Acrobat Reader)(accessed January 2004).

Syamananda, Rong. *A History of Thailand,* 6th ed. Bangkok: Thai Watana Panich, 1988.

Time-Life Books. *Southeast Asia: A Past Regained.* Alexandria, VA: Time-Life Books, 1995.

Wyatt, David K. *Thailand: A Short History.* New Haven, CT: Yale University Press, 1984.

CHAPTER TWO
The Economy of Thailand

It is often said that the twentieth century witnessed more changes—social, political, economic, and technological—than the entire previous millennium as a whole. In particular, the decades following World War II saw the surprisingly rapid socioeconomic growth of both colonial and independent nations that were once classified as "underdeveloped." Much of this development was a direct result of the demise of nineteenth- and early twentieth-century colonialism, coupled with the diverse opportunities of newly gained independence. And although it is a nation that has never been colonized, Thailand was no less a party to both the benefits and the deficits of industrialization and other forms of economic development. As noted in Chapter One, the Vietnam War years (1960–1975) afforded Thailand myriad economic opportunities from the United States, particularly in the development of basic infrastructure (e.g., construction, road systems, airfields, communications, as well as the labor forces to support them). By the war's end, the groundwork had already been laid for Thailand's transformation from a regional agrarian economy to a globalized industrial/technological economy, within which agriculture continued to play a fundamental albeit altered role. From that point on, the evolution was incessant. Following a brief period of recession in the early 1980s, Thailand became the recipient of massive foreign capital investment, particularly from Japan. By 1991, Thailand had been declared "the Fifth Tiger" of the Asian Pacific "tiger economies" (along with Hong Kong, Singapore, Taiwan, and South Korea). In 1995 the World Bank announced that Thailand had the world's fastest-growing economy—10 percent per annum in 1985–1995. By 1998, the bubble had burst: Thailand was at the epicenter of an economic crisis that enveloped all of East and Southeast Asia for the next two years.

In this chapter we will examine some of the details surrounding Thailand's rapid industrial and technological development as a global economy; its meteoric rise, fall, and recovery during the 1980s and 1990s; and what I have previously introduced as "the four pillars" of the Thai economy: agriculture, natural resources, manufacturing, and tourism.

THE RISE: THAILAND'S DEVELOPMENT INTO A GLOBAL ECONOMY

Industrial and technological development in the West has been an ongoing evolutionary process that has covered a period of approximately 225 years. But imagine the socioeconomic effects of that same process within the space of only twenty-five to forty years: this is essentially what has occurred in the Kingdom of Thailand. Within the space of a single generation, Thailand's economic system was dramatically transformed from solely agrarian to include the industrial/technological sectors as well.

Like many Third World countries in the mid-twentieth century, Thailand requested the assistance of the World Bank in order to develop a viable plan or vision for its economic development. In 1957 the World Bank's mission to Thailand recommended the establishment of a national economic planning agency. In 1959 the Thai government established the National Economic Development Board (NEDB), whose purpose it would be to undertake a continuing study of the kingdom's economy and to draw up plans for its development. The NEDB's first formal economic plan came out in 1961 and covered a period of six years. The plans that followed covered time periods of five years each; they have since been referred to simply as "Five-Year Plans." In 1972 the NEDB's name was changed to the National Economic and Social Development

Board (NESDB), as social development came to be recognized as a vital component of Thailand's overall development (Thailand is currently in its ninth NESDB Five-Year Plan).

The World Bank's early recommendations included the creation of an initial blueprint for Thailand's economic development. It was based on the principle of "import substitution," meaning that if a nation develops its own industrial capacity to manufacture more of its own goods, it will (1) become less dependent on foreign imports of those same products, and (2) increase national assets through the export of those domestically manufactured goods. Necessary to this program was a move away from strong government control, with more developmental freedom and initiative given over to the private sector. Once the program was in place, the Thai infrastructure developed as well, through funding from both the World Bank and directly from the United States, in order to service the rapid military buildup during the war in Vietnam.

The positive effects of import substitution began to level off in the mid-1970s. Following the end of the Vietnam War, this slowdown (combined with the mass departure of the U.S. military) evolved into a recession in the early to mid-1980s that was exacerbated by the Organization of Petroleum Exporting Countries' (OPEC's) increase in oil prices in the 1970s, a move that had global economic effects. To keep the wheels on the tracks, Thailand received economic assistance from the World Bank and the IMF (International Monetary Fund). Their administrators devised a short-term structural adjustment program for Thailand that was designed to stabilize the economy through reductions in government expenditures, currency depreciation, and more emphasis on privatization and government deregulation. Much of this deregulation was geared toward the energizing of the Thai export market. The Thai government, for example, reduced import taxes on raw materials that were used in the manufacturing of exported goods and made tax credits available to exporters, even going so far as to allow for 100 percent foreign ownership of domestically based foreign companies.

Due to this increased deregulation and privatization, foreign investment was beginning to pour into the country by the mid-1980s, particularly from Japan. Japanese investment was embraced by many as a quick fix that lifted Thailand out of the doldrums of recession. As a result, the IMF guidelines for a gradual recovery and a studied access to world markets were being increasingly disregarded.

What economic factors attracted foreign investment to Thailand? Generally speaking, most economic experts would say that there were essentially three:

- The maintenance of high-interest rates on loans, which translated into a higher return for the foreign investor.
- The maintenance of a fixed rate of currency exchange, a principle known as "pegging." Because the baht (the unit of Thai currency) was regarded globally as a "soft currency," that is, unstable, the Thai government "pegged" the baht to the U.S. dollar, which was regarded as a stable currency. The pegged exchange rate was twenty-five baht to the dollar. By doing so, Thailand was able to offer foreign investors a guarantee of stability. This was good for local banks as well, because they were afforded a clear projection of how much they would be repaying for loans in U.S. dollars. In order to maintain the pegged rate within a narrow window that was allowed to open only a fraction above or below twenty-five, the Bank of Thailand would buy or sell U.S. dollars from its own reserves and/or existing loans.
- The easing of restrictions on foreign investment; the lifting of restrictions allowed for not merely the lending of foreign funds to Thai banks and financial institutions but the opening of foreign-owned banks and labor-intensive branches of foreign industries. And so, when Japan's trade deficit with the United States (see p. 61), combined with rising domestic production costs, forced the country to look offshore for industrial sites where production costs—particularly labor—would be cheaper. Thailand welcomed

the opportunity. From 1994 through 1998, Japanese investment in Thailand would jump (in Thai baht) from 3.1 million to 60.5 million.

These essential factors placed Thailand on a road of economic expansion that was paved not with domestic assets but with foreign capital (for a more detailed discussion of all the developmental factors listed above, see Bello et al. 1998).

THE RIDE: A LIFE OF PROSPERITY

As previously noted, Thailand had been declared by 1991 "the fifth tiger" of the Asian Pacific "tiger economies." In 1995 the World Bank announced that Thailand had the world's fastest-growing economy—10 percent per annum in 1985–1995—due to both its profitable export market and the massive influx of foreign investment. And although so much of it was based on foreign capital and an artificially pegged exchange rate, no one seemed to notice. But instead of reinvesting that capital into long-term profitable projects (e.g., education of unskilled laborers, the continuing improvement of export quality, reduction of urban air and water pollution), the new capital was channeled into two primary directions.

The first of these was credit. The high interest rates that attracted a foreign investment appeared to work for everyone, in that the funds from a foreign loan that was given to a Thai financial institution at a rate of, say, 12 percent were, in turn, re-lent to Thai customers at a rate of 20 percent, thereby giving the bank the opportunity to collect the 8 percent difference, a "free ride," as it were, to reinvest in real estate development projects and elsewhere. As the money flowed in and out, upper- and middle-class Thais—especially those employed in the financial sector—embarked on a credit-driven shopping spree. An increasingly flagrant display of material wealth became for many middle- and upper-class Thais an almost indispensable means of establishing social position and attaining political influence.

WITHDRAWN
LIBRARY
WAUKESHA COUNTY TECHNICAL COLLEGE
300 MAIN STREET

The second channel was real estate speculation and development. As young Thai couples became more prosperous, they began to disregard traditional Thai custom by moving out of their parents' households in order to establish their own. This newly prosperous middle class and the companies for which they worked were going to buy new homes and new office buildings, and they were going to buy and establish credit accounts in new shopping malls. Expensive jewelry, fashionable clothing, European automobiles, and brand-new homes, complete with patios and decks for entertaining—came to be regarded as social necessities and visible indicators of personal financial success. In the late 1980s and early 1990s, construction projects—homes, apartment complexes, shopping malls—were rampant throughout Bangkok and the surrounding suburbs of Nonthaburi provinces. With the additional interest being garnered from loan transactions such as those described earlier, banks began to finance massive subdivision developments.

> Speculating in real estate became the order of the day. . . . It would not be an exaggeration to say that half of Bangkok's landed families became real estate developers and the other half became real estate investors and speculators. During weekends developers would set up stalls in supermarkets and department stores to market their wares and real estate associations organized roving fairs with houses for sale. Small apartments became a convenient unit of investment for mid-dle-and-high-income families and this drove up the demand. The units could be sold for a higher price, because of the enormous demand. . . . Many developers had one characteristic in common: they did very little market research, which was considered unnecessary, because the demand was everywhere. (Sheng and Kirinpanu 2000)

But the down side of the equation is that property developers began to build almost solely on projection and not on demand; that is, they produced buildings based upon the assumption that someone would come along and move into them, as opposed to producing buildings for actual individuals or companies that had previously contracted them to do so. Things were beginning to get out of hand.

THE FALL: A HOUSE OF CARDS COLLAPSES

One of the profound consequences of the attention given over to credit establishment and real estate speculation was that the health of Thailand's export market was ignored. As foreign investment mounted, the profits of the Thai export market were initially envisioned as the means by which the foreign debt would be repaid. But in 1996, export had come to something of a standstill. After export growth rates of 22.26 percent and 21.61 percent were posted for 1994 and 1995 respectively, a growth rate of –2.87 percent was posted for 1996. But the reasons for this export slowdown are not to be attributed solely to diverted attention. The slowdown was also tied to yet another factor that we have previously discussed: the artificial pegging of the Thai baht to the U.S. dollar. For ten years, the fixed exchange rate kept the Thai export market competitive. But when the dollar appreciated in 1995 and again in 1996, the baht appreciated as well. Though currency appreciation would seem to be a welcome trend at first glance, it resulted in an increase in Thai export prices on the international market. Thailand was, as they say, caught between a rock and a hard place: the pegging of the baht was benefiting one component of the economic picture (at least on the surface) while damaging another. The house of cards was beginning to collapse.

By 1997 the foreign debt stood at a grand total of US$89 billion. Due to the export slowdown and eventual standstill, confidence was waning; the baht was depreciating on the global market. In response, foreign investments were being pulled out, and loans were being called in. As pressure mounted to devalue the baht, the Bank of Thailand struggled to maintain a pegged rate of exchange that had seemingly become carved in stone. The Bank of Thailand sold off millions of its reserve dollars in a desperate attempt to protect the value of the baht.

As this text is written for the nonspecialist (in regard to Thailand specifically or to economics generally), the following analogy is intended to serve as a means of illustrating the economic principle behind what took place. Picture a gigantic old-fashioned balance scale, with flat pans on either side in which one places what one wishes to weigh. On one side are twenty-five Thai baht, and on the other side is one U.S. dollar. Regardless of the amounts, the pegged rate of "25:1" must be maintained (2,500:100, 25,000:1000, etc.) We have already seen the dilemma posed by the appreciating dollar when the baht followed accordingly. But what is to be done when the baht depreciates while the dollar holds steady? If the pegged ratio is somehow to be maintained artificially, more dollars have to be sold (either one's own reserves or those of another nation that has agreed to offer assistance) on a global market that knows that the 25:1 ratio is no longer valid. Some may exchange at that rate for old time's sake, but most will not. All of a sudden, the Thai side of the scale requires thirty-five baht, and then forty baht, per U.S. dollar. And so herein lies the dilemma: how can the scale remain balanced when the pan of Thai baht has become so much heavier than the pan containing a dwindling number of U.S. dollars? Then an inquisitive observer happens to look underneath the pan of Thai baht, and what does he see? He sees a large wooden beam that is gingerly supporting the pan in order to give the appearance that the two pans are still in a state of equilibrium. Unfortunately, the beam is starting to crack under the weight. It is inevitable that it will soon splinter, and the baht pan will have to fall, exposing its true weight.

As simple a model as it is, the preceding analogy graphically expresses the challenge that was facing the Bank of Thailand. On July 2, 1997, when it could no longer bear the weight, the Bank of Thailand had no choice but to pull out the faltering supports and let the baht "float," that is, to fall to its true level of worth. The rate of the baht to the dollar immediately dropped to 30.27; in December, the rate was 45.29. By January 1998, the ratio of the Thai baht to the U.S. dollar had fallen to an all-time low of 56:1 (averaging out at 53.81), a drop in value of more than 100 percent. Beginning with those employed in the dozens of financial and real estate development firms that were forced to close, somewhere between two and three million Thais would lose their jobs in the ensuing recession.

PICKING UP THE PIECES: THE ROAD TO ECONOMIC RECOVERY

In July 1997, the IMF was called in to offer emergency assistance (ironically, one of the causes of the current crisis was the earlier IMF economic plan that called for looser regulatory controls on investment practices back in the mid-1980s). By August, a plan was negotiated. In return for an IMF "bail-out" package of $17.2 billion, Thailand agreed (1) to maintain high interest rates on loans, (2) to cut a large number of unnecessary government expenditures in order to create a surplus in the government budget, and (3) to raise the rates of basic public utilities (electricity, water, natural gas, etc.). But probably the most important required change was an overall reform of Thailand's financial sector (banks, mortgage companies, etc.), including the shutdown of those financial institutions that were no longer productive, as well as the merging of others in order to strengthen their financial base.

Needless to say, these measures placed a strain on the Thai public at large. Within such a crisis and recovery, it was difficult for the average person to understand that the way to rebuild the economy is to stimulate its growth through increased financial activity, when the natural inclination is to step back and hold on tightly to what one still has (by way of comparison, consider the fact that for several months after the terrorist attacks of September 2001, Americans experienced the same sort of fearful ambivalence and were unwilling to invest their funds).

In February 2001, Prime Minister Thaksin Shinawatra presented a reform statement to the Thai parliament that was applauded by many financial analysts as an agenda that would go a long way in stimulating Thailand economy. Primarily directed at improving consumer confidence and encouraging investment, his agenda included the following:

- The creation of the National Asset Management Corporation (NAMC) to take over non-performing loans (NPLs) from public and private banks at a high discount of their initial value (an NPL is a loan whose repayments have fallen so far behind that it will likely result in loan default or foreclosure). In 1999, for example, NPLs in Thailand peaked at 42 percent. This relief would encourage the banking system to "wipe the slate clean," as it were, and extend new credit to its customers.
- A three-year moratorium, or grace period, on the repayment of small-scale agricultural debts in order to keep more money in the hands of Thai farmers in the more impoverished rural regions of the country.
- The distribution of a one million baht revolving fund to each of Thailand's seventy thousand rural villages and urban communities. As long as it was for the good of the community, villages could do virtually anything they wanted with this money: building projects, repair and improvement of existing facilities, and so on.
- The creation of a "People's Bank," an institution to give poorer sectors of the society better opportunities to apply for loans and financing on major purchases.

Since 1999, Thailand has done a remarkable job in recovering from a virtual economic collapse. Although the road to complete recovery is continuing, Thailand is currently enjoying its highest levels of prosperity since the 1997–1998 crisis. In 2002, Thailand had an overall GDP (gross domestic product) growth rate of 5.2 percent, with exports claiming 66.3 percent of the total GDP. And as noted previously, Thailand's rate of unemployment at the end of 2002 was less than 2 percent. A GDP growth rate of 4.5 to 6 percent was anticipated for 2003, with an export rate projected at 71.5 percent of the total GDP. In fact, the 2003 growth rate was 6.7 percent. Initially, a growth rate of 10 percent was projected for 2004, but due to the economic effects of the war in Iraq, religious unrest in Southern Thailand (see "Religion" in Chapter Three), and the early Spring 2004 health scare brought on by avian influenza ("bird flu"), this figure has been pared back to a more conservative 7 percent. In late April 2004, the Bank of Thailand projected a more specific GDP growth rate of 6.8 to 7.8 percent. The exchange rate of the Thai baht continues to hover at approximately forty to the U.S. dollar. We may never see a rate of 25:1 again, but an "unpegged" baht at a reasonably steady rate is certainly a healthier baht in the long run.

THAILAND'S FOUR PILLARS

Agriculture, natural resources, manufacturing, and tourism comprise "the four pillars" of the Thai economy, each of which presents a variety of interrelated issues and challenges. We will now look closely at how each of these pillars has been affected by twentieth-century industrialization in general and by the economic events of the 1990s.

Agriculture

Traditionally, the cultivation, processing, and export of agricultural produce has been regarded as the mainstay of the Thai economy. Indeed, had one seen nothing of Thailand firsthand but the crowded streets of Bangkok, the media-shaped imagination is nevertheless filled with romantic images of flooded green rice fields stretching to the horizon, farmers in wide-brimmed hats, and hand-driven plows hitched to water buffaloes, all working to produce mountains of jasmine rice. Although Thailand has been among the most agriculturally prosperous of Asian nations (given its historical ability to take advantage of lucrative trade agreements while still managing to avoid the pitfalls of foreign colonization), its dependence on a single crop—rice—made it exceedingly vulnerable to international fluctuations in market price and seasonal variations in harvest volume. And so perhaps the need for economic diversification was inevitable. In 2000, agricultural production as a whole (sugarcane, rice, cassava, pineapple, etc.) comprised only 7 percent of Thailand's exports, as manufacturing alone comprised an overwhelming 86 percent. Thailand's overall GDP figures are somewhat more equitable: agriculture comes in at 11 percent, industry at 40 percent, and services at 49 percent. Jasmine rice, for example, continues to be Thailand's number-one agricultural export; in fact, Thailand ranks first in the world in rice production. But note the shift that took place during the last half of the twentieth century, as indicated in Table 2.1.

Table 2.1 Quantity and Value of Exported Rice, Selected Years

Year	Quantity (tons)	Value (Thai baht)	% of Export
1956	1.2 million	2.8 billion	40.39
1966	1.5 million	4 billion	27.96
1976	2 million	8.6 billion	14.15
1986	4.5 million	20.3 billion	8.70
1996	5.5 million	50.7 billion	3.60
2001	7.7 million	70.1 billion	2.42

Source: Adapted from "Key Statistics of Thailand 2003, Table 13.7: Quantity and Value of Exported Rice 1961–2002." National Statistical Office of Thailand.

Although the volume and value of exported rice has shown significant annual increases, the rate of export has dropped dramatically as Thailand developed industrially and diversified its exportable goods into the industrial/manufacturing sector. What is surprising, however, in Table 2.1 is that agricultural production overall (including forestry) still accounts for about 45 percent of the Thai labor force, whereas manufacturing accounts for about 15 percent, with wholesale/retail trade keeping pace at about 14 percent. Compare these labor percentages to those of agriculture and manufacturing income within the overall GDP (above). The figures belie a less idyllic picture: the vast economic disparity that exists between minimal export income for agricultural produce and the size of the rural population that produces it. Though twentieth-century industrialization certainly brought Thailand into the global market, most of its financial returns—even those of agricultural production—have been fed back into urban-industrial development. In effect, agricultural production has served to subsidize more growth in industrial production than in its own sector. As a result, the economic development and income level of much of Thailand's rural-agricultural population is running far behind that of its urban-industrial population.

About 33 percent of Thailand's soil/land area is arable, that is, suitable for farming. As in many nations, the greatest challenge to Thailand's agricultural production is the sustaining of land arability and the prevention of soil erosion, not to mention the physical loss of arable land altogether, due to the urban and/or industrial expansion that it ironically supports. Not unlike biological systems, ecological systems will "wear out" if they are overworked. With more produce being demanded from less space, much Thai farmland has been completely worn out through overuse season after season. This is a good example of how a radical change in an economic base affects multiple dimensions of human experience: when a labor-intensive economy shifts to a capital-intensive economy, one's essential relationship with one's work is altered as well. The land itself, once regarded as an environmental partner with a living spirit of its own, becomes little more than a financial commodity whose worth is evaluated solely in terms of how much it can produce.

Rice Cultivation

As rice cultivation constitutes such an integral part of Thailand's economic and cultural identity overall, it would perhaps be helpful for the reader to know something about how rice is grown there. Traditionally, the rice-growing season in Thailand commences in May with the Royal Plowing Ceremony. It takes place near Bangkok's Grand Palace, in a spacious, grassy expanse called Sanahm Luahng ("the field of the King"). During the ritual, an official convener appointed by the king uses a ceremonial plow drawn by white bulls to plow a long furrow into the field. He is followed by chanting Brahman priests and by four women carrying baskets of rice seed. The women scatter the seed in the plowed furrow. Once it has been sown and the ceremony is concluded, the onlookers scramble for the rice seed in the furrow, as it is believed that if these seeds are mixed with one's own, a good crop will be ensured.

Though any large-scale agricultural endeavor is a complicated affair, rice-planting is especially so. Even with the assistance of mechanical plows and transplanting machines, it is very labor-intensive. Globally, there are several methods of planting and growing rice. Even in Thailand alone, different methods are employed, due to the variations in seasonal patterns and terrain. Generally speaking, the planting season runs from June through September (the rainy season), and harvesting takes place in December and January (the cool season). The central plains and lowlands may have two or three crops, whereas the more limited rainfall of the northeast allows for only one.

Irrigated (artificially flooded) rice fields are common in Thailand. Found primarily in the northeastern region, they are, as noted above, the source of Thailand's finest jasmine rice. The paradox is that the highest quality of rice is produced under the most challenging of circumstances: limited rainfall, poor soil, and impoverished economy. Other methods include dry seeding (in the uplands and the hills of the north), rainfall seeding (in the lowlands of the central plains), and deepwater seeding (in flooded river banks and delta regions), in which the rice plants literally float on 1–5 meters (3–15 feet) of water. Flooded fields (irrigation, rainfall, and literal flooding) comprise about 90 percent of Thailand's rice production.

As irrigated rice fields are by far the most common in Thailand, here is a very general stage-by-stage overview of what takes place:

1. Land preparation: the fields are flat but surrounded with earthen walls for water control. The field is then flooded with several centimeters of water for a few days.
2. At the same time, rice seed is soaked in water. After a few days, the seeds will sprout. Depending on the method of planting, the germinated seeds will be dealt with in one of two ways: hand broadcasting or transplanting. Hand broadcasting is simply the scattering of the germinated seeds over the water of the irrigated field. It takes a very experienced farmer to scatter the seeds evenly. The transplant method requires that the germinated seeds are temporarily planted in numerous large trays or seedbeds until they are perhaps 10–15 centimeters (4–6 inches) tall. This can take as long as one month. Then the young plants are transplanted into the submerged mud of the irrigated field. There are now machines to do this, but traditionally it is done by hand, one plant at a time.
3. During this waiting period, the irrigated field must be plowed in order to control weeds. It is essential that the weeds are plowed under prior to broadcasting or transplanting.
4. Once the seeds and/or plants take root, the water level must be maintained at several centimeters but never overtaking the tassels of the plant. It will take three or four months for the rice to mature. As there is little to do during this period, it is traditional for the younger men in the community to enter the monastery as Buddhist monks until it is time for the harvest.
5. The rice is mature when it flowers and then turns light brown in color. Once the color change has taken place, the field is drained and left to dry out.

6. When the field is dry and the rice turns to a lighter yellow-brown color, the rice is harvested and milled.

For more information about the most important types of rice in Thailand and the essential role that rice plays in Thai culture overall, see Language, Food and Etiquette.

A Sufficiency Economy

Each year on his birthday (December 5), H.R.H. King Pumipohn Adunyadayt of Thailand presents a public speech that is perhaps comparable in content and spirit to the annual State of the Union address in the United States. In December 1997, the Thai monarch addressed the economic crisis that his country was facing. To be a "tiger" in a trade economy, he said, is not as important as embodying the cooperative spirit of self-sufficiency, that is, a "sufficiency economy." To be sure, technology and international trade relations are necessary components for Thailand's growth, but it is even more important to recognize and to make the most of what is already inherently Thai, for example, land, resources, and agrarian values of communal care and self-sufficiency.

In his address, the king sought to downplay the perceived disparity between a "trade economy" (based on an exchange of goods with external entities) and a "self-sufficient economy" (in which a given comunity produces everything it needs internally). Economic practice, he said, does not have to be reduced to a question of choosing one or the other, nor does it mean that a trade economy is by definition "modern," while a self-sufficient ecomnomy is to be regarded as "primitive." On the contrary, to be self-sufficient does not mean to withdraw from the world market, but rather to preserve one's regional awareness and translate that awareness into the manner in which one conducts business. For exapple, if a rural village farming enterprise (or even an urban-based business) finds that it has a surplus of its produced goods, why not reduce transportation costs by selling it in one's own region at a reasonable price, as opposed to increasing the price of the product artificially by incorporating high transportation costs into it? Both buyers and sellers benefit when lower production costs translate into lower prices (the English text of this speech and other birthday speeches of King Pumipohn can be found at a Web site that is sponsored by the Thai Royal Government: http://kan chanapisek.or.th/speeches).

In that same speech, King Pumipohn's example of the rice market provided a graphic illustration of the consequences of maintaining a solely trade-oriented focus that sells goods outside of the region from whence they came. Rice is purchased from farmers for both the regional and global markets. However, they must sell their rice at a relatively low price in order to allow for additional costs, such as transportation and export fees, if the market price is to remain competitive. The farmers' profits are therefore minimal. If the farmer cannot afford to retain a sufficient amount of "sustenance rice" (rice for his own family's use), he is placed in the position of having to buy rice as a consumer, in which case he, too, must pay the increased market price. King Pumipohn related a specific example of how this inequity occurs even within the domestic market. Under the governance of a trade-oriented economy, rice that is produced in Northern Thailand's Chiang Rai Province is sold to marketers in Bangkok who, in turn, have added in transportation costs, thereby raising the price, before it is sold to consumers. But the puzzling part of this equation is that even though the rice originally came from Chiang Rai, consumers in Chiang Rai have to pay the Bangkok market price for it.

King Pumipohn concluded his address with a paradoxical challenge to the Thai people: in order to move forward, a backward step must be taken. Although it might seem on the surface to be regressive or self-defeating, such a step is by no means intended to deny or forsake the advantages of technolgy and global trade relations, but to recover and imple-

ment those agrarian values of communal care and self-sufficiency wherever and whenever it is possible to do so, and to
incorporate them into Thailand's global and domestic economic relationships. In essence, the king's speech served as a
belated reminder that, not only in agriculture but in national
identity overall, these are the values that have defined the
Thai people for centuries.

Natural Resources

Thailand's primary natural resources are rubber, mineral ores
(primarily tin and tungsten), and fishing/seafood (primarily
prawns), each accounting for minimal portions of the overall
GDP compared to the manufacturing sector. At one time,
hardwood timber, particularly teak, was also a major natural
resource and export commodity. But as the operative term in
that statement is the verb "was," I have chosen to focus on
what was once one of Thailand's greatest natural assets
because of the many intertwined economic issues that led to
its demise. Indeed, Thailand's diminishing forest cover falls
under the category of ecological/environmental challenges,
some of which will be discussed elsewhere in this text. But
due to its interrelationship with population, income distribution, agriculture, and industrialization, deforestation becomes
an economic issue as well.

The Royal Thai Forest Department (RFD) was created in
1896, during the reign of King Chulalongkawn (Rama V).
Prior to the establishment of the RFD, the forests were considered sufficiently abundant for people to cut timber quite
freely for their personal use (fuel, construction, etc.), except
for teak, which required the purchase of a special permit
from the local village chiefs. Though the origins of such permit practices are likely found in animistic religious beliefs
surrounding sacred places and reverence for the trees as spiritual entities, permit acquisition degenerated into more or
less of an arbitrary transaction that did little to regulate how

much teak could be removed, as long as the chief or village headman received his money (the sum of which was also unregulated). As of September 1896, the RFD placed the forests under the charge of the Thai central government and enacted regulatory policies for the collection of fees, the maintenance of state forest reserves, the creation of a trained forestry staff, and the implementation of scientific conservation techniques. But what happens when the ideals of ecological responsibility come into conflict with the realities of economic demand?

Although Thailand never suffered the indignities of outright colonialism, its international trade relationships of the late nineteenth and early twentieth centuries—and particularly those with European powers—nevertheless served to compromise its integrity to some degree. Southeast Asian hardwoods such as teak were highly prized in Europe for furniture, inlay work, and wall coverings. And as King Chulalongkawn actively sought formal diplomatic and trade relations with the many nations he had visited in Europe, the Siamese monarchy granted huge logging concessions to numerous European nations, and continued to do so through 1932. Although foreign logging concessions were phased out following the establishment of the constitutional monarchy in 1932, commercial logging had already become quite developed as a domestic enterprise. And tragically, by continuing to conduct "unofficial" financial transactions with village headmen and regional chiefs (as many of the foreign enterprises had done in the past), some of these commercial loggers succeeded in harvesting vast amounts of timber from land that was not allocated to them, even to the point of invading land that the government had already set aside as national forest reserves. Such dealings with local villages also served as an inroad for the attainment and exploitation of cheap laborers from the villages themselves.

The economics of agricultural/rural impoverishment have played a role in the deforestation crisis as well. Due to (1) the physical expansion of the industrial sector into land areas once utilized for agriculture, and (2) the plight of the landless tenant farmer who can barely subsist on what he/she profits after making payments to the landowner, many farmers from Thailand's central plains have been forced to migrate northward—ironically, to cultivate land that had already been cleared of its natural forest cover by commercial loggers. In turn, the farmers' constant need for fuel wood has consumed even more.

But there is another component to the migratory picture. As central plains farmers moved northward, northern hill populations were moving southward. As noted previously, approximately six major tribal groups comprise the hill peoples of Northern Thailand. For hundreds of years, the traditional enterprise of many of these remote groups has been the cultivation of poppies and the production of opium, an occupation that developed and grew, once again, primarily due to foreign (European) demand. From an agricultural perspective, the work is suitable to the high-altitude climate and rugged terrain of the northern mountains. As government suppression of this illegal activity has increased over the past few decades, hill people have been encouraged to move into the cultivation of more conventional crops, such as corn, cabbage, and other vegetables. But such a profound shift in enterprise also required a radical change of venue, as these crops can be grown only at lower altitudes. Forced southward out of the mountains and into circumstances that were completely foreign to their established way of life, many of the hill tribe people had little choice but to continue their practice of what is conventionally known as "slash and burn" agriculture, wherein the entire forest cover of a portion of land is simply cut down and burned off in order to make way for the planting of crops. The same land is utilized for as many seasons as the soil will allow. When the soil is no longer viable, it is essentially left for dead, as one moves on to introduce the same debilitating process to the next parcel of forested land.

In recent years, government-sponsored education programs have introduced sounder methods of land use and forest conservation to both migratory populations and commercial enterprises. The Royal Thai Forest Department has initiated reforestation projects and striven to maintain what remains of Thailand's forests in protected reserves and national parks. But the tragic fact is that so much damage has already been done, and regulatory laws and logging policies are difficult to enforce in remote areas of the country. Thailand's present forest cover is minimal. Though many sources report that forests currently cover about 28 percent of Thailand's land area, many environmental experts place the figure at less than 20 percent. Compare this to a 1961 estimate of 53 percent—a loss of at least 25 percent over a period of forty years!

Seen in its entirety, the intensity of economic necessity has resulted in environmental consequences that will be felt for a long time to come. Deforested land accounts for very unstable soil that due to its increased exposure to the elements, becomes highly susceptible to water and wind erosion, flash flooding, and mudslides. Increased water runoff due to erosion results in massive siltation of rivers, reservoirs, and canals. "*Siltation*" refers to the buildup or congestion of water-carried sediment, or "silt," that can literally choke waterways, even to the point of impeding transportation (yet another economic ramification). The best way to overcome these problems is to restabilize the soil through large-scale reforestation programs, both as ground cover and as wind barriers around cultivated land.

Manufacturing

As noted earlier, the industrial/manufacturing sector accounts for approximately 40 percent of Thailand's overall GDP and the lion's share of its exports—86 percent. Table 2.2 illustrates the itemized export value of Thailand's major manufactured items.

Table 2.2 Manufactured Items and Export Value, 2001

Manufactured Item	Export Value (Thai baht)
Computer parts	340 billion
Electrical appliances	211 billion
Textile products	189 billion
Integrated circuits	179 billion
Plastics	110 billion
Vehicle parts	101 billion
TOTAL EXPORT VALUE	**1.1 trillion**

Source: Adapted from "Thailand Economic Information Kit, Table 8: Major Export Items 2002." Thailand Development Research Institute.

The major portion of Thailand's growth in manufacturing is clearly in the area of electronics. In the 1980s and 1990s, multinational electronics corporations led the way in the establishment of foreign investment in Thailand. But as discussed previously, one of the primary reasons that foreign investment was attracted to Thailand was its favorable labor costs. And though the presence of foreign-based industry and manufacturing has certainly increased Thailand's overall GDP, the essential role of Thai industrial labor has in most cases remained at an unskilled or semiskilled level. The foreign agenda was not so much directed at developing Thailand as a technological base as it was toward utilizing Thailand's low-cost labor base to assemble, apply, or package technology whose components were created and developed in their respective home countries.

The economic statistics of almost every nation-state in the world indicate something akin to the so-called "40–60 Principle." In 1999, for example, the top two fifths of the Thai population accounted for 78 percent of the income while the bottom three-fifths of the population received only 22 percent. We have previously noted this unbalanced economic ratio as it exists overall between rural Thais and urban Thais. But expansive industrial growth led not only to the northward displacement of farmers but also to the migration of thousands of rural/agrarian Thais into the urban/industrial sector. This labor influx has created a similar economic disparity between the very wealthy and the very poor within the confines of Bangkok itself. The search for work and for a better life as a *dek tayp*, or a "Bangkok kid," carried its own consequences. If one is afforded no technological training or creative education beyond the skills necessary for running the machines, assembling already-built components and packaging them, the "vested interest" that one would experience in predominantly agrarian contexts has disappeared. Left without this vital connectedness, the worker's interest is no longer in the quality of the process/product but the quantity of the paycheck, which remains very low. In Bangkok, Thais have oftentimes found themselves simply locked into a different stratum of poverty than the one they were in before.

Northeastern Thai *loogtoong*, traditional "country music," is replete with ballads and stories of rural Thais who have come to Bangkok in search of a better lot, all the while lamenting the loss of their previous, more holistic way of life and their loved ones. But economic necessity has left them with no choice. In the following loogtoong from the early 1960s, Bangkok is presented as a foreign and malevolent place where one will encounter nothing but heartache. To be sure, this song's imaginative use of metaphor embellishes the truth, but the subjective experience portrayed is not unlike that of many rural Americans who leave home for the first time and try to "make good" in overwhelmingly large urban centers like Los Angeles or New York City:

Don't go to Bangkok!
I'm telling you, little one, I've been there already.
Don't go to Bangkok!
I'm telling you, you'll only get hurt.

Indeed, the people there may seem like the cream of the crop,
But their beautiful faces are like masks that hide a thousand
   evil intentions;
Their smooth tongues are but a cover for fast hands.
They lay in wait to do us harm, to pounce upon us;
They'll tear your heart out for a meal, and leave you like the
   walking dead.
They'll carve you up, body and spirit,
And display it before everyone, like a war trophy;
And then you'll have to return to the safety of your nest,
In a stupor that hovers between life and death.

But along with the realities of labor and income distribution, the role of manufacturing in the Thai economy has most certainly had its shining moments as well. As noted in Table 2.2, the textile industry constitutes one of the most important components of Thailand's manufacturing sector. Though many conventional textile and clothing items are produced in Thailand, any discussion of Thai textile production would not be complete without an overview of one of the kingdom's great success stories: the twentieth-century revitalization and growth of the Thai silk industry.

It is generally held that the art of sericulture (the raising of silkworms and the production of silk fabric) began in China some five thousand years ago. Because of its natural origins in the work of a living entity (i.e., the silkworm, whose single cocoon can produce as much as 1,500 meters—nearly a mile—of silk thread), the fabric that is produced from it has been regarded as virtually a sacred commodity. Silk fabric was reserved for only the most ceremonial purposes and the most important gifts. And because the Chinese guarded the secret of silk production so closely, the technique spread to other regions very slowly. Through Alexander the Great's (356–323 BCE) conquest of Persia, the establishment of diplomatic relationships and marriages between Chinese and Central Asian royalty, and even the smuggling of silkworm eggs by Buddhist monks, sericulture migrated both east and west little by little, resulting eventually in the development of the fabled "Silk Road" trade route during China's Han Dynasty (205 BCE –220 CE), which connected Western China with Central Asia (Persia, now Afghanistan) and finally the Mediterranean. In time, the perilous Silk Road gave way to maritime trade routes that connected China with Southeast Asia, India, and the Mediterranean West. Most of us are familiar, for example, with the travels of the Italian explorer Marco Polo, who in the thirteenth century returned to Italy from China with beautiful silk fabrics and sericulture technology. By the fourteenth century, Italian silk was well on its way to becoming a world-class commodity.

But in light of the preceding overview, what of Thailand? Was silk introduced to Thailand through Chinese trade? Or did Thailand have its own indigenous sericulture? Such questions are shrouded in ambiguity, due to archaeological discoveries at a site we have visited before: the ancient village of Ban Chiang in Northeastern Thailand, which is believed to date back as early as 4000 BCE. Excavations there have uncovered rolls of unwoven and undyed silk thread, which have led experts to postulate that Thailand's silk technology could be indigenous and as old as that of China.

Through both inscriptions and temple paintings, it is apparent that sumptuous and intricately woven silk fabrics were present in the royal court of Sukhothai (1238–1350) and in the northern Thai kingdom of Lanna (1259–1558). By the age of Ayutthaya (1350–1767), Thai silk was a prized commodity that was sought after by European traders. But by the eighteenth and nineteenth centuries, it was becoming ever more difficult for the Thais to compete with the growing silk trades of China, Persia, Japan, and India (not to mention Italy and France). Due to the influx of cheaper factory-produced fabrics from their Asian competitors, Thai silk production gradually devolved into a relatively small and isolated cottage industry that was most active where it began: in the villages of Eesahn, Thailand's northeastern provinces.

During the reign of King Chulalongkawn (Rama V, 1868–1910), however, attempts were made to revitalize the Thai silk industry. In 1903, the Department of Silk Craftsmen was established under royal patronage. Efforts were made to teach the art of sericulture throughout the kingdom, and new orchards of mulberry trees (the trees in which silkworms flourish and spin their cocoons) were planted in Northeastern Thailand. Weaving loom technology was improved, and by 1910 Siam was exporting annually over thirty-five tons of silk. But following the death of Chulalongkawn, silk production decreased dramatically due to lack of sustained government support as well as the ever-present competition from Siam's Asian neighbors.

But one of the fruits of the Siamese "silk renaissance" of the early twentieth century deserves specific mention. In the early 1900s, a Thai textile weaver from the northern Chiang Mai region traveled to Burma to observe local silk-weaving techniques. Seeing that they were superior to what he had previously seen, he opted to attempt his own silk production based on what he had learned from the Burmese. After some successful experimentation with weaving looms and dyeing processes, this entrepreneur, Chiang Shinawatra, founded the Shinawatra Silk Company in Chiang Mai in 1929. The reader will not be mistaken if the surname sounds familiar, for this is the family into which Thailand's current prime minister, Thaksin Shinawatra, was born in 1949 (to my knowledge, the prime minister is not directly associated with the company). Still operating today, the Shinawatra Silk Company of Chiang Mai is Thailand's oldest and longest-running silk production company.

Just after World War II a series of chance events took place in Thailand that would radically alter the global landscape of the Asian silk market. In September 1945, James H. W. "Jim" Thompson was a member of the Office of Strategic Services (OSS), the wartime U.S. intelligence agency and forerunner of the modern Central Intelligence Agency. Thompson's original mission was to enter into Northeastern Thailand and work with the underground resistance against the Japanese. But the Japanese surrender in August precluded his mission and resulted in his being assigned to Bangkok to supervise the reopening of the U.S. Embassy.

After receiving his military discharge in 1946, Thompson decided to remain in Thailand. As he sought to reestablish himself as a civilian, Thompson utilized his prewar skills as an architect by assisting in the renovation of Bangkok's famous Oriental Hotel. He traveled widely in Thailand, and eventually visited the impoverished provinces of the northeast, where he encountered what would soon change his life: the village practitioners of the isolated and almost forgotten Thai silk industry. In former times, the raw silk from this region had been sold to weaving families in Bangkok. But due to the previously mentioned rise of cheaper, factory-produced silks from other nations, this trade relationship had virtually disappeared. Thompson found but a small group of northeastern villages that still produced and wove silk for their own use. The textures, colors, and patterns astounded him. The unique handwoven character of Thai silk (described by Thompson as "humps and bumps") was nothing like the ultra-smooth and seemingly spiritless texture of factory-produced silks.

Excited by his discovery, Thompson sought to reestablish an active trade relationship between the raw silk producers of the northeastern villages and any remaining weaving families in Bangkok. He found them in a small district of Bangkok called Ban Krua. To his surprise, the weaving families that lived there were not Buddhist but Muslim. Interestingly, it was their identity as a religious minority that had preserved their existence as a closely knit community. Thompson nurtured this new "silk road" between Eesahn and Ban Krua. Although most of the Ban Krua weavers were skeptical of his vision, Thompson was able to commission one weaver to produce enough silk fabric to serve as samples that he could show to fashion editors and designers in the

H.R.H. Queen Sirikit shown with her husband, King Pumipohn
Adunyadayt, wearing traditional Thai silk apparel, July 1960.
(Hulton-Deutsch Collection/Corbis)

United States. It wasn't long before Thai silk designs were on
the cutting edge of world fashion.

Jim Thompson founded the Thai Silk Company in 1948.
Ethical man that he was, Thompson sought to ensure that the
company's profits would benefit the weaving families of Ban
Krua and the villagers of Eesahn. He allowed foreign interests
to purchase no more than 49 percent of the company's initial
stock shares, thereby retaining 51 percent control for Thai
interests alone.

By the mid-1960s the Thai Silk Company had established
a global network of representatives that covered thirty-five
countries. Among its early achievements is this: in the 1959
Hollywood epic *Ben Hur*, Thai silk from Jim Thompson's company was utilized in all of the principal costumes. In 1967 the

H.R.H. Queen Sirikit wearing modern Thai silk apparel, on a visit to Washington, D.C., on June 28, 1960. (Bettmann/Corbis)

company achieved net profits of $1.5 million. But from Thompson's viewpoint, the true measure of success dwelt not in the profits of the Thai Silk Company but in the large number of rival companies that had arisen. In that same year, there were more than one hundred competitors in Thailand.

But along with continuing global notoriety and financial profits, 1967 was a year marked by puzzling loss as well. In March, Jim Thompson disappeared while on a vacation in Malaysia. Not surprisingly, speculations concerning his fate covered everything from the probable (accidental death through a fall in the jungle, natural death due to heart attack or stroke) to the fantastic (murder by competitors, kidnapping by communists). As no body was ever recovered, his fate and/or whereabouts remains one of Thailand's great mysteries.

The vision of entrepreneurial individuals such as Chiang Shinawatra and Jim Thompson survive in their companies and in a host of others. In addition, the Thai royal family has done its part to support such vision. In the early 1960s, H.R.H. Queen Sirikit introduced her own Thai silk fashions to the United States during a state visit. Since then, she has continued to play an instrumental role in Thailand's silk revival, particularly in her ongoing support and patronage of the cottage silk industries of rural Thailand. Today, the Thai silk industry as a whole employs over twenty thousand producers and weavers throughout the kingdom. According to the Thailand Department of Export Promotion, silk exports in 2002 earned 521.65 million baht, or just over US$13 million. Top importers have been the United States and the United Kingdom, followed by Japan, Italy, and France. Although $13 million is by no means an overwhelming figure, it is nevertheless quite an achievement for a singular product that in the mid-twentieth century was little more than a cottage craft.

Tourism

In the broad sense of the term, one of Thailand's largest and most profitable "industries" is tourism. In light of all of the wonderful sights, sounds, and tastes that this remarkable country has to offer, it is no wonder that tourism is such an important pillar of the Thai economy. As noted previously, the service sector of the Thai labor force comprises about 49 percent of Thailand's overall GDP; it would not be inaccurate to suggest that a good deal of that sector (e.g., hotel, restaurant, transportation, etc.) is connected with tourism. Table 2.3 indicates some pertinent figures for Thailand's "top ten" visitors in 2003.

Table 2.3 Most Frequent Tourists to Thailand, and Duration of Stay, 2003

Tourists by Nationality	Number	Average stay (days)
Malaysia	1,340,193	3.61
Japan	1,026,287	6.96
Hong Kong	657,458	4.29
Singapore	633,805	4.48
China	624,923	6.53
United Kingdom	550,087	12.29
Taiwan	525,916	6.29
United States	469,165	10.12
Germany	389,293	15.91
Australia	284,749	9.62

Source: Adapted from "2003 Tourism Statistics." Tourism Authority of Thailand.

As should be evident from the ten statistics shown in Table 2.3, the overwhelming majority of tourists in Thailand are East/Southeast Asians. East/Southeast Asian nations accounted for 6,199,719 tourists—a 61.49 percent share—of a grand total of 10,082,109 international visitors who came to Thailand in 2003 (Tourism Authority of Thailand 2003). And although Western nations fall toward the bottom of the top ten list, it should be noted that Western tourists tend to make up for it by staying in Thailand much longer than their East Asian counterparts, whose shorter visits are likely due to the fact that their itinerary is primarily business-oriented.

After the Vietnam War ended in 1975, Thailand became an increasingly popular travel destination. Thailand had almost one million visitors in 1976; it can be assumed that the praises that were being sung by thousands of U.S. soldiers returning home played no small part in this increase (although the specific nature of some of those assessments became something of a double-edged sword, as we shall see). At any rate, over the course of the past twenty-five years, the Kingdom of Thailand has done much to raise its profile as a major tourist attraction. Throughout the world, for example, 1987 was promoted as the "Visit Thailand" year. In 1996, Thailand celebrated the fiftieth anniversary of the reign of its current and longest-reigning monarch, H.R.H. King Pumipohn Adunyadayt (Rama IX). The festivities that surrounded this auspicious occasion attracted worldwide attention. And finally, the Tourism Authority of Thailand's highly successful "Amazing Thailand" promotion of 1998–1999 helped to bring almost ten million tourists to Thailand in 1998. Indeed, even throughout Thailand's economic crisis and ongoing recovery, the tourist industry has continued to flourish.

As advantageous as a thriving tourist industry is to the economic health of a nation, there are consequences as well. A human culture is not unlike a natural ecology: its diverse components (customs, rituals, performances, spaces, social relations, etc.) are dynamically balanced to interact in a certain manner. The economics of tourism can compromise that balance. What was once a sacred space becomes a thirty-minute stop on a tour bus route; what was once a private religious ritual becomes a public performance with a ticket price; what was once a classical dance-drama of the royal court becomes an after-dinner spectacle at a Bangkok hotel. In short, indigenous culture is transformed into an economic commodity. To be sure, the economic survival of many has come to depend on such performances and exhibitions, and there are certainly those among them who deserve to be recognized as bona fide carriers of indigenous traditions and preservers of ancient sites. Yet in some cases, even the performers themselves lose touch with the cultural origins of their own performances. As an old saying goes, "They used to tie up the cat each evening in order to prevent her from drinking the milk that was put out for the gods; today, they just tie up the cat." In other words, "as long as the tourists continue to pay money to see this performance or that space, we will continue 'to tie up the cat.'"

Figure A. *A Wat Po panel from which few, if any, rubbings have been taken.* (*Courtesy of Timothy Hoare*)

Sometimes the economics of tourism can take a more graphic toll. A case in point are the famous bas-relief panels at Wat Pra Jetupohn ("Wat Po"). Wat Po is a Buddhist temple adjacent to the grounds of the Grand Palace complex in Bangkok. Its four exterior walls are circumscribed at eye level by a series of one hundred fifty-two marble bas-relief carvings that depict episodes from the *Ramakien,* the classic Thai mythological epic that is based on the Indian *Ramayana.* Each bas-relief panel is an equilateral square that measures

Figure B. *A Wat Po panel that has been damaged by too many stone rubbings. (Courtesy of Timothy Hoare)*

forty-five centimeters per side (approximately 18 inches), or about 2.25 square feet. Although the specific facts surrounding their origin remain somewhat uncertain, the panels are generally believed to have been installed at Wat Po as part of a temple renovation in 1825, during the reign of Pra Nahngk-lao (Rama III, r. 1824–1851). Particularly during the mid- to

Figure C. *A genuine rubbing taken from* Figure B *that the author found at an antique store in the United States. (Courtesy of Timothy Hoare)*

late twentieth century, tourists and historians from around the world visited Wat Po to make rubbings of the bas-relief panels. A "rubbing" is made by affixing a large piece of porous paper to the stone surface and then rubbing the paper against the stone with a soft drawing medium, such as charcoal, pastel, or soft lead, in order to transfer the stone image to the paper. Following years of successive rubbings by eager visitors, many of the Wat Po panels have been severely damaged (see photos). As a result, the practice of taking rubbings has for many years been prohibited by the Thai government.

Today, tourists can still purchase stone rubbings at Wat Po. But now they are made from a limited number of replicated panel woodblocks, created solely for the tourist industry. The tourists continue to be told, of course, that the rubbings have come directly from the temple walls.

I have mixed feelings about my own genuine panel rubbing (Figure C), which I purchased at an antique store in the United States (the reader must take my word that it is genuine). As "antiques" go, it was a great find, and it is a beautiful addition to my office wall. But it is always displayed next to a recent photograph of the original stone panel from whence it came, so that I will always be reminded of the real cost of its creation.

DOING BUSINESS IN THAILAND

Not unlike the United States, businesses in Thailand take three basic forms: sole proprietorships, partnerships, and corporations. Business interests in Thailand are both domestic and foreign. They are governed by a variety of governmental and private agencies. The Ministry of Commerce, for example, oversees business and trade practices to ensure that they are in accordance with the law. The Ministry of Industry regulates industrial and entrepreneurial development, promotes Thailand to foreign business investors, and provides assistance for their smooth entry into the Thai economic landscape. The Department of Internal Trade supports domestic businesses and companies to ensure that their goods and services are allowed to compete fairly with those of foreign interests (both imports and foreign-owned companies in Thailand). Most foreign nations (including the United States) have established chambers of commerce in Thailand to represent and support their respective businesses and to act as liaisons between the given company and the appropriate ministries of the Thai government.

Throughout this chapter we have been discussing the economy of Thailand in the rather remote language of percentages, currencies, and growth rates. At this point, let us move from the intellectual abstraction of numbers to the flesh and blood of people. How do Thais "do business," both with foreigners and with one another? Just as in other nations, there is a cultural protocol to be followed if one is to be successful in his/her business dealings. To appreciate this protocol fully, the reader is advised to refer to the sections on Thai society and etiquette in conjunction with the following.

As noted in Chapter Four, a favorite Thai phrase is *mai pehn rai,* which generally means "never mind," or "don't worry about it." But in the broader sense, it expresses the overall Thai perception of what is important and what is not. Thais are very hard-working but also very easy-going people. Therefore, linear time schedules and the making and keeping of hard deadlines are not characteristics of Thai business practice. Thai business people are more concerned about the development and maintenance of good relationships than they are about simply getting things done in a "timely manner." In short, the business relationship is not a mere vehicle for achieving an end; a good relationship constitutes an end in itself. This cultural attitude often poses a challenge for westerners who are engaged in business dealings in Thailand. But it is vital for the Western business person to understand it. In terms of the overall concept of "time," perhaps one could say that time is primarily quantitative (objectively measured) for the westerner but primarily qualitative (subjectively experienced and enjoyed) for the Thai.

In our overview of Thai history, it was noted that the identification of Thais by surnames (last names) is a relatively new development, having been instituted in 1913 by King Vajiravudh (Rama VI). But as Thai surnames are very long and difficult to pronounce (even for Thais!), they are reserved for only the most formal of circumstances. Therefore, business introductions are carried out on a first-name basis, including whatever title the person may hold. If, for example, I were meeting a Thai in a professional venue, I would be introduced not as "Dr. Timothy Hoare" but as "Dr. Tim" (the "th" sound would be avoided, as it is not an element of the Thai language and is therefore difficult to pronounce). Another important component of business protocol is the sequence of introductions. If there are several people present, the person of lowest rank or age is always introduced first. Finally, if Thai business people are being introduced to westerners, they will likely shake hands and not perform the traditional bow, or *wai,* until subsequent meetings (for a description of the wai, see "Thai Etiquette").

Like most Asian cultures, Thais place a great deal of importance upon the presentation of business cards. The business card is regarded in much the same manner as one's resume— professionally speaking, it is one's representative. It is therefore treated with great respect. For the American, it is best to have a business card that is printed in English on one side and Thai on the other. It is always presented to the most senior person first, and with both hands. Once a business card is received from another, it should never be bent, written on, or "fiddled with" in one's hands. It is best to have a portfolio that has plastic pages with individual spaces that are designed to hold business cards. Finally, under no circumstances should one ever remove one's business card from, or place a just-received business card in, the back pocket of one's trousers.

The practice of gift giving is also very prevalent in Thai business relationships, especially in early-stage meetings. But at the same time, it is advisable for a foreign visitor *not* to bring a gift to a first-time meeting, as it could prove embarrassing for the Thai recipient if he/she does not have a gift to offer in return. As business gifts, Thais appreciate such things as pen and pencil sets, liquor, or what are often referred to as "coffee table books." If, for example, the gift presenter is from the United States, a large book with color photographs of U.S. cities and landscapes would be an ideal introductory gift. It is appropriate to give flowers to a Thai businesswoman, but one should avoid certain types. Carnations and marigolds, for example, are associated with death. And though the lotus is probably the most beautiful flower in all of Thailand, it is reserved for offerings at Buddhist temples.

The establishment and maintenance of a good relationship dwells at the heart of any business transaction in Thailand. It is very common for one of the two parties involved to invite the other out in the evening for dinner, drinking, and general entertainment. Although the reason for the evening is grounded in business, it is considered impolite to discuss business with one's host. Nevertheless, the overall purpose of the evening is for the host to determine what sort of person his/her counterpart is. Is he/she friendly, outgoing, relaxed? In a sense, it is laying the groundwork for negotiations.

For one who is not culturally attuned, business negotiations in Thailand can be like trying to walk up an escalator that is going down. For both Thais and foreigners, the priority must be not to cause one's counterpart "to lose face," that is, to become embarrassed. In the United States, we tend to affirm the individual more than the group. One's ability to be direct and to say what one means—in some cases, even to the point of being confrontational—is usually regarded as a positive attribute. But the relationship is more important than the individual in Thailand. If in the process of negotiations a Thai is presented with a less-than-satisfactory business proposal, he/she will not simply say "no." In order to "save the face" of his/her counterpart, the Thai will likely smile and respond with something like, "It will be difficult," or "It will take a long time," as opposed to an outright refusal of the terms. The westerner is strongly advised to take the same approach. One should never push one's position; in time, there will be a meeting of the minds.

As I often tell my students in World Religions, when visiting another country, never dismiss the importance of religion, even in seemingly secular circumstances. In Thailand, the opening of a new business or factory will often be marked with a Buddhist ceremony to confer blessing and good fortune. If one is attending such a ceremony, he/she should bring an envelope containing 100–200 baht as an offering to the temple that is conducting the ceremony. The envelope should be presented to the host of the event.

Last, a word about corruption. There are few, if any, nations in the world whose unofficial business and/or governmental practices do not include the occasional under-the-table financial incentive in order "to get things done" in an expedient manner. Thailand is no exception. Although the Thai government has put numerous reforms in place to combat such abuses (particularly in bureaucratic relationships), the practice is an ancient one that remains deeply rooted in Thai culture at-large. Because most of the early business people, merchants, and shopkeepers in Siam/Thailand were Chinese, it is likely that their entry into the culture was accompanied by the long-established tradition of secret societies, bureaucrats, and even gangs that extorted "protection money" from them in exchange for favors such as exclusive contracts, the driving away of competitors, or exemption from licensing, inspections, adherence to local building codes, and the like:

> In pre-modern China, the merchant had an attitude of mind quite different from that of the Western entrepreneur. . . . According to the latter, the economic man can prosper most by producing goods and securing from his increased production whatever profit the market will give him. In old China, however, the economic man would do best by increasing his own share of what had already been produced . . . to control an existing market by paying for an official license to do so. The tradition in China had been not to build a better mousetrap but to get the official mouse monopoly. . . . The bureaucracy lived by what we today would call systematized corruption, which sometimes became extortion. This went along

with the system of intricate personal relationships that each official had to maintain with his superiors, colleagues, and subordinate. (Fairbanks and Goldman 1992, 181–182)

Both in China and in Thailand, corruption therefore evolved into an acceptable economic and bureaucratic institution, conducted more in the open than one might guess. Official legislation can be passed, but practices that are hundreds of years old are difficult to overcome.

THAILAND'S ECONOMIC FUTURE

Popularly referred to as "Thaksinomics" by those who both support and oppose him, Prime Minister Thaksin Shinawatra's economic reform measures appear to be paying off. In August 2003, the Thai government made its final payment—a year early, in fact—on the US$17.2 billion bail-out loan extended to it in 1998 by the International Monetary Fund. As noted above, the economic growth figures (GDP) for 2003 exceeded projections. In light of the war in Iraq and the SARS outbreak in Asia, many analysts believed such expectations for 2003 to be next to impossible. And although Thaksin was aiming for 8 to 9 percent in 2004, the more conservative projection of 6.8 to 7.8 percent is still a healthy one. In 2003, Thailand has benefited greatly from free trade agreements (FTAs) with both China and India. Thai exports to those nations have increased 30 and 20 percent, respectively.

In October 2003, the United States and Thailand began negotiations for a free trade agreement. Building on a 2002 Trade and Investment Framework Agreement, an FTA should result in the elimination of a wide array of tariff barriers and increase U.S. exports to Thailand, particularly agricultural products, machinery, and aircraft. Currently, Thailand is the eighteenth-largest trading partner of the United States, with mutual trade totaling almost US$20 billion in 2002. In regard to real estate—according to most analysts, the core of the

Thai economic crisis—homebuyers are now required to pay via their lenders a 30 percent down payment on any home valued at more than US$250,000. With only serious buyers willing to pay such funds up front, the previous illusion of consumer demand that led to a massive surplus of vacant housing likely will be prevented.

How Thailand will fare economically in the long run remains to be seen. But with hope, there is a lesson in the Thai experience, not just for the Thais but for the economic health of every nation. In the introduction to this text, it was stated that the "Thai-ness" of the Thai is not a simple thing to quantify or define, especially for an outsider. But at the same time, it was also noted that sometimes the outsider has the capacity to recognize that quality more readily than the Thai, simply because his/her cultural orientation is not blurred by the experience of living in the midst of it. From an economic standpoint, perhaps one can say that this ineffable cultural quality is what King Pumipohn was speaking about in his 1997 birthday address when he spoke of self-sufficiency and the "sufficiency economy," the recovery of agrarian values, and that paradoxical "step backwards." Perhaps the economic crisis was a "wake-up call" to the Thais, to remind them that being a "Thai" is just as important as being a "tiger," that self-sufficiency needs to be balanced with global dependency. Whether there is any direct relationship between the king's recommendations and Thailand's remarkable economic recovery is difficult to say. But it is nevertheless worth noting that King Pumipohn's vision of a sufficiency economy was incorporated into Thailand's current Ninth National Economic and Social Development Plan (2002–2006). One can only hope that the combined visions of the king and the prime minister will continue to guide Thailand into a bright and secure economic future.

References
Arnold, Wayne. *New York Times*. "Thailand Sets Path toward Better Economy." October 24, 2003. http://www.nytimes.com (Accessed Oct. 24, 2003).

Bello, Walden, Shea Cunningham, and Li Kheng Poh. *A Siamese Tragedy.* London: Zed Books, 1998.

Business Day Newspaper. "Growth on Track: Analysts." http://www.bday.net (Accessed June 5, 2004).

———. "GDP May Slip to 6%: NESDB." http://www.bday.net (Accessed June 5, 2004).

Butler, Stephen. "'It Was Too Easy to Make Money'; and Now the Thai Economy Is Barely Afloat." *U.S. News and World Report* 23, no. 4 (July 28, 1997): 41.

Channel News Asia. 2003. "Thai Economy Is Best Performing Asian Economy after China." www.channelnewsasia.com (Accessed December 15, 2003).

CIA World Factbook 2003. www.cia.gov.

Fairbanks, John, and Merle Goldman. *China: A New History.* Cambridge, MA: Harvard University Press, 1992, 1998.

Jim Thompson House. "The Silk Story." Jim Thompson House Web site. http://www.jimthompsonhouse.org./life/index.html.

Leightner, Jonathan E. "Globalization and Thailand's Financial Crisis." *Journal of Economic Issues* 33, no. 2 (June 1999): 36–73.

Parkes, Carl. *Thailand Handbook,* 3d ed. Emeryville, CA: Moon Travel Handbooks, 2000.

Royal Forest Department of Thailand. "History." http://www.forest.go.th.

Sheng, Yap Kioe, and Sakchai Kirinpanu. "Once Only the Sky Was the Limit: Bangkok's Housing Boom and the Financial Crisis in Thailand." *Housing Studies* 15, no. 1 (January 2000): 11–27. OCLC FirstSearch. http://newfirstsearch.oclc.org (Accessed Dec. 11, 2003).

Speeches of His Majesty King Pumipohn Adunyadayt. http://kanchanapisek.or.th/speeches.

Thailand Development Research Institute. http://info.tdri.or.th.

Tourism Authority of Thailand. 2003. http://www.tourismthailand.org.

U.S. Embassy in Thailand. http://www.usa.or.th.

Warren, William. *The Legendary American: The Remarkable Career and Strange Disappearance of Jim Thompson.* Boston: Houghton Mifflin, 1970.

Xinhua News Agency. June 26, 2003. "Thai Economy to Remain Stable with Good Outlook: PM." http://infotrac.galegroup.com (Accessed Dec. 11, 2003).

———. August 29, 2003. "Thai Economy to Grow 6 Percent in 2003." http://infotrac.galegroup.com (Accessed Dec. 11, 2003).

CHAPTER THREE

Social Institutions

POLITICS, GOVERNMENT, AND THE ROYAL MONARCHY

As discussed in our outline of Thai history (see Chapter One), Thailand has been a constitutional monarchy since 1932. Even though the monarchy continues to serve as the spiritual and ceremonial head of state, Thailand's actual working government is supervised and represented by a prime minister. Under the current constitution (ratified in 1997), the prime minister is elected to a four-year term, not by the people, but by the political party that holds the most seats in the House of Representatives. Similar to the United States, the Thai government is composed of three distinct branches: the executive, the legislative, and the judicial.

In 2004 the executive branch was composed of H.R.H. King Pumipohn Adunyadayt, Prime Minister Thaksin Shinawatra, and a "cabinet" of ministers to supervise the various sectors of the government. The prime minister selects a cabinet of twenty ministers, usually from the membership of the party or coalition of parties that elected him. In turn, these cabinet ministers are the administrators of twenty ministries, or departments. Thailand's ministries are similar in name and function to the federal departments found in the U.S. government, such as Ministry of Education, Ministry of Commerce, and Ministry of Defense.

Similar to the U.S. Congress, the Thai government has a bicameral legislature called the National Assembly. It consists of a 200-member Senate, directly elected by the Thai people, and a 500-member House of Representatives, 400 of which are elected by the Thai people, with the remaining 100 being drawn proportionately to the represented political parties. Currently, Prime Minister Thaksin Shinawatra's party, the *Thai Rak Thai* ("Thais love Thais"), controls an overwhelming 365 of the 500 seats of the House of Representatives (for more information on the unique nature of Thai political parties, see below).

The judicial branch is composed of three court levels: the Constitutional Court, the Courts of Justice, and the Administrative Courts. The Constitutional Court is not unlike the U.S. Supreme Court, in that it deals strictly with constitutional issues. Its members are nominated by the Senate and then appointed by the king. The Courts of Justice oversee criminal and civil cases. Within the Courts of Justice are three sublevels whose function are self-explanatory: the Court of First Instance, the Court of Appeals, and the Supreme Court. The Administrative Courts are concerned with lawsuits between private parties, as well as litigations between Thailand and other governments. It should also be noted that in Southern Thailand, where the majority of the population is Muslim, traditional Islamic law plays a role in judicial affairs. Provincial Islamic courts have a limited jurisdiction over cases concerning marriage, family, and probate matters.

Though we have seen that there are some fundamental similarities between the structures of the Thai and U.S. governments, there are some distinct differences as well. In the United States, for example, we are accustomed to partisan politics. We traditionally identify a given political party with a certain sociopolitical philosophy, regardless of who is representing that party at the time; for example, Democrats are generally liberal and supportive of strong, centralized government whereas Republicans are conservative and supportive of a more laissez-faire government. In Thailand, however, political parties are nothing like this. A party is little more than a coalition of people who have given their collective support to a particular individual. There may be dozens of political parties in Thailand at any given time. In short, Thais don't align themselves with a particular party that represents a sociopolitical philosophy as much as they give their support to a particular person who can address their immediate needs and concerns. In short, Thais are accustomed to perceiving their leaders as discrete "personalities." The prime minister, for example, is not regarded simply as an agent of a larger, more abstract political idea, but as a kind of entity unto himself. His power and influence are generated not by political affiliation but by his own individual effort and perseverance. From a cultural perspective, this rationale is quite sensible for two reasons. First, fundamental Buddhism teaches that one's karmic disposition in the ongoing cycle of birth, death, and rebirth is solely a question of one's own actions. Generating a strong political following is like accumulating "good karma" (for a detailed explanation of this Hindu/Buddhist concept, see "Religion," later in this chapter). Second, the premise of rallying around a person as opposed to a party is deeply rooted in the ancient tradition of royal court patronage and ritual. Personal charisma is deemed as being on a par with professional competency, if not more essential altogether.

In national/parliamentary elections, Thai voter turnout is relatively high. In the Parliamentary elections of 2000, for example, approximately 29.9 million votes were cast out of a registered voter pool of approximately 42.8 million, resulting in a voter turnout of almost 70 percent.

Below the national level, the Thai government also functions on a variety of regional and local levels. Thailand is divided into seventy-six *jahngwahts,* or provinces. Comparatively speaking, the American might think of a jahngwaht as a "state." Each janhngwaht is subdivided into a handful of *ahmpuhrs,* or districts. A small province might have five to seven districts, whereas a larger province could have as many as fifteen to twenty. Again, the U.S. equivalent might be a "county." In total, there are at present 794 ahmpuhrs in Thailand. An ahmpuhr is further subdivided into *dahmbohns,* or townships. Finally, a dahmbohn consists of a number of *moobahns,* or village groups. In rural areas, a moobahn is what one would understand to be a village in the traditional sense of the term; but in suburban and urban areas, a moobahn is the equivalent of a neighborhood or a residential subdivision. From jahngwaht to moobahn, every regional division is governed by an appointed administrator. A jahngwaht is ruled by a provincial governor (*poowahrachagahnjahngwaht*). Provincial governors are appointed by the Ministry of the Interior, although Bangkok (a province in its own right) elects its own. An ahmpuhr is ruled by a district administrator (*naiahmpuhr*), a dahmbohn is ruled by a town manager (*gahmnahn*), and a moobahn is ruled by a village headperson (*pooyaibahn*). Following is a brief description of what these administrators do.

The provincial governor presides over a provincial council, supervises the overall administration of the province, and coordinates the work of field staffs from the various ministries of the central government. The district administrator reports to the provincial governor, supervises the collection of taxes, maintains basic registers and statistics (e.g., births, deaths, marriages), oversees local elections at the township and village levels, and convenes monthly meetings of the township and village administrators. A town manager assists in tax collection and supervises the work of village headpersons, meeting with them on a regular basis. A village headperson serves as a conduit between villagers and district administrators, keeps village records, arbitrates civil disputes, and generally serves as the village "peace officer."

Although the administrative divisions and officials described here constitute the traditional structure of regional and local government, it should also be noted that Thailand does have many towns and cities that qualify as "municipalities," such as Bangkok. These larger municipal areas function as components within that hierarchical structure but also have elected mayors that administer their particular local affairs.

The importance of these administrative divisions is not limited to bureaucratic matters alone. Rather, anyone who mails a letter or rides a public bus in Thailand needs to be aware of the various provinces, districts, townships, and villages within the country. And as often as regional boundaries change (rezoned townships, new suburban villages, etc.), it is vitally important to stay on top of it all. If, for example, I want to mail a letter through the Thai postal system, this is how the envelope address would look (a former address of one of my Thai relatives):

Khanittha S (name)
108/409 (house number)
Gritsadanakawn 10 (moobahn)
Bahngrahkpattana (dahmbohn)
Banhgbuatawng (ahmpuhr)
Nohntaburi (jahngwaht)
11110 ("zip code")
Thailand (country)

In addition to these primary administrative positions, the civil service in Thailand employs thousands of men and women in low, middle, and high-level positions throughout the multiple facets of regional government, as well as in the various ministries and departments of the central government. Despite complaints about the inadequacy of government salaries, or the personal politics that inevitably come into play as one makes one's way through the labyrinth of professional advancement, a civil service career is still considered to be among the most desirable career routes to financial security and social status. The benefits of government employment are excellent: employees and their families receive complete medical coverage, expense-free education, and very comfortable pensions. However, professional security has a way of devolving into professional complacency. While this may perhaps be said of any bureaucracy in the world, one of the most common complaints that one hears about Thai government bureaucracy is how long it takes to get things done, particularly at the points of contact between the government official and the Thai public at large. As noted in our discussion of the Thai economy, corruption and bribery have become all too common methods of expediting bureaucratic transactions.

How have Thai women fared in political administration? Thai women were given the right to vote and to hold public office through Thailand's first constitution, in 1932, but women were not elected to Parliament until 1949. Recent studies (2000) indicated that Thai women comprised approximately 10 percent of the membership of the Thai Senate and 6 percent of the House of Representatives. But elected women at the municipal, district, and provincial levels combined amount to no more than 10 percent. Women also reportedly hold over 18 percent of the top administrative positions in the various ministries of the Thai government, although most of these positions are limited to what many would consider to be "gender-traditional" areas, such as the ministries of education and public health. It was not until 1995 that women were appointed to the positions of provincial governor and district administrator for the first time. On the local level, women have better opportunities to become involved in political administration. There are eighty-one female mayors of Thai towns and cities, and 209 female city clerks.

What role does monarchy play in Thailand's government? As noted in our previous discussion on early Thai history, the kings of Sukhothai, most notably Ramkahmheng (r. 1275–1317), ruled in the spirit of the dhammaraja, that is, in accordance with the concept of the compassionate and paternal king who is guided by the wise and ethical teachings of the Buddha. In stark contrast, many of the kings of Ayutthaya inherited the ancient Indian concept of devaraja, or "god-king," primarily through the Khmer civilization. They were perceived (and perceived themselves) as much more remote and inaccessible figures who were, as far as the Thai people were concerned, shrouded in transcendent mystery. The kings of the Chakri Dynasty (1782-present) recovered, for the most part, the Sukhothai model of the paternal king who was guided in his reign by the Buddhist concept of virtue. This is especially true of the current and longest-reigning monarch of Thailand, H.R.H. King Pumipohn Adunyadayt (Rama IX).

Despite the fact that the Thai monarchy has had neither absolute nor constitutional power since the advent of the constitutional monarchy in 1932, the king continues to be regarded by the Thai people as the head of state, the defender of the faith, and the very personification of the Thai national identity. Just as the Thai national flag's colors of red, white and blue represent nation, Buddhism, and monarchy, so also the king is the embodiment of those three facets of the Thai consciousness. With no constitutional authority per se, his personal intervention has nevertheless brought even the most violent coups and revolutions to an end.

> As ceremonial head of state, the monarch is endowed with a formal power of assent and appointment, is above partisan affairs, and does not involve himself in the decision-making processes of the government.... [The King remains] the nation's most respected figure because he was popularly perceived to be the embodiment of religion, culture, and history. He [ensures] political stability and unity by lending legitimacy to important government actions and, in potentially destabilizing situations . . . by discreetly signaling his support of the incumbent government. (Library of Congress 1987: 186–187)

And so even in the twenty-first century it would be no exaggeration to say that in many Thai hearts and minds, the king continues to be lifted up as something of a devaraja, but at the same time is embraced as a virtuous and paternal dhammaraja. As such, King Pumipohn is not regarded as a mere representative of the royal monarchy as an abstract idea; rather, in his very person, the king *is* the monarchy in all its power and virtue.

One of the more overt ways in which this unique identity is affirmed is through the use of language. When one makes verbal reference to the king or to any member of the royal family, one must employ *rachasahp,* or "royal language." This is a high language composed primarily of verbs, nouns, and pronouns that are reserved only for them. The use of rachasahp applies not only to the protocol of formal circumstances but to TV/radio news broadcasters who are simply reporting the king's public activities on any given day. Even when making reference to an action as mundane as eating or walking, special verbal forms must be employed.

Unless it is commemorating a particular event or occasion, virtually every postage stamp in the Thai postal system bears a portrait of King Pumipohn. Though such a convention is hardly unusual for a monarchy, I was surprised to learn on my first visit to Thailand that many traditional Thais hold the monarchy in such high esteem that even the very idea of licking the back of a stamp that bears the king's image would be an act of great disrespect (at least in public view). Today this is a moot issue, as Thailand's post offices now carry self-adhesive stamps.

Whether in Thailand or in a foreign nation, one would be hard pressed to find a Thai home or business that does not have elegantly framed portraits of King Pumipohn and Queen Sirikit hanging on the wall. Oftentimes, one will also find a portrait of Chulalongkawn (Rama V) nearby, as he is still revered as the "father" of modern Thailand. Among the numerous social and technological advancements achieved during his reign (1868–1910), King Chulalongkawn decreed that persons in the presence of the king would no longer be forced to prostrate themselves on the floor but be permitted to sit in normal postures. Nevertheless, it continues to be a fundamental component of royal protocol that no one's head should be higher than that of the king. But for all of the effort that is traditionally devoted to the lifting of the royal monarchy to a level of "paternal transcendence," the current

H.R.H. King Pumipohn Adunyadayt (Rama IX), 1946–present, accompanied by his daughter, H.R.H. Princess Maha Chakri Sirintawn. May 8, 1987. Bangkok, Thailand. (Michael Freeman/Corbis)

monarch and his family are remarkably present to the Thai people and actively involved in their cultural development and economic welfare.

King Pumipohn was born in 1927—not in Thailand, but in Cambridge, Massachusetts, where his father, Prince Mahidohn of Songkla, was studying medicine at Harvard. The reader will recall that Pumipohn's older brother, Ananda Mahidohn, was initially chosen to be the next king, following his childless uncle's abdication in 1935. The kingship was

H.R.H. Queen Sirikit. (Courtesy of the Royal Thai Government)

thrust upon Pumipohn unexpectedly at the age of nineteen, in the wake of Ananda's mysterious death in 1946. Prior to his formal coronation in 1950, he returned to Switzerland to finish his education, quickly changing his major from natural sciences to political science and law. But his talent and continuing interest in both the arts and the sciences was nevertheless destined to become a vital component in King Pumipohn's role as Thai monarch.

King Pumipohn is known for a wide array of talents. In addition to being an avid photographer, painter, and sailor, he is a talented musician and composer, particularly in the field of jazz. Due to his Western education, he is fluent in three European languages. But alongside all of these personal talents, King Pumipohn is most known for what he has done directly for the Thai people. Having come to power at such a transitional time in Thai history and in world history at large, he was faced with the challenge of how to address the needs of a society that was simultaneously grounded in ancient tradition and on the brink of industrial/technological transformation.

In the past, the opportunity for a typical Thai citizen to speak to or even to see his/her king was rare indeed, especially outside of Central Thailand. After all, what did the course of events taking place in an urban center like Bangkok have to do with the day-to-day lives of rice farmers in the northeastern provinces of Eesahn? Did it really matter who was in charge? In response to generations of isolation, one of King Pumipohn's most pivotal decisions was to bring the monarchy into direct contact with the provincial people, especially those of the northern and northeastern regions (he is, in fact, the first Thai monarch to have traveled to every province in Thailand). By so doing, the king has been able to witness firsthand the challenges faced by rural communities. It is in this context that King Pumipohn's continued interest in science, technology, and engineering has come into play. He has addressed and in some cases even personally financed the development of scientific methods to improve crop pro-

duction, water conservation, reforestation, and a much-publi-
cized program in cloud-seeding for improved rainfall. Even on
the grounds of his home in Bangkok, King Pumipohn has constructed fields of experimental rice, a dairy farm, and a series
of ponds in which he has raised several fast-breeding species
of fish that have been used to replenish the freshwater food
fish population in provincial rivers and streams.

The ongoing commitment to the welfare of the Thai people
does not end with King Pumipohn; other members of the
royal family are actively engaged in similar projects and
endeavors. Queen Sirikit, who travels with her husband on
many of his visits to rural and mountainous areas, has over
the years taken a special interest in the revival of Thailand's
ancient arts, such as weaving, metalworking, woodworking,
rattan ware, and, as we saw in the previous chapter, silk production. She has helped to organize, fund, and provide a market for cottage industry cooperatives, especially those that
provide employment opportunities for rural women. Such
cooperatives have proven to be vital for the financial support
of rural villages that have suffered from poor crop seasons.

King Pumipohn and Queen Sirikit have four children: one
son and three daughters, all of whom are now adults. Though
the crown prince and the princesses each support their
father's agenda in varying capacities, the most notable among
them is Princess Maha Chakri Sirintawn. Born in 1955,
Princess Sirintawn is a remarkable woman. She holds multiple academic degrees, lectures in two of Thailand's most prestigious universities, serves as head of the Thai Red Cross, and
is engaged in numerous developmental projects and educational programs for Thailand's poor. Her title, *Maha Chakri,* is
particularly significant. Conferred in 1981 in acknowledgment of her tireless service to Thailand, it translates loosely
as "great lord." But the implication of the title is more than
honorary. Essentially, *Maha Chakri* identifies Sirintawn as
the crown princess of Thailand. In light of the fact that there
is already a crown prince, would one be mistaken in reading

some subtle controversy into the question of royal succession? Not necessarily. Although Crown Prince Maha Vajiralongkawn is the traditional heir apparent to the Thai throne, Princess Maha Chakri Sirintawn is so loved by the Thai people that her succession to the throne as the first female monarch in Thai history is a very real possibility. Although it is more than likely that the crown prince will inherit the throne, only time will tell.

EDUCATION

When King Ramkahmheng of Sukhothai created the first Thai alphabet in 1283, the initial benefactors of this new literary tool were the Buddhist monks, for they could now translate ancient Buddhist texts from Pali (the original language of the Theravadan Buddhist scriptures) into a textual language of their own. In turn, they could educate themselves and the laity in a variety of subjects through both the spoken and the written word. The farmers and peasants who comprised the vast majority of Thai society, however, saw little need for literacy and formal education. As was the case with many agrarian-based cultures, history, folklore, popular religious beliefs, and basic day-to-day information were transmitted orally. And so, prior to the late nineteenth century, opportunities for formal education in Thailand were limited to the economically privileged members of the aristocracy and the royal court. Education was acquired not in schools and universities but through the priesthood of Buddhist temples and monasteries. Therefore, not unlike early medieval European society, the religious institutions were the first centers of literacy and education.

As noted in the previous outline of Thai history, the mid- to late nineteenth and early twentieth century Siamese monarchs Mongkut (Rama IV, r. 1851–1868), Chulalongkawn (Rama V, r. 1868–1910), and Vajiravudh (Rama VI, r. 1910–1925) were instrumental in establishing the foundations of Thailand's formal educational system. The reader will recall Mongkut's contracting of a European teacher (Anna Leonowens) for the children of the royal household in 1862; this was followed by Chulalongkawn's creation of the first state-sponsored school for the children of princes and courtiers in 1871, as well as opportunities for Thai students and scholars to study abroad (including Chulalongkawn's own son, the Crown Prince Vajiravudh). Through such circumstances, Western-inspired models for teaching and learning were gradually introduced and assimilated into Thai society. In 1892, the Ministry of Education was created and placed in charge of overseeing the development and implementation of an educational system that would be accessible by all sectors of Thai society. It was to be structured around two interrelated paths: the academic and the vocational. During Vijaravudh's reign, a formal system of elementary, secondary, and postsecondary institutions was created, including colleges of teacher training, civil service, law, medicine, and engineering. The initial purpose of these postsecondary institutions was to train qualified personnel for government service in Thailand's growing bureaucracy. By the time the constitutional monarchy was established in 1932, a formal educational system was in place that came to be recognized as essential to Thailand's continuing development as a modern nation-state.

Thailand is a member of the Southeast Asian Minister of Education Organization (SEAMEO). Member nations follow a basic curriculum structure in their respective educational systems. The components of Thailand's educational system and their distribution have evolved over the years and continue to do so. At present, the Thai educational system and its curriculum are constructed in the following manner:

1. Pre-primary education is for 3–5-year-old children and is more or less equivalent to the Western model of preschool and/or kindergarten. It emphasizes the integration of physical, intellectual, emotional, and social development prior to formal education. Because attendance at this level is not compulsory, most of its institutions exist within the private

sector and are supervised by the Office of the Private Education Commission, a subsidiary of the Ministry of Education.

2. Primary education is provided for children aged 6–11 years. It is compulsory and free of charge. Loosely equivalent to grades one through six in the West, its curriculum emphasizes literacy, arithmetic, and communication/language skills. "Language skills" means more than learning to read and write in Thai. As early as the primary level, students are exposed to the fundamentals of English vocabulary and grammar. These parallel paths of language study will continue for as long as the student remains in formal education. Because student backgrounds vary according to the unique cultural elements and ethnicity of the given region of the country, the national curriculum embodies a certain degree of flexibility. Government primary schools are under the supervision of the Office of the National Primary Education Commission, Ministry of Education, although there are some demonstration schools (i.e., training schools attached to teacher's colleges and universities) that fall under the supervision of the Ministry of the Interior.

3. Secondary education is divided into two sections of three years each, called "lower secondary" (equivalent to Western grades seven through nine) and "higher secondary" (equivalent to grades ten through twelve), respectively. The secondary education curriculum covers five core areas: language, science/mathematics, social studies, character development, and work education. As a component of the language core, English-language courses are mandatory. The lower secondary level emphasizes moral ethics and basic academic skills. It also offers a wide variety of both academic and vocational subjects so that the student can explore and discern his/her particular interests and strengths. Once the student's interests and strengths are identified, the upper level provides academic and/or vocational courses that correspond to those interests. If a student wishes to enter directly into a specialized field, such as business accounting, a basic computer-related profession, or a vocational/technical field, he/she is required only to complete the lower secondary level. The student will then enroll in a

training institution that specializes in the given field. But if the student intends to enroll in a postsecondary academic institution, that is, a college or university, he/she must also complete the higher secondary level. Secondary education, though strongly encouraged, is not compulsory at either level. As we shall see, this in itself constitutes a fundamental problem for the overall health of Thai education.

4. Tertiary or higher education focuses on the full intellectual and social development of the student and his/her advancement into a specialized professional field. Thailand's sixty-five colleges and universities are supervised by the Ministry of University Affairs. There are about 150 additional vocational training colleges under the supervision of the Ministry of Education. Thailand's first state university was Chulalongkawn University, founded in 1917 by King Vijaravudh in honor of his father. Chulalongkawn University continues to be Thailand's most prestigious educational institution. In Thailand, the perspective toward university education is markedly different from that with which a westerner is likely accustomed. State universities have what is referred to as "closed" (restricted) enrollment whereas private colleges and universities have "open" enrollment. State universities are therefore considered the most desirable, and admission is extremely competitive. Admission to state universities is attained only through a competitive national university entrance examination that is given in April of each year by the Ministry of University Affairs. By June, the results of the examination are broadcast on national television. It is a very stressful time for students and their families, for if one's name does not appear on the screen with the school to which he/she has applied, it means that he/she did not earn a satisfactory grade on the national exam. If this is the case, one must apply to one of the private colleges or universities, whose admission requirements are more "open" and therefore less rigid. But unfortunately for the financially responsible party, they are also much more expensive!

Although it sounds strange to the Western ear, the combination of high expense and low status is perhaps indicative of the low percentage of students enrolled in private institutions of higher learning. But on the primary and secondary levels, the private school perspective is somewhat different. Though the vast majority of primary and secondary students attends public government schools, there are a handful of very fine private institutions, most of them affiliated with a denomination of the Christian church. But they, too, are quite expensive. In 2000, for example, private primary schools accounted for about 13 percent of the primary enrollment.

Because Thailand still considers itself to be a developing country on the global stage, it should not be surprising that students are generally encouraged to follow educational paths that center on science and technology, as well as business. As we have seen, both the primary and secondary curricula are geared in that direction, whereas the arts and humanities tend to take a back seat (if not discouraged altogether) as far as career direction is concerned. To be sure, Thailand's fine-arts heritage is revered; but from a practical perspective, the kingdom's future is seen as being hinged on its ability to keep pace with a global network whose information and communications technology seemingly evolves on a daily basis. Nevertheless, there are formal educational channels for the creative and artistic spirits of Thailand, most notably Silapakawn University. As the academic branch of the government Department of Fine Arts, Silapakawn was founded in 1943. It offers formal programs of study in studio art (painting, sculpture, etc.), performance art (theater and dance, both classical and contemporary), interior design, architecture, and archaeology. Secondary though they may be, the traditional visual and performing arts of Thailand will always constitute the soul of the kingdom, and it is to the credit of the Thai government that they have not been forgotten.

It is not difficult to spot a primary or secondary student in Thailand. As all public schools are supervised by the Thai government, students are, for the most part, required to wear uniforms. Boys wear navy blue trousers (short or long, depending on the age of the student) with short-sleeved white

Thai primary school children. (Anuchit and Khanittha Chaiarsa)

shirts; girls wear navy blue pleated skirts with short-sleeved white blouses and blue ties. Although Thai school children are spared the competitive fashion battles that all too often plague public school dress codes, student self-esteem, and family budgets in the West, the purchasing of mandatory uniforms nevertheless places a significant financial burden on many Thai families, especially in rural areas. As figures cited below will indicate, the expense that accompanies the enrollment of a child in school is high on the list of reasons for nonattendance, even during the compulsory years. For such circumstances, the Thai government has implemented financial assistance programs that are designed to subsidize education-related expenses for families in need.

At virtually all levels of education in Thailand, the Thai classroom has traditionally been regarded as an environment of reasonably strict conformity, not creative individuality.

Thai secondary school children. (Courtesy of Anuchit and Khanittha Chaiarsa)

Teachers and professors normally present their material in a traditional lecture format that doesn't provide much opportunity for student response or participation. Students are taught from a very young age simply to accept what a teacher or professor says without question, as anything less would be deemed disrespectful. At the same time, however, it should be noted that Thai educators, particularly in the upper secondary and postsecondary levels, have begun in recent years to adopt more participative teaching models, such as interactive discussion groups and student-led presentations. Nevertheless, when Thai students travel to the West to attend a college or university, it is often very difficult for them to become accustomed to the premise that teacher-student interaction in the classroom is expected and encouraged.

Extracurricular activities play an important role in Thai

education. Interscholastic sports such as soccer, track and field, volleyball, tennis, swimming, and even basketball are quite popular. But one of the most pervasive extracurricular activities for both boys and girls is scouting. First introduced to Thailand in 1911 by King Vajiravudh (Rama VI), it began initially as a kind of adult reserve paramilitary force called *Sueah Bpah*, or the "Wild Tiger Corps." Designed to assist legitimate military forces on the homefront in the event of emergencies or natural disasters, the Wild Tiger Corps was modeled after the British Volunteer Corps that Vajiravudh observed during his university study in England. Later, Vajiravudh created a junior branch, appropriately called *Loog Seuah*, or the "Tiger Cubs." Eventually a branch for girls was created as well. Thailand is the only nation in the world in which a scouting program was directly founded by a monarch. It continues to be supported by royal patronage.

In Thai primary and secondary schools, the scouting program functions on three levels: the Cub Scouts (primary years 1–4), the Scouts (primary years 5–6), and the Senior Scouts (secondary years 1–2). As contemporary scouting activities are quite similar worldwide, Thailand is no exception. Objectives include such things as development of national pride and identity, public service, physical fitness, environmental awareness, and practical skills such as map reading, first aid, use of tools, and camping. Thursday is "Scout Day" in Thai schools, and students come to school wearing their scout uniforms. They attend local and regional meetings and work toward the attainment of proficiency badges in areas such as those listed above. Now a part of the worldwide scouting program, Thailand hosted the Twentieth World Scouting Jamboree in 2003.

Thailand's educational system has both its successes and challenges. On the plus side, literacy rates in Thailand are quite high. For Thais aged fifteen and over, males have a 96 percent literacy rate, and females have a rate of 91.6 percent. This is a very significant increase from 1970, when the overall kingdom literacy rate was 88.9 percent for males and no more than 74.8 percent for females. In typical Thai classrooms, the ratio of students to teacher is quite good as well: in primary schools the ratio is about 20:1, and in secondary schools, about 25:1.

Recent studies, however, have indicated figures that are less than encouraging. In 2002 the overall rate of matriculation from primary to secondary schools stood at about 90 percent. But with a compulsory requirement of only six years—the completion of the primary/elementary level—the dropout rate in secondary schools is considerable, particularly in rural and/or impoverished communities. The circumstances for dropping out vary, but the vast majority of them are financial. In 1997 a study was conducted among approximately 2.5 million Thai youth aged 13–19 (1.3 million males, 1.2 million females) who had dropped out of secondary school. Of that total, 44.8 percent had discontinued their education due to lack of financial support, and 23.4 percent had to go to work to earn a living. Within those figures, female dropout percentages ran approximately 5 percent higher than males in both categories. As a result, the average completion rate among Thai adults is 6.5 years, little more than the compulsory requirement.

In a 1990 study, the percentage of Thai males aged 15–24 who were enrolled in secondary or tertiary (postsecondary) schools stood at only 17.9, and the female percentage among the same age group was 17.3. The percentages for the year 2025 are projected at 20.9 and 22.8, respectively. These percentages are among the lowest in Southeast Asia. If current educational trends do not improve, Thailand could be facing a grim scenario, in that the vast majority of its working adults will have little more than a primary education. Without the continued presence of a skilled workforce that is qualified to function in a high-technology environment, Thailand will no longer be able to keep pace with competitive economies in the region. A 90 percent rate of progression from primary schools to secondary schools is encouraging, but how does one keep them enrolled when the more immediate concerns of farming and/or working simply to make ends meet for their families become the priorities? One can only hope that through a combination of increased government subsidy and heightened public awareness, or "education about education," more students and their families will be able to appreciate the larger picture without having to make a choice between educational preparation for their future and financial survival in the present.

One facet of Thai education that is in continual need of attention is the promotion of more substantial educational choices and opportunities for women. Today, it is not so much a question of opportunity; educational opportunities for women have increased substantially over the past few decades. In 1975, for example, 22 percent of Thai women attended secondary school (high school), and only 3 percent went on to college-level education. But in 1995, 37 percent attended secondary school, and 20 percent went to college. Thailand's National Statistical Office (NSO) concluded that "the present generation [both male and female] generally has equal access to education. However, gender inequality still remains in terms of major fields of study. Women tend to enroll in courses such as liberal arts and home economics that conform to their socially defined roles" (Social Statistics Division, National Statistical Office). Thus, improved education for women in Thailand today is interpreted not so much as a question of establishing new educational opportunities per se but of overcoming the long-held social assumptions that seem to mask those opportunities for many Thai women. But despite the NSO's assertion that equal gender opportunity exists, it can most certainly be argued that the very presence of "socially defined roles" constitutes a lack of educational and/or professional opportunity.

Teachers have always been highly respected in Thailand. In former times, teachers in Thailand worked for no pay; they

Thai theater and dance students performing Pitee Wai Kru, or "the rite of paying homage to teachers." (Courtesy of Timothy Hoare)

simply taught their students in a spirit of service and kindness. At the conclusion of each year or session, grateful students would hold a ceremony to express their appreciation. Even though teachers are now paid salaries like every other working person, one of the more unique features of the Thai educational system continues to be *pitee wai kru,* "the rite of paying homage to teachers." Performed at each and every educational institution in Thailand at the end of the school year, pitee wai kru is a solemn, highly ritualized event in which all the students of the given school assemble to show their collective appreciation and respect for their teachers. Sometimes small gifts are given, but normally students present their teachers with flowers and/or fruit and then bow before them (see the custom of wai, discussed in the section "Thai Etiquette"). Pitee wai kru also provides special remembrance and commemoration for those teachers who have passed on, both recently and long ago. Even though they are no longer living, the enactment of the ritual invokes their spiritual presence.

Essentially, the student-teacher relationship in Thailand is one that never ends. Even after one has graduated, become an adult, and entered into a profession, one's teacher will always be one's teacher. If a Thai person has the occasion to meet with one of his/her teachers again at any time in the future, that teacher will still be shown the same degree of respect as in the past when he/she was a child. And so, in a sense, pitee wai kru continues to be enacted throughout one's life.

RELIGION

The role of religion in contemporary Western cultures such as the United States has been shaped by fundamental principles of individualism and the separation of church and state. As such, religion is usually regarded as a private matter of one's own conscience, as a personal choice among many within a cultural landscape that is predominantly secular.

In most Southeast Asian cultures, however, the role of religion in the life of the people is not so sequestered. It is much more public, in the sense that religion is not simply a question of one's individual belief system but of an overall cultural character. As noted earlier, the white stripe in Thailand's national flag represents the prevalence of its primary religion: Buddhism. Not surprisingly, approximately 95 percent of the Thai population is Buddhist; 4 percent follows Islam (to be addressed presently); and the remaining 1 percent accounts for Christianity, Hinduism, and other belief systems, some of which will be addressed as well. But before discussing Thai Buddhism in particular, I offer a brief overview of the historical Buddha and what he taught.

Who was the Buddha? First and foremost, the Buddha was not a god, but a man. Siddhartha Gautama (ca. 563–483 BCE) was born in Northeast India—in what is now Nepal. He was a prince in a high-caste family and therefore lived in an exceptionally affluent and protective environment. At his birth, it was prophesied that he would grow up to be either a great king or a great redeemer. His father, of course, opted for the kingly direction and did everything he could to shield Siddhartha from any pain and suffering. But as this prophecy had two possible paths, destiny took its course. As we are told in *The Legend of the Four Passing Sights,* Siddhartha experienced a radical transformation when the sound of some beautiful music lured him outside the palace walls. Along the road, he witnessed an elderly man, whereby he learned the reality of age; a person ravaged by disease, which showed him the reality of sickness; a corpse, which stunned him with the reality of death; and finally, a community of monks with their begging bowls, which taught him the reality of want.

Age, sickness, death, and want; is there any realm, asked the shaken Siddhartha, in which human beings are freed from these facts of human existence? And so he set off on a journey, leaving behind his affluence and royal identity (as well as his wife and child). He studied with Hindu ascetics for six years, living at times on only a few grains of rice per day. Such self-denial and austerity almost killed him. Realizing that the path of extreme asceticism was as pointless as his previous path of decadence, Siddhartha sat under a tree to meditate, determined not to arise until he had achieved enlightenment.

During the next forty-nine days and nights, Siddhartha was subjected to a variety of visions and temptations from Mara, an Indian equivalent of Satan. In one tradition, we are told that in the midst of these visions, an angel appeared to him. The angel carried a three-stringed musical instrument and began to play it. The first string made no sound, because it was tuned too loosely. The second string broke, because it was tuned too tightly. The third string, however, played a beautiful tone, because it was tuned just right (does this sound familiar?). From this experience, Siddhartha realized the truth he had been seeking. One must seek not the extreme paths of austerity or affluence but the way of temperance,

which the Thais call *tahng sai glahng,* or "The Middle Way."
It was at this point that Siddhartha became *buddha.* The
word *buddha* comes from the Sanskrit verb *budh,* which
means "to wake up" (*budh ta,* past participle "to have woken
up"). For example, upon being asked by some curious inquirers, "Are you an angel, a prophet, a god?" the Buddha simply
replied, "I am awake." The Buddha, therefore, is the one who
is enlightened, or "awake."

What did the Buddha teach? Among his most important
teachings are the Four Noble Truths:

1. *Dukkha,* or "suffering": life and its experiences are unsatisfactory and impermanent. All things and experiences change;
   nothing remains the same. Everything that we regard as
   lasting and independent is in fact simply an effect of a
   previous cause, which will, in turn, serve as a cause for a
   subsequent effect.
2. *Tanha,* or "desire": despite this state of impermanence and
   constant change, we still crave and lust after what life has to
   offer. Suffering and desire, therefore, are inextricably linked to
   one another. No matter what we want, be it an object or an
   achievement, it will inevitably result in the realization of its
   inherent impermanence, thereby leading to desire once again.
   This cycle of "dependent origination" is called *karma.* Unless
   broken, the karmic cycle continues on and on.
3. Desire must therefore be overcome; the cycle must be broken.
   No desire means no suffering.
4. The prescription for overcoming desire is "The Eightfold Path":
   right understanding, right aspiration, right speech, right
   conduct, right livelihood, right endeavor, right mindfulness,
   and right concentration. Each of these is a meditative step
   along the path to enlightenment.

One's personal disposition or situation within the cycle of
suffering and desire, and ultimately of birth, death, and
rebirth, is known as karma. Karma literally means "work" or
"action." Any action that one does, or any thought that one
thinks, generates positive or negative karma. Ultimately,

then, how one lives one's life shall determine the disposition of his/her rebirth. Therefore, karma may be thought of as a kind of moral monitor. It is based on neither luck nor predetermined destiny, but on the fundamental relationship of cause and effect. The individual him/herself alone is responsible. It is for this reason that Thais often speak of "making merit," that is, of performing kind and generous acts in order to generate good karma. The accumulation of good karma leads one toward the ultimate goal of Buddhist enlightenment: the release from the karmic cycle of birth-death-rebirth, or *Nirvana*. Nirvana comes from the Sanskrit verb *nibbati*, meaning "to extinguish," as a breath of air or the wind extinguishes a flame. Thus Nirvana is the void, the negation of experience and one's misperception that anything that we want or have is "real." Indeed, this does not strike the Western consumer-oriented mind as "liberation." But we must keep this within the context of the Buddha's teaching. If "every thing" is impermanent and unsatisfactory, then the only "thing" that is permanent and satisfactory is "no thing." It is for this reason that in many styles of Buddhist art and architecture, simplicity, emptiness, and space are the most important characteristics.

Though the preceding overview has presented the origins and fundamental teachings of Buddhism, it must always be kept in mind that a religion not only shapes a cultural identity but is also *shaped by* the culture in which it is practiced. So also, Thailand has shaped and seasoned Buddhism with its own unique cultural ingredients.

Traditionally, Thailand acknowledges the year 543 BCE as the year in which Siddhartha began his spiritual journey—when he was about twenty years of age. If one adds this number to the current Western year (as of this writing, 2004), the sum is 2547. Thus, the current "Buddhist year" in Thailand is 2547. Most other Buddhist cultures determine the Buddhist year by basing the equation on the accepted year of his birth, 563 BCE.

Along with every other Southeast Asian nation except Vietnam, Thailand practices a form of Buddhism known as Theravada, or "the way of the elders." As discussed in Chapter One, King Ramkhamheng of the first Thai kingdom of Sukhothai (1275–1350) established diplomatic relations with the island kingdom of Ceylon (contemporary Sri Lanka). In what can only be described as a kind of Buddhist revival, Ceylon had become the center for Theravada Buddhism for a variety of reasons. After state-sponsored Indian Buddhism undertook its mission to East and Southeast Asia under King Ashoka (273–232 BCE), a new form of Buddhism had begun to develop and evolve by the first century CE; its adherents called themselves *Mahayana,* which means "larger vehicle." Dismissing some of the earlier Buddhist teachings and monastic lifestyles as too strict, introspective, and ascetic, the Mahayanists taught a revisionist version of Buddhism that was, to employ a contemporary term, more "user-friendly" for the popular laity. In turn, they derisively referred to their archaic predecessors as *Hinayana,* or "smaller vehicle." Whereas the Mahayana tradition took hold in China, Korea, and Japan, the Theravada Buddhists can be more or less regarded as a subgroup of the so-called Hinayana that, in response to the Mahayanist reformation, attempted to recover the Buddha's teachings in their "pure" form (this was, of course, a kind of revisionism in its own right). By the Sukhothai period, Buddhism had come and gone in India, Hinduism had reemerged as the mother religion of India, and the Muslim conquest of India had dispensed with them both. Ceylon had become, in effect, the last refuge of the Theravada Buddhists. Sukhothai's Ramkhamheng, already a devout Buddhist, invited Theravadan monks from Ceylon to Sukhothai to purify the Khmer-influenced Buddhism that was being practiced. In turn, delegations of Sukhothai monks traveled to Ceylon to study the newly revised Theravadan scriptures. In summary, Theravada (Hinayana) and Mahayana Buddhism can be compared in the following manner. Theravadan Bud-

A local wat (temple) in Nontaburi Province, west of Bangkok.
(Courtesy of Anuchit and Khanittha Chaiarsa)

dhists regard the Buddha as a human teacher, albeit an extraordinary one, from whom one can learn the path to enlightenment. One must work out his or her salvation within oneself as an individual. A meditative, disciplined, and monastic lifestyle is emphasized. Mahayanists, on the other hand, perceive the Buddha as a divine savior whose universal compassion and accessibility are such that anyone can offer prayer to him. Therefore, the monastic community is not emphasized as being above or beyond the laity.

For these reasons, Theravada Buddhism in Thailand is focused primarily on the well-being of the monastic community and the *wat,* or "temple," in which they reside. There are thousands of wats throughout Thailand. The relationship between the lay community and the priesthood of the local wats is very symbiotic, in that they take care of one another in myriad capacities.

To many people, the very notion of a monastic lifestyle comes across as a very solitary, reclusive, and even selfish road to follow. Indeed, the Buddhist path to enlightenment is primarily one of introspection and self-examination. But as I often tell my students, to be "centered on the self" is not the same thing as being "self-centered." As we shall see, this monastic community is in fact very public and, by his very identity and the work that he does, the Buddhist monk himself serves as an ethical example for people to emulate.

The Thai wat is hardly a secluded institution. In addition to providing essential religious services for the lay community, such as weddings, funerals, and new home/new business blessings, the wat serves as an educational center for both children and adults, a social gathering place for the local lay community, and a strong support center for environmental awareness. In recent years, many Thai Buddhist temples have become, in partnerships with local doctors and nurses, innovative pioneers in hospice care for the terminally ill, which has become particularly important in the wake of AIDS in Thailand.

In a manner similar to that of the medieval West, adolescent boys in Thailand, if so inclined, may choose to leave their worldly lives and enter the temple monastery as novice monks. They might stay as little as a few months or as much as several years. Or, if they and the temple abbot so decide, they might be ordained at age eighteen and live their entire lives as Buddhist monks. It is, in fact, a normative rite of passage for a Thai adolescent of approximately thirteen years to enter the temple as a novice monk for a minimum of three months if it is economically feasible for the family to give him up as a working contributor to their finances. While I was in Thailand in 1991, I attended one of these festive celebrations for a coworker of my sister-in-law at the Ministry of Industry. Close to thirty years old, he chose to do this as a gift for his mother, because his family could not afford for him to be away when he was thirteen. The celebration lasted two days, and the family's entire neighborhood as well as most of the young man's coworkers were involved. This was, of course, a prime opportunity for the visitors to meet the *sangha* (the community of resident monks), to tour the temple grounds, and to make material/financial offerings to the temple.

It is an honor of the utmost proportions for a Thai family to see their son go through this rite of passage, particularly if he makes the decision to stay. Even as a novice, the boy more or less gives up his identity as a "son" and becomes, in a spiritual sense, higher than even his parents. But if he opts to return to his secular life in three months or three years, he may do so freely, with no social stigma attached.

The Thai Buddhist monk is certainly easy to recognize. He wears an orange-colored robe, with no shoes or sandals. For the sake of simplicity, his head and eyebrows are shaven at the time of ordination. But monks who have been ordained for some time will often have allowed their hair to grow back to the length of a closely cropped "crew cut." The life of a Thai Buddhist monk is relatively ordered and disciplined. He follows several precepts (e.g., celibacy, abstention from alcohol, respect for all living things, no contact with money), one of which is not to eat after midday—that is, he must have his meal of the day in the morning. Generally speaking, monks live on the daily offerings of the lay community. One of the primary ways that this is carried out is

A Thai mother and daughter giving alms to a Buddhist monk.
(Courtesy of Anuchit and Khanittha Chaiarsa)

through the food collection rounds that the monks will make each day to receive offerings from individual households in the village or neighborhood that is served by the temple. In both rural and urban areas, a queue of six or eight orange-robed monks walking silently down the side of the road is a common early morning sight. They each carry a large, deep covered bowl made of wood or metal in which they receive food offerings from the local homes. Most conscientious householders will be waiting at their front doors with food that they have prepared early in the morning just for this purpose. When the monks arrive, there is no verbal greeting or overt eye contact. As the monks stand in a row before the house, the resident will come forward, bow to them, and then simply place the food in their bowls one by one. Once the ritual is completed, the monks will move silently on to the next house. This daily ritual of almsgiving is called *dtahk bahdt,* which literally means "to dip large spoonfuls (of food) into a bowl."

One of the more colorful "skeletons" in my closet involves dtahk bahdt. Having just arrived in Thailand for the very first time in 1986, I was alone in my mother-in-law's house, for she and my wife had gone shopping. Two men with shaven heads and orange robes appeared before the gated driveway. Always eager for opportunities to work on my Thai language skills, I approached them, and the three of us had a nice conversation. Before they went on their way, I had given them all of the loose change in my pockets, as well as some cigarettes and candy that I had on hand. Being very proud of both my conversation skills and my meritorious actions, I later told my wife and mother-in-law all about it. To my surprise, they were horrified, as these two men were not monks at all but criminals or beggars who were posing as monks! Coming from a professor, it serves as an amusing story for my students; we were all young and naive at one time or another. . . .

Another way in which the laity can support the temple is through a specific ritual offering known as *tahm boon.* This phrase means "to make merit," in the sense that any benevolent or generous action toward a Buddhist monk or temple is understood as an asset to one's personal disposition or karma. As explained previously, the accumulation of good karma leads to a good rebirth on the long path toward Nirvana. Strictly speaking, tahm boon is usually carried out by going directly to the temple to make the offering. Such visits may occur on a regular monthly basis or to mark significant events, such as the new year, a wedding anniversary, a birthday, the commemoration of a deceased loved one, or to celebrate one's graduation from university.

One specific type of tahm boon takes place at both the beginning and the ending of the rainy season. During the rainy season, monks cannot make their daily rounds to receive offerings and are therefore restricted to the temple monastery. The laity will bring all sorts of gifts to the temple to see them through this period of seclusion. These gifts include practical items such as soap, towels, toothbrushes, medicines, writing paper, and pillows, as well as money that can be used by lay temple assistants to purchase additional items as needed. Each person gives according to his/her capacity, and so it is quite normal to see many of the laity rubbing their hands on every offering, so that even if one could afford to give only a little, he/she will be a part of all of it. At the end of the rainy season, a similar event will take place to welcome the monks out of seclusion. In addition to the traditional offerings, the monks will usually receive new robes.

Not unlike many religious traditions, the concept of making individual "merit" to build up good karma sometimes overshadows the doing of the benevolent act for its own sake. An interesting aspect of this merit-making transaction is that as Thai Buddhist monks have become more and more actively involved in sociopolitical causes (such as protests against environmental abuse, political corruption, etc.), they have created their own subtle albeit powerful way of expressing their displeasure. The Thai phrase *kwahm bahdt* means "to turn one's bowl upside down," in the sense that an inverted bowl will not accept any offerings. Suppose that a politician under the influence of special-interest groups or the head of a questionable logging company has come to the temple to make an offering. The monks at the temple can "turn their bowls upside down." This act severs the merit-making transaction, thereby placing the person's karmic disposition in great jeopardy. Unless the individual is willing to make the necessary amends, he/she is, for all intents and purposes, "excommunicated" from a religious transaction that is, for the devout Buddhist, essential.

There are about 200,000 ordained Buddhist monks in Thailand today. But the Buddha's teachings also promoted and supported an ordained role for women as nuns. At present, the Buddhist nun population in Thailand numbers somewhere between seven and ten thousand. Nuns have shaven heads just like the monks; but instead of wearing orange robes, their robes are white. There has been, however, considerable controversy in Thailand surrounding the question as to whether the Buddhist nun should be recognized as "ordained" in the same formal sense as the Buddhist monk. Is not the role and service of a Buddhist nun in Thai society as vital as that of her more prevalent male counterpart? Because this controversy is more about gender than religion, we shall address it more fully in the following chapter, Thai Society and Contemporary Issues.

Albeit in no compulsory sense, Buddhism is the "state religion" in Thailand. But other traditions are observed and practiced as well. Though they are certainly in the minority, the various indigenous traditions of animism and ancestor worship that are practiced by the previously mentioned northern hill tribes warrant some mention. Generally speaking, animism centers on the belief that objects and phenomena of nature, such as trees, mountains, rivers, storms, and winds have living spirits within them that require sacrifices and offerings in order to keep them under control. Similarly, ancestor worship is practiced as a way of showing respect and reverence for family or community members who have passed on, but whose souls are believed to be lingering about in and around the community. Through necromancy (ritual practices through which one communicates with the dead), offerings are made to keep the ancestral spirits content. If such sacrifices are not made, there can be considerable discord within a given family or community. As one commentator put it, ancestors can live in one of two places: in your bloodstream or on your back.

Such traditions should not be simply written off as mere superstition; animists have a profound respect for nature and the environment, and ancestor worshipers keep the honor and memory of past family members and communal heroes alive in their hearts and minds. Regardless of whether one actually believes that spirits do in fact infuse one's natural surroundings, the notion that something holy and sacred is so immediately present to one's lived experience and physical location is an honorable one. Indeed, one could say that animism is perhaps the earliest form of heartfelt environmental awareness.

One of the more unique aspects of Thai Buddhism is its "popular religiosity," or its assimilation of some of these ancient indigenous folk practices that predate Buddhism altogether. These practices include astrology, divination, fortune-telling, the maintaining of spirit houses, and the collecting of amulets. Though fortune-telling might perhaps be compared to the popular practice of paying particular attention to one's daily horoscope in the West, it is for the most part taken more seriously and on a wider scale in Thai society. Professional fortune-tellers are not hard to find in Thailand; in fact, even though most Buddhist monks tend to disapprove of such practices, there are actually monks who will perform the service. Many Thais seek out fortune-tellers for guidance on matchmaking, upcoming business decisions, lottery tickets, and the like. For an additional fee, a fortune-teller will even come to one's home.

Most Thai homes have spirit houses in their front or back yards or, if there is no yard, a spirit house might be attached to the outer wall of the actual house. More Chinese than Thai in origin, a spirit house is a "residence" for local ghosts (some of them not so congenial), or more likely for the ghosts of one's ancestors. About the size of a small Western dollhouse, some of them are so ornate and beautifully constructed that they rival the real houses in whose yards they reside! In order to maintain familial accord or household harmony, one must not only provide a nice residence for these ghosts but also take care of them through sacrifices and offerings. These offerings are usually in the form of a daily "meal" of rice, fresh fruit, and perhaps a small glass of liquor, accompanied by sticks of burning incense.

Thai amulets. (Lindsay Hebberd/Corbis)

But perhaps the most intriguing aspect of popular religion in Thailand is the almost cultic attention given by many to the collecting of amulets. Usually measuring about one-half to one inch in size, amulets are small images of an endless array of human and divine figures, ranging from revered Buddhist monks from the distant past to countless Hindu deities, or even the Buddha himself. They may be made of clay, lead, bronze, or even gold.

If one goes to Sanahm Luahng, a large, open park-like expanse near the Grand Palace in Bangkok, one can find literally hundreds of street merchants who deal solely in the buying, selling, and trading of amulets. There are probably many Thais who collect these amulets simply as religious relics that will likely increase in value; but for many more, an amulet is like a charm or talisman that is believed to contain power and good fortune—it might be worn on a chain around the neck, or simply be kept at home on the altar next to one's Buddha image.

Although most Buddhist monks do not condone any of these practices, they are more or less content to tolerate them. Indeed, those who do practice such things would definitely be insulted if anyone, monk or otherwise, suggested that they were anything but good Buddhists.

Any discussion of religion in Thailand would not be complete without addressing Islam, the religion that has historically shaped and more or less dominated the cultural landscape of Southern Thailand. Thai Muslims account for about 4 percent of the population, making them Thailand's largest religious minority. They reside primarily, though not exclusively, in the three southernmost provinces bordering Malaysia, a nation where Islam is the predominant religion. In fact, most Thais of this region are of Malay descent. Not unlike the manner in which Eesahn and Lao cultures are intertwined with one another in Northeastern Thailand, the Thais of these southern provinces share a common cultural heritage with the Malays of the region. This is evident not only in religion, but in language patterns, food, and dress. For example, Muslims in these three provinces speak Yawi, a dialect of Malay spoken in Malaysia, rather than Thai. As such, Muslims in Southern Thailand maintain a unique identity within the kingdom's diverse cultural landscape.

But as noted above, the Thai Muslim population is not limited to the southern provinces alone. In total, there are some two thousand mosques in Thailand, and approximately one hundred of them are located in Bangkok. Associated with many of these mosques are parochial schools that offer both secular and religious instruction. In acknowledgement of their culture and identity, King Pumipohn has done many things to support the Muslim sector of the Thai population. With his own funds, for example, he financed the translation of the Qur'an, Islam's holy scriptural text, into the Thai language. In addition, the king (or one of his representatives) presides at the annual celebrations commemorating the Prophet Muhammad's birthday. He also appoints a member of the Muslim religious community to serve a term of office as *chularatchamondri,* the national representative for Islamic affairs.

Other provisions have been created to benefit Thai Muslims more directly. Muslim employees of the Thai government are given a full month's leave with pay during the Islamic month of Dhu al-hijrah, so that they may participate in the *hajj,* the pilgrimage to the Great Mosque in Mecca, which is Islam's holiest site in Saudi Arabia. In provinces with considerable Muslim populations, legal cases that are concerned with family or inheritance matters may be handled, if so desired, according to traditional Qur'anic law, with a Muslim cleric serving as judge.

Despite such provisions, the relationship between the Muslims of Southern Thailand and the Thai government (particularly on the regional/local levels) has historically been tense, and continues to be so. Some Muslims of Southern Thailand claim, for example, that they have become victims of discrimination in both employment policies and educational opportunities. They often feel subjugated by the Thai Buddhist majority. In their quest for more sociopolitical autonomy and self-determination, some have even pressed for the creation of a separate Muslim state in Southern Thailand.

The unstable climate has pushed some Southern Thai Muslims toward militancy and extremism. But taking into account the entire Muslim population of Thailand, such extremism has a very limited following. On the other hand, many Thais suspect that external militant/terrorist factions have in recent years attempted to enter Thailand in order to set up "grass roots" training operations and cells in the southern provinces in much the same manner as communist insurgents did in the north and northeast during the Vietnam War years. Compared with Malaysia, Indonesia, and the Philippines, many fear that Southern Thailand has become a safe haven for similar operations to be carried out, as well as an environment in which extremists are able to live and work in relative anonymity. Although direct links to organized global factions are not suspected, recent violence in the southern provinces (particularly in January and April of 2004) has only increased fears of insurgent activity. In 2004 alone, confrontations and skirmishes between police/soldiers and Muslim extremists in Southern Thailand have resulted in the loss of over 150 lives. But once again, it must be emphasized that the overwhelming majority of Thai Muslims live and work in complete harmony with their Buddhist neighbors.

Islam pervades the southernmost provinces of Thailand, and animistic beliefs and rituals live on in the hill tribes of the north (as well as in the popular religious practices of Thai Buddhism). But we must also give some attention to the presence of Hinduism in Thailand. Indeed, there are both indigenous Thais and Indian immigrants who are Hindus; but at the same time, Hinduism plays a role in the lives of Thai Buddhists as well. Perhaps most surprising is Hinduism's seemingly incongruous presence in the ritual protocol that has for centuries surrounded the Thai royal court.

As Buddhism evolved from its Indian/Hindu context in the fifth century BCE, it is natural that there should continue to be a relationship between them. For example, although Buddhism flourished outside of India as a missionary-driven religion, there are still very significant Buddhist sites in India. And because Hindus came to regard the Buddha as simply one aspect of their multifaceted perception of divinity (i.e., that vast multitudes of gods comprise the singular ultimate reality of Brahman), they give the Buddha the same respect that they give to their traditional deities. In a sense, the practice of Hindu devotion by Thai Buddhists can be explained in much the same way. Though the Buddha had little to say about the Hindu deities, he did not simply renounce or deny their existence, nor did he claim a divine status for himself. Prior to the arrival of the earliest Buddhist missionaries, Hinduism permeated Southeast Asia in the pre-Thai kingdoms, and particularly in the Khmer Empire of Cambodia. Even after the Kingdom of

Sukhothai embraced Theravada Buddhism once and for all as its "state religion," Hindu deities like Indra (the chariot-driving wielder of thunder and storm) or the cyclical "trinity" of Brahma (the creator), Vishnu (the maintainer), and Shiva (the destroyer) simply remained on the scene as familiar and secure facets of the Thai religious landscape.

Bangkok is home to several well-known Hindu images and shrines that are patronized by Hindu and Buddhist alike. The famous Erawan Shrine, for example, displays a four-faced image of Brahma. As Erawan is the name of Brahma's three-headed elephant on which he rides, small teakwood elephants may be purchased at nearby stalls to bring to the shrine as offerings, along with flowers, money, and incense. Perhaps more unusual than the shrine itself is the fact that it sits at a busy intersection in downtown Bangkok in front of the Erawan Grand Hyatt Hotel (see also "Erawan Shrine" in Significant People, Places, and Events). Another Hindu deity is found at the formal entryway to Wittayalai Nadasin, the National College of the Performing Arts. Here one will see a large image of Ganesha, the elephant-headed son of Shiva. In traditional Hinduism, Ganesha is "the overcomer of obstacles"; at Nadasin he is the "patron deity," as it were, of the performing arts. Due to his capacity as a remover of obstacles, Ganesha (or as the Thais call him, Pra Pi Kanayt) is very popular with high school and university students who are facing major exams. At final exam times, his shrine will be covered with flowers and other offerings that range from the hopeful to the desperate!

But as stated at the outset of this subject, the most intriguing dimension of Thailand's Hindu-Buddhist plurality is that which has for centuries enveloped and defined the Thai monarchy. The reader will recall from Chapter One that the Khmer Empire (802–1431) was a Hindu culture. Its leaders supported the Indian concept of the devaraja, or "the god-king," meaning that the king was literally held to be an avatar (a god in human form) and therefore a being so remote and inaccessible that even one's shadow passing over him could result in grave consequences. The elaborate rituals surrounding such royal events as coronations, births, marriages, and funerals were conducted by Brahmin priests. The early Thai kingdoms were strongly influenced by the Khmer culture in art, architecture, religion, and politics. This was especially so for the Kingdom of Ayutthaya (1350–1767). It inherited and enforced the concept of the devaraja and the Brahminic ritual protocol that supported it. For the Thai as well as the Khmer, the legitimacy and sacredness of both rule and ruler were manifested in the enactment of the ritual. It was, in essence, a choreographed dance of power.

Here is a vivid example. Dated at 1450, palace records from the reign of King Trailok of Ayutthaya describe an outdoor ritual that was performed in conjunction with royal coronation ceremonies. On a grand theatrical scale, the performers enacted a famous Hindu creation myth known generally as "the churning of the ocean." In this myth, the gods and the demons have discovered that a divine elixir known as *amrit* (similar to the "ambrosia" of Greek mythology) lies at the bottom of the ocean. This amrit will confer immortality on the recipient. The gods and demons are told by Indra that they will have to engage in a contest to determine who will receive it. In the midst of the ocean stood Mount Meru, around which was coiled the great *naga,* or snake, Vasuki. Indra instructed the gods to pull back and forth on the tail of the snake while the demons pulled on the head. Because Vasuki was still coiled around the mountain as they pulled, this motion turned the mountain in a circular motion (like an agitator in a modern washing machine) that violently churned up the ocean. The churning action raised the amrit from the depths of the primordial waters, as well as the innumerable pieces of the created world as we know it.

Thais refer to this Hindu myth as *chahk nahk deuk dahm bahn,* or "the pulling of the dragon." In its ceremonial performance at Ayutthaya, the amrit that was churned up from the bottom of the ocean represented a kind of pure and untouched creative potential that was to be conferred upon the newly-crowned or renewed king. The amrit symbolized his absolute power, which could be a blessing or a curse to his administration: it was his to use with wisdom and forethought for the sake of his kingdom.

Although this particular ritual is no longer performed, Hindu-influenced rituals of this nature carried over into the Rattanakosin period (1782–present). And though the monarchs of the Chakri Dynasty from Chulalongkawn up to the present have become exceedingly more accessible and "human," the monarchy of King Pumipohn continues to be surrounded by elaborate Hindu pageantry.

All human beings enjoy and even need ceremony at one time or another. But what makes such seemingly archaic ritual continue to be meaningful in the twenty-first century is evidenced by the sort of person it surrounds. For King Pumipohn, the most accessible and selfless king in Thai history, the purpose of the pageantry is to lift up and celebrate the monarchy as a sacred and social institution, not the monarch as a sacred and divine being.

THAI LITERATURE: THE SOCIAL IMPORT OF THE *RAMAKIEN*

At first glance, it perhaps seems unusual to classify a work of literature as a "social institution." But in the case of the *Ramakien,* the chapter would be incomplete without it. The *Ramakien* is the Thai version of the ancient Indian Hindu epic, the *Ramayana* (yet another example of how Hindu thought has been assimilated into Thai culture). It tells the story of Pra Ram, the crown prince of Ayutthaya (not to be confused with the actual Thai kingdom of Ayutthaya). Ram is newly wedded to his beautiful consort, Nahng Seeda. But through a court conspiracy, he is forced to renounce his rightful throne and go into exile along with Seeda and his brother, Pra Lak. While in exile,

Seeda is abducted by Totsagan, the powerful demon king of the Island of Longkha. All of this serves as something of a prologue to the central body of the tale, in which Ram, aided by a vast army of monkey warriors, lays siege to Totsagan's island kingdom and demon army. Following innumerable adventures and battles, Ram emerges as the victor, and both Seeda and his lost throne are restored to him.

Sometimes referred to as "the Odyssey of Asia," the *Ramakien* resembles just that: Homer's *Iliad* and *Odyssey*, not to mention the medieval *Lancelot Cycles* of Chretien de Troyes, and even George Lucas's *Star Wars*. Moreover, the story of a heroic figure dispossessed of what is rightfully his, combined with the abduction and rescue of his love interest— both of which are depicted against the larger backdrop of an ultimate confrontation between good and evil—is to be found in a host of novels, films, and folk tales throughout the world.

The *Ramayana* (the original Indian version) dates back to the third century BCE, and its variants exist in virtually every country of Southeast Asia. As noted in the chapter on Thai history, the Thai version was penned by King Ramathibodi (Rama I) in 1798, and it was adapted specifically for dramatic performance by his son, King Puttalaytia (Rama II), between 1809 and 1824. As a performance art, the *Ramakien* constitutes the sole repertoire of the *Khon,* or the classical masked dance-drama of Thailand.

Why should this epic tale of Indian origin play such a pervasive role in Thai culture? As a Thai creation, it is likely that the *Ramakien* served to validate the new Chakri Dynasty in the wake of the utter destruction of the real Ayutthaya in 1767 (named after the kingdom depicted in the Indian *Ramayana*). This may explain why a literary epic of Hindu mythology should be embraced by a Buddhist culture: it placed the monarchy as well as the nation into a relationship with the gods.

The Ramayana was composed as . . . a work designed to augment and perpetuate the transitory glories of the monarch's origin, conquests and court by making them the subject of a work of literature. By the talismanic qualities inherent in a work of art, it was further to guarantee the king's claim to identity with Rama, and through him the godhead. The Ramayana, in other words, was the "Great Seal" of the king's divinity. (Cadet 1970, 31)

That relational identity remains so strong that there are those Thais who even today will point toward the ruins of *their* Ayutthaya and declare that this is in fact where it all took place, at some point in premonarchic history.

Though not all Thais may be familiar with the formal story, the spirit and imagery of the *Ramakien* is deeply embedded in the Thai culture. Beyond the Thai classical theater, the story appears in grade school texts and even in comic books. Its diverse characters—divine heroes, monkey warriors, and demons—serve as immediately recognizable icons in venues that extend from the formal visual arts to advertising media. Indeed, "Buddhism alone is a more pervasive religious influence, but even Buddhism takes second place to the *Ramakien* where the arts are concerned" (Cadet 1970, 24).

References

Cadet, J. M. *The Ramakien.* Bangkok: Kodansha International, 1970.

Hoare, Timothy. *Pulling the Siamese Dragon.* Lanham, MD: University Press of America, 1997.

Keyes, Charles F. *Thailand: Buddhist Kingdom as Modern Nation-State.* Boulder, CO: Westview Press, 1987.

Library of Congress. *Thailand: A Country Study.* Washington, DC: Federal Research Division, Library of Congress, 1987.

National Identity Board of Thailand. *Buddhism in Thai Life,* 3d ed. Bangkok: National Identity Board, Office of the Prime Minister, 1984.

National Statistical Office of Thailand. http://www.nso.go.th.

Office of the Prime Minister. *Thailand in Brief.* Bangkok: Foreign News Division, Public Relations Department, Office of the Prime Minister, 1982.

Parkes, Carl. *Thailand Handbook,* 3d ed. Emeryville, CA: Avalon Travel Publishing, 2000.

Rahula, Walpola. *What the Buddha Taught,* 2d ed. New York: Grove Press, 1974.

Royal Thai Government. Home Page. http://www.thaigov.go.th/index-eng.htm.

Scouting in Thailand. http://www.thaiscouting.com.
Southeast Asian Minister of Education Organization. http://www.seameo.org.
U.S. Embassy in Thailand. http://www.usa.or.th.
Yupho, Dhanit. *The Custom and Rite of Paying Homage to Teachers.* Thai
     Culture Series, No. 11, 5th ed. Bangkok: Fine Arts Department,
     1990.

CHAPTER FOUR

Thai Society and Contemporary Issues

THE THAI IDENTITY

Over the course of the past century, Thai society was pro-
foundly influenced and shaped through its exposure to an
ever-evolving global diversity of intellectual ideas, social values, and scientific technologies. To be sure, the day-to-day
lives of the Thai people have most certainly been enhanced
by the fruits of modernization, which include such things as
state-of-the-art communication technologies, scientific agricultural methods, industrialized production, and improved
healthcare and education, as well as an increased awareness
of women's rights. However, as is so often the case when
worldviews collide with one another, benefits come with consequences. Modernity has also brought about widespread
commercial development, environmental pollution, the separation of home and workplace into isolated spheres of experience, radical changes in traditional family dynamics, rampant
consumerism, and the seemingly constant need to be enter-
tained by an ongoing array of audio-visual media. Therefore,
any discussion of Thai society, popular culture, and contemporary issues must take this dichotomy into account: "what is
held to be so" (tradition) and "what is done" (practice) are
not necessarily the same things.

Be that as it may, the essential "Thai-ness" of the Thai
identity remains as pervasively present in the cosmopolitan
streets of Bangkok as it is in the traditional villages of the rural
north or northeast. A vital facet of that identity is reflected

through the Thai expression *mai pehn rai,* which means "nevermind" or "think nothing of it." Generally speaking, this oft-heard phrase reflects the rather cool-headed disposition for which Thais are known. Although life is fraught with twists, turns, and reversals of fortune, Thais tend not to over-react to them. Things simply happen, and they will be dealt with in due time, in the appropriate manner, and with a calm heart. This perspective holds even if the circumstance is a positive one: an overt expression of joyful elation in response to good fortune is uncharacteristic as well. Along these same lines, Thais will go to great lengths to avoid confrontation in both personal and professional life, preferring to seek and maintain harmonious relationships whenever possible. Typically, the Thai will respond to difficult situations and difficult people with little more than an enigmatic smile. The "Thai smile" is famous throughout the world and yet is probably more misunderstood and misinterpreted than any other characteristic of Thai behavior. For a more detailed discussion on this subject, see the reference section on Thai etiquette.

Two other very common Thai expressions are the idiomatic phrases *sabai sabai,* which means "relax and don't take things so seriously," and *sanook sanahm,* which essentially means "enjoy your life." The combined spirit of the two phrases would be equivalent to the English expression "take some time to smell the roses." With that spirit in mind, Thais try to enjoy their work as much as they enjoy their play. Like most people, Thais value hard-earned money and the wise use of it. Their work ethic is very strong. But unlike in the West, the typical Thai workplace is not "goal oriented" or overly concerned with productivity, the meeting of deadlines, and the like. As noted in Chapter Two, it is more "process oriented" and focused on maintaining a harmonious working environment and respectful relationships between employers, employees, and customers. The presupposition is that such a working environment will, by definition, achieve what is supposed to be achieved in the course of a working day. And so if a foreigner, Western or otherwise, came into a Thai place of business and made a service request that was prefaced with the words "I need it yesterday" (an aggressive phrase that is all too familiar to most westerners), it is quite likely that his or her request would be unfulfilled.

It would not be inaccurate to say that Buddhist teachings are foundational in one way or another to all of these aspects of the Thai identity. A strong emotional reaction to an event or circumstance, for example, is indicative of one's material attachments and/or relational dependencies. As we have seen in our previous overview and discussion of religion in Thailand, Buddhism teaches one to "let go," to attain a spirit of detachment, as all of these things we desire to attain and control are impermanent and insubstantial. By following *tahng sai glahng,* or "the Middle Way," one practices temperance and moderation, thereby avoiding all extremes in one's lifestyle and behavior. Nevertheless, Buddhist ethics teach that life and its gifts are to be enjoyed while we have them, as long as our actions are carried out responsibly and do not bring harm to others. One should exhibit compassion for all living things, which, by extension, applies to how one conducts oneself in both personal and professional relationships.

THAI FAMILY LIFE

Everybody in Thailand is somebody's something—brother, sister, son, daughter, parent, cousin, and so on. Perhaps it is for this reason that "the family" serves as a kind of standard model by which all other relationships in Thai society are measured. It is within the dynamics of family life that Thai children learn and internalize the basic codes of conduct that will inform and guide them throughout the rest of their lives.

Contemporary Western culture, for example, generally defines a family as a discrete household unit consisting of one or two caregiver/parent figures and a number of dependents, that is, children. In traditional Thai society, however, a family encompasses much more. In addition to parents and children, it is not unusual for a single Thai household to include grandparents, an aunt or an uncle, and perhaps a cousin or two. In addition, it is traditional for young newly married couples to live in the home of one set of parents, at least for a while. In any case, grown children are morally obligated to take care of their parents when they become too old to take care of themselves. But as it is becoming more common in Thailand for grown children (married or not) to move out and live on their own, this usually means that the parents will eventually be absorbed into the grown child's household (usually that of the oldest child). If the grown child never moved away in the first place, the parent's home becomes, in effect, the child's. Although this moral tradition is more prevalent in rural villages, it continues to be the norm (generally) for many urban/suburban households as well. In the latter case, however, it is often a practical matter of economic necessity as much as a cultural expression of tradition. In recent decades, for example, Thailand has seen a growth in the development of retirement condominiums and assisted-living communities in urban areas, but they are very expensive and there continues to be something of a stigma attached to them. Because grown children in Thai society are traditionally required to be as responsible for their aged parents as their parents previously were for them, some Thais feel that even if the elderly residents of such retirement communities are physically and financially comfortable, it nevertheless suggests to the public that their children have shirked their responsibility and cast them aside.

But as noted above, the opposite will occur as well. Instead of the elderly moving into retirement condos, it is becoming more common to see young middle-class professional couples moving away from the central family altogether, and into their own homes as they become more prosperous (as discussed in Chapter Two, this is one of the sociological trends that led to the Thai housing boom of the 1980s and 1990s). But again, it is still likely that when their respective parents become too old to take care of themselves, they will be absorbed back into the couple's home.

The traditional Thai family is an environment in which status and its accompanying responsibilities are acquired by age and experience. A child comes to know his/her place in the family hierarchy very soon, not just in regard to parental figures but also in relation to older/younger siblings. Older siblings are responsible for younger siblings, an obligation that under some circumstances (e.g., financial responsibility, courtship matters) may very well carry over into adulthood. Conversely, it is common practice for a young man or woman to initiate a discussion with his/her older sibling over important matters or decisions, even to the point of asking the older sibling for "permission" to take this or that path. It is simply understood that regardless of age, the relationship of older to younger will always be there. At the same time, however, increased exposure to the value that westerners place on individuality and self-determination has led many Thais—young and old alike—to see this tradition as something of an obligatory prison from which they would both be happy to be set free. But generally speaking, the awareness of and the respect for age and seniority that one learns as a child will come to shape virtually every aspect of one's personal and professional relationships.

Aside from age, another important element in Thai family dynamics is gender. The Thai family (as well as Thai society at large) is, for the most part, patriarchal, that is, male-dominated. But having said this, it must be emphasized that such a statement is indicative of Thailand's cultural traditions but not necessarily every Thai person's cultural practices or norms. As noted earlier in this chapter, "tradition" and "practice" are not always synonymous. But generally speaking, it can be said that the male partner (spouse/father) tends to be cast as the head of the household, the primary wage earner, the major decision maker, and to be afforded more leisure time (usually with professional or personal peers outside of the home environment). The paradox that comes in play here is that if the male does have an abundance of leisure time at his disposal, it is likely due at least in part to the fact that he has given control of the "details" (e.g., household management, financial planning, primary care-giving, etc.) to his spouse. In turn, the wife/mother may work very hard, but she has at the same time been afforded a great deal of authority over what takes place in the household (and perhaps more than her husband may realize!).

Oftentimes, the raising of children follows this same traditional pattern. As they grow older, sons tend to be given more freedom and behavioral leeway than daughters. As an adult, the son may also acquire the authority to assist in the making of major decisions, regardless of whether he continues to reside with his parents. As explained previously, it is likely that his parents will eventually be absorbed into his household anyway. But in today's culture, it is just as likely for a daughter to acquire that role, both as a decision maker and as a parental care-giver, especially if she is the oldest sibling in the family.

Last but not least, it is not unusual for an urban or suburban Thai family—even one on a moderate income—to have a live-in housekeeper. A *dehk rahp chai,* or a "serving child," is usually a young adolescent girl from the countryside. Most often coming from the economically impoverished northeast (Eesahn), these girls are paid a minimum wage to assist the host family with such things as housecleaning, cooking, and childcare. Oftentimes, an arrangement has been made to send the bulk of her monthly earnings to the girl's family. The familial relationships with housekeepers vary; some are treated in an impersonal employer-employee manner whereas, in more liberal households, they are essentially regarded as additional members of the family. They may eat meals and spend leisure time with the family and even go on outings and holidays with them. If the relationship is long-term—for example, five years—the younger children of the family may come to identify with the dehk rahp chai as their primary caregiver, more so than their own mother.

Under the most ideal circumstances, a truly good relationship with a dehk rahp chai may even evolve into a kind of unofficial "foster care," for want of a better term. It is not unheard of for a host family to go so far as to make arrangements for the girl to attend secondary school and even college, the latter a life-changing opportunity that would be unlikely at best if she had remained in her rural village.

THE THAI HOME

Due to the limitations of space, most residents of highly concentrated urban centers like Bangkok live in apartments, townhomes, or high-rise condominiums. Individual family dwellings are found primarily in the more suburban areas that surround the city. They are grouped into "villages" (*moobahn*) that remind one of modern American subdivisions. Based on a handful of pre-designed models that vary in square footage and amenities, the modern suburban Thai home more or less resembles those that one might find in the subdivisions of Southern California and Florida. Ranging anywhere in price from modest to affluent, all of these homes have ceramic tile roofs and white stucco exteriors to reflect the tropical sun. They are usually two stories, with two to four bedrooms. Garages are rare, as are basements (at least in the Bangkok region, due to its very soft sea-level soil). Almost every house in a suburban Thai village has a small front and back yard. The entire lot is usually walled, with a gated driveway. But even though the yards are small, most every home will have an impressive garden, with a wide variety of lush green plants, bright flowers, and perhaps a fruit tree. Many suburban Thai villages also have small shopping centers, restaurants, and banks within their boundaries. Some of the larger ones will even have their own community centers, complete with tennis courts and swimming pools.

A contemporary suburban village street in Nontaburi Province.
(Courtesy of Anuchit and Khanittha Chaiarsa)

Although virtually every private motor vehicle in Thailand has air-conditioning, only the most affluent homes are centrally cooled, as electricity is very expensive. But many middle-class homes have "hotel-style" air conditioning units in one room, usually the master bedroom. And although all suburban village homes have indoor plumbing and modern kitchens/bathrooms, all water that is used for drinking or cooking is bottled, and must therefore be purchased on a weekly or monthly basis.

In the villages of the rural provinces, family dwellings are naturally more traditional in style. Depending on one's income and family size, some can be quite large and may even be composed of multiple buildings that form a kind of family complex around an interior courtyard of sorts. In the northern provinces, for example, the traditional "Thai-style" homes are easily recognized by the unique design and rhythmic lines of their steeply pitched roofs. Although single-story,

A traditional northern Thai home design. (Courtesy of Anuchit and Khanittha Chaiarsa)

the house itself is generally raised, resting on a series of wooden piles or pillars (approximately eight to ten feet tall) that protect the interior from flooding during the rainy season (as well as from uninvited nocturnal visitors from the forest). The house is accessed via a steep wooden stairway. In the midday heat, the patio-like space underneath the house remains relatively cool and therefore serves as a primary gathering place for family and friends. Traditionally, this space also serves as the kitchen, so that heat from cooking will be diffused outside. This traditional architectural style is often adapted into contemporary home designs.

The typical single-family village farmhouse of the northeastern provinces is much more basic in design. It is usually a single-story structure made of wood, also raised above the ground, with a roof that is constructed from a combination of thatched palm leaves and corrugated sheet metal (which can be very noisy in a hard rain!). It will have two to three rooms at most. The majority of rural village houses today have electricity and at least communal access to running water. As far as basic telephone service is concerned, a rural village home with its own telephone would be a rare thing indeed. But for those villages that have telephone service, it is usually a single public phone in a communal location, such as a post office. As noted earlier, basic telephone service is yet to be established in many rural Thai villages.

In rural regions such as Eesahn, where rainfall can at times be very intense but at the same time very short-lived, it is essential that every house have a large concrete reservoir or ceramic tank for catching and keeping rainwater (*ohng gehp nahm*). Rooftop guttering systems are designed to collect and direct rainfall to these reservoirs.

POPULAR CULTURE
AND "WESTERN" VALUES

The word *popular* is an adjective that means "of the people." To address the "popular culture" of any nation or region, one must necessarily consider that curious dichotomy to which we previously alluded: "what is held to be so" (tradition) and "what is done" (practice) are not necessarily the same things. In the case of Thailand, such a question depends largely on where one finds oneself. In Thailand's rural regions, "practice" remains very much aligned with traditional Thai values, such as those presented earlier. Religion and family, accompanied by a good-natured approach to life's hills and valleys, are fundamental to one's social assumptions and worldview as to "how things are." But in major urban centers such as Bangkok or Chiang Mai, it would be accurate to say that mainstream popular culture is more or less grounded in a subtle variation of that dichotomy: the tension that exists between one's *cultural* identity as a Thai and one's *personal* identity as an individual. And in many ways this individuality is shaped, for good or for ill, by Western values and assumptions.

The contemporary urban/suburban Thai not only lives daily with the conveniences of modern communications and information technology, rapid mass transit (sometimes more "mass" and less "rapid"!), and fast food restaurants, but he/she is also inundated daily with Western-inspired media images that promote consumerism, affluence, fashion consciousness, youthfulness, sexuality, and time for leisure as expressive channels of individual freedom. How have these images played out in Thai popular culture?

Consumerism and Affluence

Bangkok is the indisputable shopping capital of Southeast Asia. And although it is by no means unusual to see westerners exploring its sprawling mega-malls and shopping districts, most of these complexes were developed primarily for the Thai consumers. Indeed, the Thai tendency toward consumerism and the amassing of material wealth sometimes appears to border on obsession. In Bangkok, the logos of Mercedes Benz, Rolex, and Gucci pervade the merchandising landscape. But does this tendency not also stand in direct contradiction to those Buddhist principles of temperance and restraint that were previously lifted up as being fundamental to the Thai identity? In most instances, the Thai-as-consumer and the Thai-as-Buddhist are actually two very separate facets of that singular identity. It does present the outsider with something of a paradox. But it is a paradox that must be viewed within the framework of the larger picture of what it means for the Thai to be "modern." The school-age Thai adolescent or young adult may equate being modern with being Western, which, in turn, simply means that it is important to be fashionable or "with it." Western children are not that much different in this respect. But for the average Thai middle-to-upper-class professional, the relationship between consumerism and modernity goes considerably deeper. Many of the conveniences that Western nations have come to take for

Some advertising transcends language barriers! (Courtesy of Anuchit and Khanittha Chaiarsa)

granted—automatic home appliances, privately owned cars, vast shopping malls, ready cash in one's pocket, consumer credit—are still relatively new for the average Thai. As "indicators" of modernity, such things have come to demonstrate, both to one another and to the world at large, that Thailand is economically, socially, and politically developed as a respected member of the global community. It is not surprising, therefore, that many Thais take offense at being referred to as "third world," or as an "underdeveloped" nation state. Consumerism has become for the Thai a means of breaking free from that reference.

The social, political, and economic impact of the Vietnam War played a significant role in the development of this mindset. Generally speaking, it can be said that Vietnam served as the West's introduction to the region of Southeast Asia as a whole; very few Americans knew anything at all about Southeast Asia until it started appearing in the evening news on

Sometimes no translation is necessary. (Courtesy of Anuchit and Khanittha Chaiarsa)

their televisions. But one of the countless tragic and bitter consequences of that experience is that most westerners also came to regard all Southeast Asians as being more or less the same (an especially challenging dilemma, for example, for postwar immigrants to the U. S. from Vietnam, Laos, and Cambodia, as well as from Thailand). Once the war had ended, Thailand was in a position to take advantage of the seeds of economic development that had been planted by the massive U.S. military presence of the previous fifteen years. Thais had seen the fruits of westernization; now they were determined to keep pace with it and to rise above the cultural stereotype that had been imposed upon them. And so in a sense, the Thai consumer, both in-country and abroad, as both tourist and tourist host, is asserting, "I am not Vietnamese, Cambodian, Laotian, or Burmese; I am Thai." And although rampant consumerism may seem to some an unusual way of asserting one's "Thai-ness," it is simply where they are and what they do. It is not so strange if one compares this trend to the consumer boom that took place in the United States following World War II: for good or for ill, consumerism became a kind of cultural hallmark of American spirit, individualism, growth, and global identity. In essence, then, Thailand has been doing in the 1970s, 1980s, and 1990s what the United States was doing in the 1940s, 1950s, and 1960s.

At the same time, however, it is important to note that affluent consumerism in Thailand often means more than just self-identity. It is also a matter of how one regards others. As a whole, the Thais are among the most gracious people that I have ever had the pleasure to encounter. In both personal and professional venues (meetings, dinner parties, informal gatherings and the like), Thais will go to extraordinary lengths to provide their guests with the very best they have to offer. They do so not to display or flaunt their wealth but to honor their guests and to welcome them into their homes or places of business.

Sexuality, Dating, and Marriage

Bangkok's notoriety for nightlife and prostitution (see below) could easily give the first-time visitor the impression that Thai popular culture is somehow sexually liberated; however, nothing could be further from the truth. Thai society at large is, in fact, quite conservative in this respect. Even with constant media exposure to Western fashions and social behavior, some elements of traditional Thai demeanor have remained intact. Western clothing fashions, for example, are quite prevalent in urban department stores and, just as in the West, are geared primarily toward adolescent boys and girls, as well as young professionals. But apparel that is worn in the public venue, especially during daytime working hours, still tends to be somewhat on the modest side (especially among women), so as not to draw undue attention to the wearer (for more on this subject, refer to the later discussion on Thai etiquette). But in practice, much of this tends to be determined by age and/or gender group. As the reader might guess, the younger sectors of the Thai population are pushing the fashion boundaries. And this is to be expected, especially when one considers the fact that virtually all Thai boys and girls who are enrolled in school spend the bulk of their weekdays clad in generic government school uniforms!

Dating relationships between boys and girls tend to develop within the context of a larger group of friends. Even after the couple is "officially" acknowledged as such by their peers, the group continues, for the most part, to serve as the essential social context of the ongoing dating relationship. Although this communal form of dating remains prevalent in Thai society, Thai parents today are finding that they are as little-informed as to what is going on in their children's social lives as Western parents are. But there was a time in Thailand when this was not the case. Consider, for example, a memory of my wife, who grew up in Bangkok. When she was in high school, a boy came to pick her up for an arranged date. Accompanying them on their date was not only her mother but also her little sister. And the poor boy had to pay for all four of them!

Except for walking hand-in-hand, public displays of affection between men and women are generally frowned upon, as physical affection, even a kiss on the cheek between a husband and wife, is a private matter. As far as "hand-holding" is concerned, it is not unusual to see adolescent girls or even young women walking hand-in-hand, nor is it unusual to see this among adolescent boys. By no means is it an indication of sexual orientation; it is simply a Thai social behavior among casual friends, and one that is evident in many Asian cultures.

Buddhist marriage and wedding practices in Thailand involve a variety of traditional rituals, some of which are not unlike those that one might encounter in other cultures. If a couple wishes to marry, it is the responsibility of the man to make a formal visit to the woman's parents in order to ask for her hand and their blessing. But this is also a negotiation, as the man is required to offer the parents a *sin sawt*, or a "bride price," in exchange for her. In former times the sin sawt would most likely be material goods—for example, land, livestock, or crops. Today it is, for the most part, monetary.

Depending on the economic status of the parties involved, it can range anywhere from the equivalent of hundreds to tens of thousands of dollars. Despite the fact that this practice tends to portray the woman as little more than a piece of property, it is not unusual for a good deal of bargaining to take place, particularly if the parents do not regard the man as their ideal choice for a son-in-law. But not unlike early European culture, traditional Thai marriages used to be little more than the outward demonstrations of larger political or economic transactions: the creating of new alliances, larger kingdoms, and the like.

Once the sin sawt is negotiated, the couple will go to the local Buddhist temple to make arrangements for the wedding. For the most part, it is up to the monks to select the proper day. Employing traditional rituals that fall outside of Buddhism proper, such as astrological readings, fortune-telling, and ancestral divination, the monks will determine the most auspicious day for the particular couple.

On the wedding day, it is traditional for the man to gather together his family and friends into a parade—like procession that will make its way to the woman's home. If the bride and groom live in the same village or neighborhood, the parade route may be little more than a few hundred yards; but if the groom is from a different village, it is customary for him to bring them all together at the outskirts of the bride's village and then to make their way to her house. While en route, the parade will likely encounter two or three of the bride's younger brothers or sisters, who will be holding a rope or chain across the road to block their way. This is part of the fun: they will demand that the groom pay the bride price up front before he can proceed any farther. Initially the groom will offer them an envelope containing a minimal amount of money. Quite naturally, they will tell him that this is hardly sufficient; he might go through four or five envelopes containing increasing amounts of money before they will allow him to proceed. Once the parade arrives at the bride's home,

Ceremonial wedding conch shell. (Courtesy of Timothy Hoare)

it is important to make a good deal of noise and music to mark the occasion. This is partly for celebration, and partly to make it known publicly that the daughter of the household is having a proper wedding and did not elope.

When all parties are assembled at the bride's house, they either will hold the wedding ceremony there or will proceed to a larger public space, such as a village community building or, if it is an urban affair, perhaps a hotel. There they will *tahm boon,* or make monetary and food offerings to the monks of the local temple who have come to perform the ceremony.

The wedding ceremony itself is quite beautiful. When everyone is assembled, the couple will come forward and sit before a small altarlike table. After some initial prayers, the senior monk will then place two circles of woven threads on the heads of the bride and groom. Symbolically uniting the couple, the circles are joined together by a length of thread or string. On the table in front of the couple is a large bowl filled with holy water from the local temple. An ornately gilded conch shell is used to dip into the water. In a ceremony called *pitee roht nahm* ("water-pouring ritual"), the couple will place their folded hands over the bowl. Then, while saying words of blessing, the senior monk will dip the shell into the water and pour it over their hands. Following this, every friend and family manner present is invited to come forward and do the same. The couple is now husband and wife. It is not customary for the Thai wedding ceremony to include an exchange of rings, but many Thai couples today will purchase them on their own.

Following the ceremony and the reception (which, like most wedding receptions around the globe, involves a great deal of food and music), it is the responsibility of the oldest couple present—the couple within either family who has been married the longest—to prepare the room (either at the home or at the hotel) where the couple will spend their first night. Traditionally, this preparation involves making up the bed with new linens and pillows and sometimes even sprinkling the bed with rose petals. Once the room is prepared, both sets of parents will escort the bride and groom to the room and give their final blessings to the couple.

Asian cultures overall tend to view marriage as a permanent arrangement, and Thailand is no exception. Although divorce rates are rising, they are still extremely low compared with Western cultures. But a low divorce rate is not necessarily indicative of marital harmony; it may also be masking the fact that if a Thai man does happen to find someone else with whom he desires to initiate a relationship, he is statistically more apt to incorporate her into his life as a *mia noi* (a "little wife," or mistress) than to terminate his primary marriage.

As observed in the previous chapter, the modest rise in educational and professional opportunities for Thai women has led to a rise in the average age of marriage for women and men alike. In turn, both men and women have less reason to worry that they will "miss the boat" if they wait even into their early thirties to marry. This trend is evidenced by the fact that the percentage of single persons in Thailand aged 15–24 is growing (this being regarded as the "traditional" age range for marriage). In 1950, for example, approximately 77 percent of the males and 56 percent of the females within this age group were single. It is projected that by 2025, those respective figures will have increased to the levels of 96 percent and 93 percent.

Thailand is, as stated previously, a predominantly patriarchal culture. Therefore, the conflict between traditional gender roles and an increasing awareness of women's rights has in recent years come to constitute an arena of some controversy in both the private/personal and public/professional venues of Thai society. As these are issues of significant social concern, some examples of them will be addressed later in this chapter.

Leisure and Entertainment

The karmic cycle of birth, death, and rebirth not withstanding, most Thais would concur with the perspective that life is for living, and so one might as well have a good time doing so. Thais have a very strong work ethic, but when it comes to leisure, their "play ethic" (if there is such a thing) is just as vibrant. In the Thai language, the catch-all phrase is *bai teow,* which simply means "going out." From midday shopping and a movie to midnight club-hopping and karaoke, it's all bai teow.

In Thailand, bai teow is almost always a group activity. Even though Western modes of individual expression have become a very visible part of Thai popular culture, Thais tend not to do things by themselves. The individual still tends to find his/her self-identity within the social context of the larger communal group. This group consciousness applies to serious dating relationships as well as to casual socialization between school acquaintances or professional colleagues.

What do Thais like to do when they bai teow? For the most part, they enjoy the same types of things that westerners enjoy doing. Movie theaters are always full, as are restaurants and clubs with live music, and a wide array of professional sports venues. Very pervasive, for example, is the "karaoke bar," a Japanese invention. Although karaoke bars came to Thailand primarily for Japanese businessmen in Bangkok, they have since become extremely popular with Thais as well (many affluent Thais even have karaoke systems in their homes for entertaining guests). But generally speaking, the most pervasive and popular entertainment media in Thailand are cinema, music, sports, and, of course, television.

Thais love movies as much as Americans do. In fact, Thais love American movies as much as Americans do. New-release American films are not difficult to find in Bangkok. Naturally, they are subtitled in Thai, and sometimes even dubbed over with spoken Thai. But Thais also enjoy their more regional cinematic art as well. Films from Chinese and Indian cinema are quite popular, particularly among those ethnic populations who live in Thailand. And, of course, Thailand has its own film industry, although most of its output is geared toward the melodramatic action and thriller genres (which also tends to determine the type of American films that are usually shown in Thai theaters). Just as the United States has a long tradition of films about "the Old West," so also Thai audiences enjoy epic tales of love and war that are set in the ancient Siamese capitals of Sukhothai and Ayutthaya. The recent internationally released film *Suryothai* (2002), the rambling but nevertheless fascinating account of the famous heroine of Ayutthaya, is a good example. And like the Chinese films that the Thais enjoy, many of these epics usually include a considerable amount of martial-arts action as well. But just as the United States has filmmakers whose work rises above the tastes of the masses, so also has Thailand produced some internationally acclaimed films that combine excellent writing, acting, and cinematography with socioeconomic issues, such as corruption, rural/urban poverty, and prostitution. Unfortunately, though such films are certainly celebrated for their artistic achievement, their artistry is all too often overshadowed by their inability to make money at the broad base of popular culture.

In addition to movies, Thais of every age and generation love to listen to music. Just as in the United States, every Thai adolescent has his/her favorite recording artist (a Thai in most cases), as well as the CDs and cassettes to support the claim. But unlike in the West, contemporary Thai popular music tends to be of a singular, mainstream style. It has a kind of manufactured sound to it that is rarely dissonant, loud, or offensive. In other words, Thai pop music, while very slick and well produced, is never "dangerous." In a sense, this is a reflection of that fundamental conservatism that subtly permeates Thai culture. If one wants to hear music that is lively, sensual, and passionate, then there is only one answer: *loogtoong*, or country/provincial songs. Like American country music, the subject matter of loogtoong usually centers on lost love, infidelity, or some other form of personal despair (recall the example of loogtoong in Chapter Two). And like American country music bands, its technical presentation has become quite sophisticated. But here the similarities end. Loogtoong is more about the singer's voice than the band's music. It has a "primal edge" to it that is difficult to describe. Often quite melancholy in tone, loogtoong has a unique quality about it that must be heard in order to be appreciated. At times haunting, it can evoke a trancelike atmosphere for the performer and listener alike. Not limited to the rural provinces, loogtoong is performed in nightclubs throughout Bangkok.

Falling into a musical category of its own is Karabao, an internationally known Thai rock-style band whose songs are incisive commentaries on Thailand's socioeconomic and environmental problems. The word *karabao* refers to a particular

Students studying khon, *the classical masked dance theater of Thailand. (Courtesy of Timothy Hoare)*

species of water buffalo, and probably serves as a cultural metaphor for the hardworking Thai people. The members of the band come from Thailand's rural provinces and therefore have firsthand knowledge of such things as the vast economic discrepancy that exists between Thailand's rural poverty and urban wealth, or the environmental consequences of irresponsible land development. Regarded as champions of Thailand's farmers and provincial working class, Karabao promotes a kind of grassroots socialism through its music, and at the same time encourages consumers to boycott imported goods and "buy Thai."

The traditional Thai performance arts continue to draw a very significant patronage. These forms include *khon, lakawn,* and *likay.* Khon is a classical masked dance/theater form that is based solely on the Indian *Ramayana,* called the *Ramakien* in Thailand. The *Ramakien* is a mythological tale of love, abduction, conquest, and deception known throughout Southeast Asia, and every country in the region has a tra-

A khon mask of Hanuman. (Courtesy of Timothy Hoare)

ditional way of interpreting it theatrically. Khon is performed only by males. Wearing ornate masks and costumes, the actors perform the narrative tale in a stylized system of movement and gesture that had its beginnings in ancient India.

Lakawn is a classical dance-drama performance art that has two traditional forms: *lakawn nai* ("inner court theater") and *lakawn nawk* ("outer popular theater"). Both forms are stylized dance-dramatizations of age-old tales, such as *chahdohk* (or *jataka*, traditional stories of the Buddha), as well as

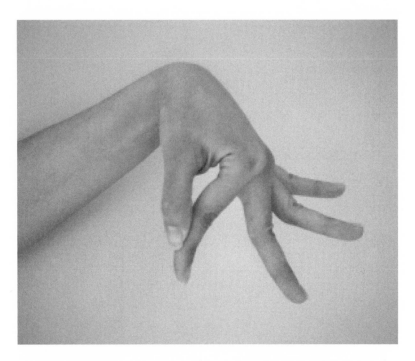

A hyper-extended hand position of Thai classical dance. (Courtesy of Timothy Hoare)

popular narrative themes of royal intrigue, forbidden love, infidelity, betrayal, and the like. Once a seldom-seen and all-female dance form of the inner royal Thai court, lakawn nai is the more refined of the two, and most noted for its graceful postures and gestures, particularly the exquisite hyperextension of the hands and fingers (see photo).

There are dozens of these hand positions in Thai classical dance. Taught from early childhood, the unusual positioning of the fingers expresses a fundamental characteristic of the Thai aesthetic sensibility. The particular position (shown above) is called *chahng brasahn gnah,* or "the elephants lock their tusks in battle." If one imagines that the dancer's index finger is the tusk of the elephant, the remaining fingers represent the thrusting movement of the tusk. They are like mul-

Dusit Hall of the Grand Palace, Bangkok. (Courtesy of Stephen and Panchat Hoare)

tiple images of one moving object seen simultaneously. This aesthetic relationship of line and space can be seen in numerous examples of Thai visual arts and design. For example, compare the hand of the Thai dancer with the photo of the Dusit Hall at the Grand Palace complex in Bangkok. Note that the multiple roof lines of this building are very similar to the multiple lines created by the fingers of the Thai dancer. They both create an illusion of rhythmic movement that compels the eye to follow.

But probably the most popular of the traditional performing arts is *likay*. Essentially a parody or satirical rendition of the nobler lakawn, the content of likay is broadly comic and farcical. Likay plays will often make use of their particular performance site by embellishing the basic storyline with topical humor and outrageous (but good-natured) references to local people or issues.

No overview of Thai entertainment media would be complete without at least a cursory glance at that most pervasive of all popular media, and one that does not involve bai teow: television. According to 1998 figures, there were an estimated 42 million television sets in Thailand. With a total population of approximately 63 million, that translates *per capita* into about 67 television sets for every 100 people. Five years later, one can only assume that the ratio is even closer. Thai television offers a wide array of game shows, children's programming, and news broadcasts. But by far, the most popular programming on Thai television is the screenplay genre known as lakawn.

Television lakawn is at once identical to and distinct from the traditional dance-drama of the same name. The age-old narrative themes remain: wealth, power, forbidden love, infidelity, and betrayal. But the context has changed from royal palaces to high-rise condominiums, from servant-drawn carriages to chauffeur-driven limousines, from aristocratic princes to corporate executives, from hand-delivered secret messages to e-mail delivered by cell phones. In essence, television lakawn is "soap opera." Like Western soaps, lakawn screenplays are serialized, in that one storyline can continue on for months. They are very melodramatic, and the characters are usually played in a very broad, two-dimensional manner, so that there is no question as to who is "good" and who is "evil." But in contrast to most Western soaps, lakawn is always prime-time evening fare, which may account for much of its popularity: the vast majority of television viewers work during the day and are home in the evening.

In a very insightful article entitled "Everyday Dramas: Television Soaps Operas in Thailand" (2003), Sara Van Fleet points to another reason for television lakawn's popularity. At the level of mainstream society, Thailand is, as noted previously, a very conservative culture. But lakawn screenplays seem to provide a safe and acceptable channel for expressing and discussing, *via the dramatized lives of its characters,* real-life social issues, such as infidelity, prostitution, corruption, and even AIDS.

Given their *sanook sanahm* ("enjoyment") attitude toward life, it is no surprise that Thais are avid sports fans. Although soccer is their number-one spectator sport, they also enjoy a number of traditional Thai sports. *Dtagaw,* for example, is a game that can best be described as a unique combination of volleyball, basketball, and soccer. It employs a grapefruit-sized ball that is made of rattan (woven strips of bamboo). Without allowing the ball to hit the ground, the players can hit and pass it with any part of their bodies except their hands. Depending on which form of dtagaw is being played, the object is either to (1) get the ball into a small suspended basketlike goal (as in basketball), or (2) get the ball over a net to the opposing team (as in volleyball). Dtagaw is very physical, as players throw themselves into the air to make contact with a rattan ball that does not simply "bounce off" when contact is made.

Another traditional and very ancient Thai sport is *muay thai,* or, loosely translated, "kickboxing." Essentially a martial art, muay thai can be quite brutal and dangerous, as the fighters are allowed to use feet, knees, and elbows to make contact with the head, midsection, and upper thighs of their opponents. In former times, muay thai fighters would wrap their hands tightly with rope or leather strips, dip them into a sticky resin, and then press them into a box filled with sharp gravel or shards of broken glass. Today they wear gloves that are similar to Western boxing gloves. Many Thais like to gamble on muay thai contests.

A seemingly more benign but still very competitive Thai sport is kite flying. Most foreigners think of this as more of a pastime than a legitimate sport, but the achievement of innovative designs and overwhelming size can become quite competitive. Thai boys enjoy flying kites in general, but as they grow older, many become involved in more serious competitions whose sole aim is to engage an "opponent kite" in battle

and bring it down. Usually these fighting kites will be controlled by strings that have been covered with a glue or resin
and then coated with ground glass or even small pieces of
metal so that it can be used to damage an opponent's kite or
cut its string. I have never witnessed a kite-fighting competition, but I have seen how dangerous they can be; my wife has
a small scar on her jaw that resulted from being accidentally
hit in the face by the glass-covered string of a fighting kite
when she was a child.

Thai sports fans are very enthusiastic about their country's
presence in the global sports venue as well. In the Summer
Olympic Games, for example, the Thai presence has traditionally been very strong in the firearms-shooting competitions. And recently (2003), Paradorn Srichaphan was ranked
among the top ten male tennis players in the world. Some
may recall that Paradorn carried the Thai flag for his team in
the opening ceremonies at the 2004 Summer Olympics.

HOLIDAYS

Traditional festivals and holidays continue to play a major
role in Thai popular culture. Dozens of days throughout the
year are set aside for religious, cultural, and national celebrations, but two of the most important are *Songkrahn* and *Loi
Gratohng*.

Songkrahn is the Thai New Year. It takes place on April 13.
Nevertheless, Thais being Thais, they often devote an entire
week to its celebrations. The most common rituals involve the
throwing of water on one another. Water symbolizes cleansing,
sometimes from debts, sometimes from accumulated sin, so
that one may begin the new year with a clean slate and a pure
heart. Among children and teenagers, the neighborhood water-
throwing rituals may rapidly progress from cups and bowls to
buckets and garden hoses. But Songkrahn is also a time for the
giving of blessings to one's elders. Therefore, a more age-appro-
priate ritual is enacted, in which a family's children will gather

in a circle around their parents and/or grandparents, and then slowly pour small amounts of water over their open hands. But whether it is a ferocious drenching of one's friends or a solemn blessing of one's parents, Songkrahn is a time for celebrating the renewal of life. And, as Songkrahn takes place during one of the hottest months of the year, a good soaking can be a welcome surprise!

The festival of Loi Gratohng is a lunar calendar-based holiday. It takes place on the evening of the first full moon in November, when the rainy season has ended and the water level is high. The story of Loi Gratohng dates back to the Sukhothai period. Nappamaht was a royal consort, or wife, to a Sukhothai king. In return for the blessings of life-giving water and fertility, she made a special sacrifice to the Water Goddess. She constructed a small lotus-shaped boat from banana leaves and, after placing in it a bouquet of flowers with a few incense sticks and a lighted candle, set it afloat in the river. The word *loi* means "to float," and a *gratohng* is a small, lotus-shaped boat. Although the festival dates back to Sukhothai, its origins are found in Hinduism and the sacrificial rituals of Brahmin priests. Today, people gather together by rivers, canals, and ponds throughout Thailand and launch candle-lit gratohngs into the water. It is believed that the gratohngs carry away suffering, sins, and bad luck, and that in a spiritual sense the gratohngs will return to them, carrying blessings and good fortune. Loi Gratohng has also become something of a romantic festival, perhaps comparable to Valentine's Day in the West. Couples will set their gratohngs afloat side-by-side and watch to see if they continue to travel along the same path. If they do so, it is a sure sign that the couple is destined to be together! As romantic and visually stunning as the Loi Gratohng festival is, it has made an unfortunate environmental impact as well. Although traditional gratohngs are handmade from natural substances like banana leaves and flowers, it has become quite convenient for many simply to purchase "ready-made" gratohngs that have been constructed from styrofoam and plastic. As these materials do not break down naturally, they have contributed to a good deal of environmental pollution in Thailand's waterways.

There are other important Thai holidays that have a more nationalistic character, such as Chulalongkawn Day. Chulalongkawn, it will be remembered, reigned as Rama V from 1868 to 1919. On October 23 (the anniversary of his death in 1910), Chulalongkawn is remembered as the monarch whose farsightedness and public service were instrumental to Thailand's transformation into a modern nation-state.

Two other notable celebrations are the birthdays of Thailand's current reigning monarch, King Pumipohn, and his wife, Queen Sirikit (December 5 and August 12, respectively). The Thai people hold the king and queen in remarkably high esteem, even to the point of regarding them as the metaphorical "parents" of the nation. This sentiment becomes wholly evident on their birthdays, as these dates are also officially designated throughout the country as *Wahn Paw* and *Wahn Maa*, or "Father's Day" and "Mother's Day."

SOCIAL ISSUES AND PROBLEMS

Human cultures and natural environments each carry their own particular sets of variables. Their introduction to one another will inevitably create conflicts and issues. As culturally rich and pleasurable as Thailand is, the kingdom is nevertheless plagued with its share of social and environmental challenges. For the remainder of this chapter, we will examine three of these issues—urban environmental concerns, Thai women and patriarchalism, and HIV/AIDS—as well as what, if anything, is being done to address them.

Congestion, Pollution, and Poverty in Bangkok

In the opening chapter of this text, I made the observation that Bangkok is the best and also the worst of Thailand, at once the most fascinating and most unnerving city this author has ever visited.

Bangkok is home to about ten million people and approximately 80 percent of the nation's motor vehicles. Bangkok continues to grow in terms of both density and area, but because there has been no serious attempt at urban planning over the years, the growth pattern is more like a haphazard, uncontrolled sprawl. As will be recalled from our overview of economics (see Chapter Two), industrial expansion into what was once fertile Central Plains farmland forced many Thai farmers to migrate northward. This rural displacement was also the result of housing development. As highways were constructed to connect Bangkok with the adjacent provinces in the 1970s and 1980s, it was inevitable that new housing developments would pop up along those highways, followed by shopping malls and other facilities to support and serve the new suburban population. For example, the adjacent province of Nonthaburi essentially became a part of Bangkok seemingly overnight. Indeed, the construction was done so rapidly that oftentimes construction codes were simply ignored for the sake of expediency, resulting in a few building collapses that made international headlines. These instant moobahns (villages) were part of the frenzied boom in real estate development and speculation that contributed to Thailand's economic crisis in the late 1990s.

Most major cities allocate about 25 percent of their space to a semi-logical grid of streets and major thoroughfares. Within the city proper, Bangkok's drivable streets comprise about 6 percent of its overall area, although some sources estimate this figure to be as low as 2.5 percent (Bello et al. 1998). As a result, the city's traffic jams are legendary. The Thai expression for traffic gridlock is *roht dtit,* which literally means "vehicles touching one another," as in bumper-to-bumper. It has been estimated that Bangkok's rush-hour traffic moves at about 4 kilometers (2.5 miles) per hour, while the average pedestrian walks at a pace of about 5 kilometers

Traffic gridlock in downtown Bangkok. (Courtesy of Michael Smail)

(3 miles) per hour. As referred to earlier, the recently completed rapid-transit skyway train system has relieved some of the congestion along major traffic arteries, but with so many people still unwilling to stop driving their personal automobiles, the skyway has yet to fulfill its potential.

As in many congested urban centers, it is quite likely that the bulk of daily business is transacted not in workplaces but on cell phones while one is confined to one's car in traffic. Having personally experienced numerous daily commutes from the suburbs to downtown Bangkok via both public and private transportation, I believe it is safe to assume that the average commuter devotes a minimum of three hours to the round trip. As a result, the average middle-class Thai commuter has had to adapt him/herself to a more limited time allotment for family or personal agenda. As environmental psychologist Helen Ross has suggested, if there is only one vehicle with which to transport family members to work, school, shopping, and so on, the space of the automobile itself becomes the artificial context for many traditional domestic activities (e.g., school homework, "quality time" with spouse and/or children, and even meals) (see Ross 1995, p. 131–151). Of course, mass transit is always an option. But as there are no apparent policies in place to govern the maximum number of people allowed on a public bus, the experience of a two-hour public commute can be overwhelming, even for the seasoned American mass-transit patron. I myself have made numerous rush-hour bus commutes into Bangkok with literally half of my body hanging outside the overfilled vehicle, one arm wrapped around the frame of a doorless entryway, while holding a briefcase in my "outside" hand. On the rare occasions in which an actual seat was available, my shoulder has served as an impromptu pillow for an exhausted and/or sleeping primary school child for a good part of the journey.

The 80 percent concentration of motor vehicles in Bangkok accounts for more than the city's traffic gridlock. A major environmental concern is their cumulative effect on Bangkok's air quality. Included in that 80 percent concentration, for example, are some two million motorcycles, most of which are "motorbikes" with small two-stroke engines (similar to a lawn mower) that produce about five times more toxic emissions than conventional automobiles. Although motorbikes and cycles are designed to accommodate one passenger, it is frighteningly common to see an entire family of four (husband, wife, and two small children) wearing no helmets and sitting astride a machine as small as 250 cubic centimeters as it weaves daringly in and out of busy traffic lanes. In addition to being exceedingly dangerous in the immediate sense, the prolonged exposure to vehicle exhaust fumes is responsible for a wide array of respiratory problems, especially among young children. Another environmental culprit is the famous *roht dtuk dtuk,* a kind of three-wheeled motorbike-taxi that can carry two or three passengers. A virtual icon of Thai urban culture, tens of thousands of dtuk dtuks are available for hire in Bangkok's streets. The Thai words *dtuk dtuk* refer to the choppy sound of their two-stroke engines.

A roht dtuk dtuk. (Courtesy of Anuchit and Khanittha Chaiarsa)

Between motorbikes, dtuk dtuks, and conventional motor vehicles, the level of CO_2 (carbon dioxide) emissions in Thailand overall is quite high. In fact, according to 1999 figures from the World Resources Institute, Thailand's output ranked second—and a very high second—among its Southeast Asian neighbors (see Table 4.1).

From a global perspective, these amounts are minimal, even for Asia; the 1999 CO_2 emissions levels of India, Japan, and China approached and, in the case of Japan and China, even surpassed the billion mark. But from a regional perspective, the ratio of CO_2 emissions to land mass in Thailand is high and therefore warrants environmental concern.

Once romantically known as "the Venice of the East," Bangkok has a vast network of canals and waterways that extend into the city and suburbs like tree branches off the mighty Chao Praya River. These canals were once Bangkok's

Table 4.1 Amount of Carbon Dioxide Pollutants in Selected Asian Nations, 1999

	CO_2 Pollutants (metric tons)
Indonesia	244.9 million
Thailand	155.8 million
Malaysia	101.3 million
Philippines	66.3 million
Singapore	53.2 million

Source: Adapted from "Climate and Atmosphere 2003." World Resources Institute.

primary transportation routes. They were filled with barges, ferries, and boat taxis. But as early twentieth-century road development and importation of land motor vehicles gradually made water transportation more or less obsolete, most of the ferries and boat taxis disappeared. Although one can still take a lively boat taxi ride to several parts of the city and even into the suburbs, many of these canals are no longer even navigable. Some have been filled in with concrete in order to make way for new construction projects. Others have become so polluted with everything from industrial to human waste that they have become toxic health hazards. Exacerbating the problem is the fact that as migrant populations pour into the city in search of jobs in factories and construction sites, the canals have often become the sites of impoverished slum communities. Alarmingly, the canals have been simultaneously utilized as sources for drinking/cooking water and as depositories for garbage and human waste. Needless to say, the collective risks to human health, wildlife, and water quality are considerable. Poverty in itself, therefore, is another major issue in Thai society. As noted in our overview of the Thai economy (Chapter Two), the chasm that exists between the rural poor and the urban rich is wide, with the top two-fifths of the population receiving 78 percent of the income, and the bottom three-fifths receiving only 22 percent. In Bangkok alone, the vast economic chasm that exists between established affluence and migrant poverty is sometimes shocking, particularly because it is not unusual to see both extremes simultaneously—and sometimes literally side-by-side—in such a densely-populated, microcosmic environment.

What is being done to address these environmental issues in Bangkok? Elsewhere in this text I describe the efforts of Thai Buddhist temples to enforce "pardon zones" in the forests and waters that run adjacent to their temples (see "Phra Boonsong Panyawutho," in Significant People, Places, and Events), as well as reforestation efforts that have been taking place in the rural provinces to repair the damage done by abusive logging practices. But the urban environment itself presents a formidable challenge simply because of the population density. In a city the size of Bangkok, the compliance with regulatory ordinances is sometimes regarded as optional, in that official policy and public practice are very often two different agenda. Just as in the United States (and depending on where in particular one happens to be), legislative wheels turn very slowly, and it is unfortunate that the influence of special-interest groups and outright bribery play such strong roles in determining which way they turn.

But some headway has been made. Leaded gasoline has been obsolete in Thailand since 1996. Many of Bangkok's major thoroughfares now have "Bus Only" lanes, which have improved the flow of mass transit. Also, the Thai government is actively encouraging large industrial corporations to set up operations in other regions of the country in order to ease the rural migration into Bangkok. But even with the offer of tax reduction incentives, compliance has not been easy to achieve, as relocation would also entail increased transportation and shipping costs in order to conduct business in the urban areas in which they currently reside.

Thailand has achieved substantial success in many environmental venues, such as reforestation and wildlife preservation, and is doing what it can to improve the quality of urban life. But until Bangkok's continuing growth can be regulated and more conscientiously zoned, significant environmental change will be difficult to achieve. This issue is of the utmost importance for Thailand, because the city of Chiang Mai, once Thailand's idyllic and best-kept secret getaway in the north, is slowly falling prey to the urban/suburban developer as more and more tourists "discover" its northern charms.

And finally, how does Bangkok keep its head above water when it is sinking? According to Thailand's Department of Mineral Resources, Bangkok is, quite literally, sinking about five centimeters (two inches) per year. The problem is that Bangkok is built over a vast swamp. In former times the city endured the annual floods of the rainy season, as those seasonal waters replenished and maintained the volume of ground water that lies beneath. But as suburban housing and industrial development increased during the 1980s and 1990s, much of that groundwater has been pumped out and utilized because it is cheaper than tap water. As a result, the soil has contracted and sunk, taking the city with it. It is estimated that Bangkok could be below sea level by 2050. If that happens, the rainy season could lead to catastrophic flooding. As noted earlier, many of Bangkok's canals, either stagnant or paved over with concrete, are no longer in any condition to serve as an effective means of water disbursement. As one writer phrased it, "Once known as the Venice of the East for its multitude of canals, Bangkok may soon resemble another fabled city: Atlantis" (*The Economist* 2000, 39).

The Thai Woman, "Patriarchalism," and the Sex Industry

Although Thai society continues to be predominantly patriarchal, the status of Thai women has improved somewhat over recent decades, at least in the urban sector. As we have previously seen, due to increased educational opportunities and a wider diversity of professional career paths, Thai women have been able to achieve a somewhat higher degree of socioeconomic independence. More and more women are finding that they do not have to be defined through a male figure—that is, a father or a husband. Today, marriage competes with education and career as options for Thai women. If a woman does choose to marry (and most still do), statistics indicate that the average age of the Thai bride is increasing as more time is devoted to education and to the establishment of a career. In 1999, for example, half or more of the female population aged fifteen to sixty-four in every major country of Southeast Asia were employed in all of the major sectors (agricultural, industrial, clerical, service, and professional). In Thailand, the figure was 68 percent, although the most highly concentrated sector was still agricultural. Currently, the average age of marriage for Thai women falls between twenty-five and thirty, whereas not so long ago it averaged between fifteen and twenty, particularly in rural communities.

And one must also recall the example that has been set by the princesses of the Thai royal family, particularly Maha Chakri Sirintawn. Her academic accomplishments and untiring service to her country have demonstrated that given the opportunity, the Thai woman is fully capable of achieving any goal to which she sets her mind (for more information on Princess Sirintawn, refer back to the section entitled "The Thai Monarchy and Royal Family" in Chapter Three).

But at the same time, it must also be acknowledged that even immoral practices and human rights abuses die hard if they are tied to tradition; when it comes to women, many of Thailand's social assumptions and cultural practices continue to be governed by a male-dominated, patriarchal mindset. In spite of the modest advancements that Thai women have been able to achieve in education, government, and vocation, many women are still victimized by "the glass ceiling": being able to look up and see the fruits of social and professional advancement, but at the same time being unable to break through in order to acquire them.

Thai Buddhist nuns in meditation. (Courtesy of Anuchit and Khanittha Chaiarsa)

"Patriarchalism" (my term for the process and practice of patriarchy) exhibits itself in some unexpected places. In the previous chapter, for example, it was noted that a controversy exists as to the legitimacy of the role and status of the Buddhist nun in Thailand. Some thirty years ago, the Thai Nuns Institute (TNI) was founded in order to provide spiritual, moral, and financial support for nuns. But because Thai Buddhist nuns are not officially recognized as "ordained" persons on a par with Thai Buddhist monks, there is no government allocation to assist them or the TNI in their mission work and community service. In Western terms, they are essentially regarded more as "volunteers" than "clergy," even though what they do constitutes their vocation and livelihood. They do receive some support from nongovernmental organizations, such as the Thai Inter-Religious Commission for Development. But the issue is not so much one of available finances as it is of underlying patriarchalism, even among the monks of the Buddhist monastic community. There are, for example, accounts of Thai Buddhist nuns who, under the supervision of a local temple, have been called to do teaching or social work in a given village or neighborhood, only to be terminated from their duties because their successes and achievements were regarded by the monks as a threat to their own integrity and standing in the lay community. For monk and nun alike, how can one serve a community well when spiritual calling and the fundamental compassion of Buddhist ethics are compromised and tainted by gender-centered politics?

Even more fundamental perhaps is the fact that the vast majority of Thai Buddhist nuns come from rural backgrounds, and often from impoverished family circumstances. Statistically, it is women from these same population groups who fall into the snare of low-paying urban factory work or, worse yet, prostitution. If young, rural Thai women who become Buddhist nuns are denied the institutional legitimacy and official sanction to support their spiritual callings, are these their remaining choices for economic survival?

Finally, one cannot discuss women and patriarchalism in Thailand without giving at least a cursory assessment of the harsh realities of what we shall loosely refer to as the sex industry. Although organized prostitution has existed and thrived throughout the world in countless modes and venues, Thailand has garnered—through more fault than its own—a reputation of almost mythical dimensions.

Like most Asian cultures, Thailand has had a tradition of royal concubinage and polygyny that is centuries old. Although such practices have been outlawed for some two hundred years, they nonetheless set the stage for a fundamentally patriarchal sexism that remains deeply rooted in the Thai culture. Although he may or may not be literally married to a second wife, it is not unusual for a Thai man of means to keep a mistress. Such circumstances are generally accepted silently by Thai women, who have little say in the matter.

As a social element of the overall cultural landscape, organized prostitution has developed into an unofficial component of the Thai economy. Recent figures indicate that prostitution is responsible for 3 percent of the overall economy, the equivalent of about US$4.3 billion a year. A visit to a brothel is something of a male rite of passage that may or may not become a lifelong mode of leisure. Although prostitution is officially illegal, it is nevertheless tolerated by the general population, and local authorities are often financially remunerated for their acquiescence. Tragically, much of it is grounded in the harsh realities of rural poverty, particularly in Northern and Northeastern Thailand. As noted previously, thousands of rural Thais migrated to Bangkok in search of a better economic future, only to find themselves mired in urban poverty as well. For many female migrants, prostitution presented itself as a way out. Even more tragic is the practice of impoverished rural families finding themselves forced literally to sell their daughters into prostitution in Bangkok. The price that is paid by the brothel to the family must be worked off by the girl, often at an outrageous rate of interest that is virtually impossible to overcome. Every now and then there are proposals to legalize prostitution, so that girls and women can be protected from such abhorrent abuse. Legalization would also allow for proper health care, insurance, and even taxation. But as one would expect in such arguments, the balance between the achievement of a social gain versus the maintenance of a social ill remains ambiguous at best.

But regardless of Thailand's patriarchal foundations, the massive proliferation of the sex industry in contemporary Thailand is by no means a product of its own doing. It is by and large a result of the Vietnam War era (1960–1975). As the American military presence in Thailand increased, so also did the demand for sexual services. This demand was met, as it merely fed into the economic needs of the impoverished villages of Northern and Northeastern Thailand that had been supplying so many young women to the urban brothels all along. Once the Vietnam War ended in 1975, the U.S. soldiers who returned home carried with them, no doubt, alluring accounts of sexual adventurism that were vivid blends of fact and fiction, reality and myth. Such tales, combined with the preexisting Western orientalist imagination, led to a rapid increase in postwar tourism and to the flourishing of such notorious nightspots as Bangkok's Patpong District, or Pattaya Beach on the Gulf of Thailand, both of which bring millions of dollars, legal and otherwise, into the Thai economy. The international attraction of such activity shows little sign of diminishment, if tourist profiles are any indication. In 2003, and thus far in 2004, the male-female tourist ratio is holding steady at about three to two.

To summarize, if the sex industry in Thailand today is "prolific," it is my contention that prior to the Vietnam War, it was no more so than that of any other culture, oriental or occidental. But due to economic circumstances, the Thais simply responded to a combination of military demand for sexual services and an exotic orientalist folklore that had been dispersed throughout the Western world following the end of the war in Vietnam. In essence, then, the Thais were victimized by a Western mythos that was imposed back upon them.

If this curious component of Thai society were not controversial enough already, in due time it would be revealed that it was carrying an additional piece of baggage that was unprecedented. In the sex industry of any culture or region, sexually transmitted diseases (STDs) are more or less regarded as an inconvenient fact of life. But the advent of HIV/AIDS in Thailand in the mid-1980s would grow into an epidemic that would alter the very social fabric of the nation.

As more and more Thai women are able to gain the educational, professional, and governmental footholds that are necessary for the achievement of meaningful systemic change, one can only hope that their socioeconomic situations will continue to improve. But again, in a society that continues to structure itself on an essentially patriarchal foundation, the challenge that remains for Thai women in both the educational and vocational venues is essentially a systemic one: it is a question of the underlying social assumptions that tend not only to govern the Thai man's perception of the Thai woman but also to shape the Thai woman's perception of herself.

HIV/AIDS

Numerous interrelated factors have contributed to the HIV/AIDS crisis in Thailand. Asia's first case of HIV infection was reported in Thailand in 1984. Over the next few years, a pattern of growth was determined that involved the following sectors of the Thai population, both as individual groups as well as through their interaction with one another: the gay community, intravenous drug users, sex workers (prostitutes) and their male clients, and those same male clients and their girlfriends, wives, and subsequent children. The scope of the danger was exacerbated when other variables were added into the mix, such as the number of male tourists from both the West and from other Asian countries who seek out sexual services, as well as the fact that a significant number of women who work in the Thai sex industry are illegal immigrants (primarily from Myanmar) who would therefore be afraid to access any legitimate medical care should they become infected.

HIV infection rates of 40 to 80 percent were found among intravenous drug users (due primarily to needle-sharing) in urban areas of Thailand, and early studies estimated that one in ten contacts between prostitutes and infected clients led to HIV transmission (East-West Center 2002). It was determined that HIV/AIDS, if left unchecked, could become a national, if not an altogether Asian, epidemic. But over the past twenty years, Thailand has taken the Southeast Asian lead in the aggressive promotion of HIV/AIDS awareness, and it has succeeded in doing so where it counts the most: not merely in the legislative halls of policymakers but at the popular level of Thai society.

In Thailand, prevention programs for sex workers and their
clients, in combination with heightened public awareness,
had a quick and dramatic impact on risk behavior. After the
heterosexual outbreak in 1989, condom use in sex work
increased from less than 30 percent in 1990 to more than 90
percent in 1997. Between 1990 and 1993, the percentage of
men using sex services declined by half. As a result, STI [sex-
ually transmitted infection] levels fell by more than 90 percent during the 1990s. HIV prevalence among young men
peaked at 4 percent in 1993 and then declined steadily, falling
below 1 percent in 2000. In pregnant women, HIV peaked at
2.4 percent in 1995 and fell to 1.1 percent in 2001. (East-West
Center 2002, 76)

One of the more interesting personalities to gain notoriety
through these prevention campaigns and educational programs was Meechai Viravaidya, a one-time government economist who founded the Population Development Association
in 1974 to educate Thais about overpopulation and family
planning. In the 1980s, Meechai directed his efforts toward
HIV/AIDS education. In so doing, he almost single-handedly
altered the Thai popular attitude toward sexuality and AIDS
prevention, particularly among the teenage population.
Through his honest and open approaches toward sex education, combined with his outrageous advertising stunts (such as
painting condom ads on the sides of water buffalo), Meechai
has earned the name Khun Toong Yahng, which translates as
"Mr. Condom." It is a name of which he is proud, for it indicates that his consciousness-raising efforts are paying off.

In light of Thailand's generally conservative identity, the
success of such programs is quite remarkable. Many other
Asian nations have been hesitant to pursue such policies and
educational programs in an open and aggressive manner,
because the content is simply deemed too "explicit" for popular consumption. In Thailand, however, it is estimated that
"without rigorous prevention programs, national HIV levels
would have reached 10 to 15 percent of the adult population

instead of the current level of roughly 2 percent. These prevention programs averted more than 5 million additional HIV infections" (East-West Center 2002, 73).

If the sex industry is officially illegal, why not just close it all down as a way of combating HIV/AIDS? Illegal as it is, this dimension of Thai society is so culturally engrained that the government decided to take a more pragmatic approach. By creating cooperative partnerships between health workers, the police, and the women themselves, they chose simply to address the reality of the sex industry as a part of life-as-lived that they had the capacity to make safer. Anything less would serve only to force it underground, which would result in conditions that are even more dangerous. And so because of their willingness to deal with the sex industry on an even playing field, as it were, the HIV/AIDS awareness programs have had considerable success.

But for these very same reasons, the same cannot be said as of yet about the overall effectiveness of such programs with the gay community and with intravenous drug users. Although it can be said that prostitution is illegal but "accepted," illicit drug use is both very illegal and very unaccepted. Similarly, homosexuality, though not "illegal," is nevertheless the object of considerable discrimination in Thai society. These two groups have already, in a sense, been driven underground. Therefore, until the already existing social barriers against them are eased, a cooperative partnership with them will remain difficult to achieve.

What is being done for those who are already infected with the AIDS virus, or for those who are suffering from AIDS-related terminal illness? In Thailand, hospice care (a form of healthcare whose primary aim is to maintain for as long as possible the comfort and quality of life of the dying) has yet to be recognized and actively developed as a vital dimension of mainstream healthcare practices. It has, however, become a major facet in the work of many Buddhist monastic communities across Thailand. Several communities of monks have realized that a core challenge in dealing with HIV/AIDS is ignorance about the condition among both sufferers and the general public, and that a grassroots/hands-on approach is the most effective way of getting the message out. For the monks, a crucial part of the process of overcoming this ignorance was the establishment of a direct and active relationship with those who suffer from AIDS. This includes, for example, the daily acceptance of food as *tahm boon* ("the giving of alms") that has been prepared for them by AIDS sufferers. This relational act alone is vitally important from both a social and a religious perspective. And so in profound contrast to their traditional role of living in relative seclusion from the secular world, Buddhist monks who are trained in AIDS awareness have become quite active in community work. Similar to the government programs described earlier, monks are running workshops and seminars to teach people how to avoid high-risk sexual behavior. Temples are providing care and education for many of the 300,000 children who have been orphaned by AIDS (some of whom are infected themselves). In addition, monks have provided AIDS sufferers with occupational training in new job skills so that they can become more economically self-sufficient. As a result of their compassionate efforts, many Buddhist temples in Thailand have gained the additional designation "HIV/AIDS-friendly."

In July of 2004, the 15th International AIDS Conference was held in Bangkok. Although Thailand continues to be at the cutting edge in the Asia/Pacific region in its efforts to provide basic AIDS awareness, education, hospice care, and economical prescription drugs, it was revealed that much more needs to be done. As noted above, the number of children orphaned by AIDS is staggering. The grandparents of many of these AIDS-orphaned children are being forced to take on the roles of parents and primary caregivers for the second time. They likely face a caregiving commitment of ten years or more, a daunting prospect for older adults who have limited financial resources even for themselves. With these issues in mind, the Conference directed much of its focus toward those segments of society who are not so much "infected" as "affected" by AIDS: the very old and the very young.

When all is said and done, Thailand's most formidable social challenges can be overcome through the continued development of its most valuable asset, that is, the Thai people themselves. Although such things as direct economic, technological, and medical assistance will always be essential for the short term, ongoing human development originates from one source alone: education. As we have previously seen, Thailand's educational challenges remain daunting. But the ultimate resolution of Thailand's social ills demands that those challenges be addressed. An educated population is more likely to make educated decisions when it comes to the future and the welfare of its nation: its natural environment, its vital health, its families, and its heritage, all of which constitute one of the most remarkable cultures in the world.

References
Bello, Walden, Shea Cunningham, and Li Kheng Poh. *A Siamese Tragedy.* London: Zed Books, 1998.
Brandon, James. *Theatre in Southeast Asia.* Cambridge, MA: Harvard University Press, 1967.
———. *The Cambridge Guide to Asian Theatre.* London: Cambridge University Press, 1993.
Chadchaidee, Thanapol. *Essays on Thailand,* 3d ed. Bangkok: D. K. Today, 1995.
East-West Center. *The Future of Population in Asia.* Honolulu: East-West Center, 2002.
The Economist. "Bangkok Gets That Sinking Feeling." U.S. edition, April 29, 2000, 39.
Khuankaew, Ouyporn. "Thai Buddhism: Women's Ordination or More Prostitution?" In *Women and World Religions,* ed. Lucinda Joy Peach, 87–95. Upper Saddle River, NJ: Prentice Hall, 2002.
Library of Congress. *Thailand: A Country Study.* Washington, DC: Federal Research Division, Library of Congress, 1987.
National Identity Board of Thailand. *Thailand in the 80s.* Bangkok: National Identity Board, Office of the Prime Minister, 1984.
Ross, Helen, and Poungsomlee, A. "Environmental and Social Impacts of Urbanization in Bangkok." In *Counting the Cost: Economic Growth*

and Environmental Change, 131–151. Singapore: Institute of South-East Asian Studies, 1995.
Van Fleet, Sara. "Everyday Dramas: Television Soap Operas in Thailand." *Education about Asia* 8, no. 1 (Spring 2003): 12–16.
World Resources Institute. http://www.earthtrends.wri.org.

PART TWO
REFERENCE MATERIALS

Key Events in Thailand's History

4000 BCE   Earliest Neolithic settlement at Ban Chiang in Northeastern Thailand. Evidence of developed bronze metallurgy and sericulture.

2000 BCE   Bronzeware culture in Chao Praya River Valley of Central Thailand.

Second Century BCE   Indian King Asoka sends Buddhist missionaries eastward into China and Southeast Asia.

First Century BCE   The pre-Thai kingdom of Dvaravati is established in North Central Thailand. The Davaravati are the first to be introduced to Buddhism from India.

Seventh Century CE   The pre-Thai kingdom of Srivijaya is established on the Southern Thai/Malay Peninsula.

651 CE   The tribal group known as the Tai unite and settle in what is now the southernmost Chinese province of Yunnan.

802–1431   The Khmer Empire, based at the Cambodian city of Angkor, is established; the Khmer will dominate Southeast Asia for several centuries to come.

1238–1350   The Sukhothai period—the first truly independent Thai kingdom to challenge and break away from the Khmer. Missionaries from Sri Lanka firmly establish Theravada Buddhism at Sukhothai.

1253   The Tai of Yunnan are driven farther southward into Thailand through Kublai Khan's conquest of China.

1259–1558	The Northern Thailand kingdom of Lanna is established.
1275–1317	The reign of Ramkahmheng, Sukhothai's most famous king.
1283	Ramkahmheng creates the first written Thai alphabet.
1292	Ramkahmheng's stone inscription of Sukhothai's earliest formal law.
1350–1767	The Ayutthaya period.
1350–1369	The reign of U Thong (Ramathibodi I), the founding king of Ayutthaya.
1431	The Khmer capital of Angkor is conquered by King Ramesuan, son of Ramathibodi I.
1512	The Portuguese are the first European traders to make contact with Ayutthaya.
1569	Ayutthaya is overrun by the Burmese and becomes a vassal state.
1590–1605	The reign of Naesuan the Great, who drove the Burmese occupying forces out of Ayutthaya.
1656–1688	The reign of Narai; Ayutthaya begins a "golden age" of cultural development and international relations.
1763–1767	Ayutthaya is reconquered and completely destroyed by the Burmese.
1767–1782	The Thonburi Interim. The defeated Siamese forces regroup under Taksin and expel the Burmese forces from Ayutthaya. A new capital is established at the mouth of the Chao Praya River.
1782–present	The Rattanakosin (Bangkok) period; the capital is moved to the east side of the Chao Praya River, the seat of the current Chakri Dynasty.

1782–1802   The reign of Chao Praya Chakri (a.k.a. Ramathibodi) (Rama I).

1802–1824   The reign of Putthalaytia (Rama II), who creates the first dramatic version of the *Ramakien (Ramayana)*.

1824–1851   The reign of Nahngklao (Rama III).

1833   The printing press is introduced to Siam; first printed Thai script.

1851–1867   The reign of Mongkut (Rama IV), who ushers Siam into the modern age. He also is noted for his association with Anna Leonowens, English tutor to the royal household.

1855   The signing of the Bowring Treaty, through which Siam opens formal trade relationships with the West.

1867–1910   The reign of Chulalongkawn (Rama V), the first Siamese monarch to travel to Europe.

1905   Chulalongkawn abolishes slavery in Siam.

1910–1925   The reign of Vajiravudh (Rama VI), founder of Chulalongkawn University.

1925–1935   The reign of Prajadhipok (Rama VII), the first constitutional monarch.

1932   Constitutional monarchy is established in Siam. First prime minister, Manopakawn Nitithada, is appointed.

1935–1946   The reign of Ananda Mahidohn (Rama VIII).

1939   The Kingdom of Siam's name is changed to Thailand: "Land of the Free."

1941   The Japanese Empire attacks Pearl Harbor, Hawaii, on December 7. On December 8, the Japanese invade and occupy Thailand. Thailand signs a treaty with Japan whereby the Japanese acknowledge Thailand's territorial integrity.

1946–present	The reign of Pumipohn Adunyadayt (Rama IX), Thailand's longest reigning monarch.
1950–1975	The beginning of Thailand's infrastructural and industrial development, which intensifies due to United States military presence during the Vietnam War.
1973	Student-led revolution against the military-based rule of Prime Minister Thanom Kittika-chorn. More than four hundred lives are lost in the ensuing riots on October 14. This day is still commemorated as Wan Maha Wippa-sok ("the most tragic day").
1992	Ratification of new constitution that places strong limitations on the military's power to wield political influence.
1995	Thailand's first truly legitimate parliamentary elections are held.
1997	Ratification of new and current Thai constitution that reforms voting practices and creates a "checks and balances" regulatory system to oversee the practices of government agencies.
1997–1998	The Thai economic crisis; by January 1998 the devalued Thai baht reaches an all-time low of fifty-six to the U.S. dollar.
2001	Thaksin Shinawatra is elected prime minister of Thailand. His economic recovery plans revitalize the Thai economy and restore the nation's economic growth levels to competitive rates once again.

Significant People, Places, and Events

Adunyadayt, H.R.H. Pumipohn (Rama IX, r. 1946–present).
If for nothing else, King Pumipohn Adunyadayt is remarkable for his longevity alone. He is the longest-reigning monarch in Thai history. But the length of his reign has given him the opportunity to become Thailand's most accessible monarch since the days of Sukhothai and one of Thailand's most prolific public servants. In spite of Thailand's checkered political history of revolutions and military coups in recent decades, King Pumipohn has never ceased in his active devotion to the social welfare and economic development of the Thai people, particularly those of the more impoverished northern and northeastern regions.

Ayutthaya.   Ayutthaya was the second major Thai kingdom (1350–1767), located about 50 kilometers (31 miles) north of what is now Bangkok. Very influenced by Khmer culture, Ayutthayan kings adopted the Khmer/Hindu monarchic model of the *devaraja,* or "god-king." In stark contrast to the more paternal ruling style of Sukhothai, Ayutthayan kings therefore became very inaccessible and distant. Nevertheless, Ayutthaya saw the development of widespread international trade relations and numerous building projects (particularly Buddhist temples). By the late seventeenth century, Europeans were describing Ayutthaya as a city of incomparable size, beauty, and wealth. One can therefore see not only Khmer but European influence in Ayutthaya's architectural remains. Ayutthaya was destroyed by the Burmese in 1767. The still-impressive ruins stand as a testimony to its greatness and are an easy drive from Bangkok.

Ban Chiang.   Ban Chiang is a renowned archaeological site in Northeastern Thailand. The work of archaeologist Chester F. Gorman (d. 1981) at Ban Chiang in the 1970s revealed a fully developed bronze metallurgy that was concurrent with the previously known bronze culture of Shang Dynasty China (c. 1750–2000 BCE) and perhaps even with that of Mesopotamian culture. These discoveries at Ban Chiang suggest that there was an early indigenous culture in Thailand, as opposed to the traditional hypothesis that the earliest "Thais" originated in the Yunnan Province of Southern China, and did not migrate southward until the thirteenth century BCE.

Bowring Treaty (1855).   Named after Sir John Bowring, the envoy from Hong Kong who came to Siam as a representative of the British government, the Bowring Treaty established the first formal trade relationship between Siam and European nations. Although King Mongkut (Rama IV, r. 1851–1868) conceded sovereignty over British subjects and landowners living in Siam, he succeeded in preserving his kingdom's independence (the only nation in Southeast Asia to do so) while increasing trade profits and establishing Siam as a modern nation-state.

Chulalongkawn (Rama V, r. 1868–1910).   Aside from the current king, Chulalongkawn is the most revered king of the current Rattanakosin period. He fulfilled his father Mongkut's visions of Siam as a modern nation-state by developing the Siamese infrastructure, creating the first Siamese postal and telegraph services, adopting European models of government and education, and abolishing slavery. Chulalongkawn was the first Thai monarch to travel to Europe. The anniversary of his death (October 23) is still celebrated as Chulalongkawn Day, one of Thailand's most important national holidays.

Constitutional Monarchy (1932).   When King Vajiravudh (Rama VI) died in 1925, he left no male heir to the throne. His younger brother, Prajadhipok, was chosen to ascend the throne as Rama VII. Trained primarily as a military officer, Prajadhipok never had the opportunity—nor did he foresee the need—to develop the administrative knowledge necessary for such a responsibility. His reign, therefore, was not a smooth one. Due to the effects of global economic depression in the 1930s, Prajadhipok was forced to cut salaries and raise taxes, thereby alienating many within both civilian and military circles. And so, on June 24, 1932, seven hundred years of absolute monarchy came to an end in a bloodless coup, which had, in effect, begun two decades before with the attempt to overthrow Vajiravudh's government in 1911. Siam's first prime minister, Praya Manopakawn Nitithada, was appointed in 1932; Prajadhipok remained on the throne as Siam's first constitutional monarch. But when his disputes with the government over royal prerogatives versus constitutional limitations reached a stalemate, Prajadhipok graciously abdicated in March 1935.

Creation of the Written Thai Script (1283). As the most prolific of the Sukhothai kings, one of Ramkhamheng's greatest achievements was the creation of the written Thai alphabet in 1283. Although spoken Thai evolved from the languages of Sanskrit and Pali, the written language was based on previously existing Mon and Khmer scripts. A shared written language became the cultural glue that joined the scattered city-states into one Thai nation with an identity of its own. The modern Thai alphabet of forty-four consonants, over thirty vowels, and five tones has changed minimally since its inception. Evidence of this achievement is preserved in Ramkhamheng's famous 1292 stone inscription, in which he declares, "This Sukhothai is good. In the water there is fish, in the field there is rice. . . ."

Erawan Shrine. One of Thailand's most well-known Hindu shrines, Erawan contains a four-faced, seated image of

Brahma, and is patronized by Hindus and Buddhists alike. Erawan is the name of Brahma's mount, a three-headed elephant. Located in the middle of downtown Bangkok in front of the Erawan Grand Hyatt Hotel, it was built in 1956 when a series of mysterious accidents began to occur during the construction of the hotel. A Hindu seer was brought in to evaluate the situation, and he declared that the shrine must be erected in order for the accidents to cease, which they did, according to popular accounts. Devotees bring offerings of small teakwood elephants, flowers, money, and incense on a daily basis.

Establishment of Bangkok as Capital of Thailand (1782). Following the sack of Ayutthaya by the Burmese in 1767, the Thais moved southward toward the delta of the Chao Praya River and set up a new capital at Thonburi, a small town on the west bank. Wary of future aggression from Burma, the capital was moved to the relative safety of the east bank. The site was a small trading village called Bang Makok ("the place of hog plums"), or Bangkok. The proper Thai name is Grungtayp Mahanakawn, which essentially means "The Great City of Angels." For its full-length, record-setting name, see "The Geography of Thailand" in Chapter One.

Fall of Ayutthaya to Burma (1767). Over the course of Ayutthaya's history, there were numerous conflicts with the Kingdom of Burma. Following Ayutthaya's seventeenth-century "golden age" of cultural development and creativity, Thai eyes that should have been politically watchful were turned inward. The Burmese invasion began in 1763, and their forces swept across Northern/Northwestern Thailand. They reached the walls of Ayutthaya in 1766, and in April 1767, after a fifteen-month-long siege, the Burmese overran Ayutthaya, destroying virtually everything in sight. Thousands were killed, soldiers and civilians alike, and the city was burned to the ground. Buddhist temples were torn down and stripped of their gold, and even images of the Buddha were melted down. Along with the immense human toll, an incalculable repository of literary and artistic work was lost forever.

Golden Triangle. Located on the Mekong River at the point where the boundaries of Thailand, Laos, and Myanmar come together, the Golden Triangle is the infamous region of smugglers, opium warlords, and mercenary armies. It is also home to some of Thailand's most notable hill tribes. Although the triangle's history is the stuff from which adventure stories are penned, today one will find considerably less "Indiana Jones" and more "Indiana tourists."

Gorman, Chester (d. 1981). A renowned figure in archaeological research in Thailand, Chester Gorman was associated with the University of Pennsylvania Museum of Archaeology and Anthropology. He did seminal research in the 1970s at the now-famous archaeological site known as Ban Chiang in Northeastern Thailand.

Grand Palace. Located in Bangkok, the Grand Palace is actually a rambling, walled complex of over thirty impressive structures, including reliquaries, temples, residential palaces, and ceremonial reception halls, that date back to the beginning of the current Chakri Dynasty (1782). An eclectic mixture of both traditional Thai and neoclassical European architecture, the complex was expanded and renovated by successive monarchs up through Vijaravudh (Rama VI, 1910–1925). Although the Grand Palace complex no longer serves as the formal residence of the king, three or four of the buildings, including the famous Wat Pra Gaow (see below), continue to function as sites for royal ceremonies and for the official reception of foreign dignitaries.

Hill Tribes. The six primary hill tribe groups in Northern Thailand are the Ahka, the Hmong, the Karen, the Lahu, the

Lisu, and the Mien. For more specific information about each group, see "The Demographics of Thailand" in Chapter One. Over the course of the nineteenth and twentieth centuries, these groups migrated to Thailand from Myanmar, China, Tibet, and Mongolia. Over the years, they have been persecuted by the Thai majority, exploited by tourism, and coerced to forsake their traditional ways by the pressures of a market-based economy. But throughout it all they have maintained their distinctive cultural identities and independence. The hill tribes are known for their exquisite handicraft work, particularly in textiles and silver, as well as for their friendly natures. The economic reality being what it is, however, some of them are also traditionally known for being among the foremost cultivators and producers of opium (which grows well in mountain altitudes), the raw source of heroin to both Asia and the West. But in recent years, royal-sponsored cooperatives have been created to enable the hill tribes to manufacture and market their handicraft goods to Thailand and to the world. And in an effort to lessen their economic dependence on the production of opium, many are being encouraged to cultivate alternative cash crops.

Jim Thompson House.   One of the finest examples of traditional Thai style and decor is found in the shape of a unique home that was designed and decorated by a *farahng* (foreigner) in 1959. Jim Thompson, the American entrepreneur who revitalized the Thai silk industry in the mid-twentieth century, purchased six traditional wooden houses from various places in Thailand, disassembled them, brought them to Bangkok, and then reassembled them into a singular structure of his own design. An avid collector, Thompson decorated his home with high-quality pieces of Southeast Asian art. Following his mysterious disappearance in 1967, the Jim Thompson House was opened to the public as a museum. More information, including history, pictures, and even downloadable driving directions for your Bangkok taxi, can be found on the Internet at http://www.jimthompsonhouse.org (see also Thompson, Jim, on page 221).

Kanchanaburi. On December 8, 1941, the day following their attack on Pearl Harbor, Hawaii, the Japanese invaded Thailand. Kanchanaburi Province of West Central Thailand is the site of the infamous River Kwaa Bridge and the "Death Railway" (the name of the river is pronounced "kwaa," and not "kwai," as depicted in the well-known Hollywood film). Intended by the Japanese as a vital transportation/supply link between Burma (now Myanmar) and Thailand, the construction was carried out in 1942–1943 by forced slave labor consisting of Allied prisoners of war as well as Thai and Burmese citizens. Disease, starvation, and literally being worked to death cost the lives of approximately 12,500 allied prisoners and as many as 80,000 Thai and Burmese, for whom no official records exist. The remains of many but not nearly all of those who died are buried at the Kanchanaburi War Cemetery and the Chong Kai War Cemetery. In the same area, one may also visit the Australian War Museum and the JEATH War Museum (JEATH is an acronym for Japan, England, America/ Australia, Thailand, and Holland), where numerous building tools, weapons, and documentary photographs may be seen. "A life for every sleeper" is the memorialized phrase at this profound site ("sleeper" is a euphemism for a wooden railroad tie).

Leonowens, Anna (1834–1914). The celebrated English governess and tutor to the royal family of King Mongkut (Rama IV), Leonowens was born in India, although in her writings she claims to have been born in Wales. She married Thomas Leonowens, a British army clerk, and traveled with him to Singapore (he was not an officer, as she further claimed in her writings). After his death, Anna started a school for young children in Singapore, but it failed. In 1862 she took a position in Siam as governess and tutor to the royal family of Mongkut, which she held until 1867. In 1870 Leon-owens published her now-famous (or infamous?) account, *The English Governess at the Siamese Court*. Among the several questionable assertions made in this book was her claim to have been the inspiration for Mongkut's modernization projects; but the truth is that her appointment as a Western tutor was part of Mongkut's own existing vision of Siam as a modern nation-state. To her credit, however, it has come to light through some recently discovered letters of King Mongkut that the two of them did confer—and sometimes heatedly—on various social and political issues, such as human slavery (see "The History of Thailand" in Chapter One).

Mongkut (Rama IV, r. 1851–1868). Mongkut was one of the most famous kings of the current Rattanakosin period. Forty-eight years old when crowned, Mongkut had spent the previous twenty-seven years as a Buddhist monk. He was an avid reader, devoted to lifelong learning in numerous fields of study, and is regarded, along with his son Chulalongkawn, as the king who initiated Siam's transition into the modern age. In the West, he is primarily remembered for his association with Anna Leonowens, English governess and tutor to the royal family. Mongkut's favorite subject was astronomy, and he successfully predicted the date and time of a total solar eclipse. But while on a field expedition to view the eclipse, Mongkut contracted malaria and died one month later.

Naresuan the Great (r. 1590–1605). Naresuan was one of the most revered kings of the Ayutthaya period. Following Ayutthaya's initial fall to the Burmese in 1569, Naresuan (while still a prince) organized an army and defeated the Burmese in 1584. Naresuan became king in 1590 and over the next three years successfully defended Ayutthaya against five full-scale Burmese invasions. By the time of Naresuan's death in 1605, Ayutthaya was so strong and unified that it would be another 160 years before the Burmese would pose another significant threat.

National Museum. Located in Bangkok, the largest museum in Southeast Asia also houses the most comprehensive collection. Exhibits include archaeological artifacts, royal jewelry and ceremonial regalia, ancient weaponry, musical instruments, Hindu and Buddhist sculpture, Buddha images from every major period, and a wide array of other period visual art media including textiles, lacquerware, wood carving, silverwork, ivory carving, and painting. Organized tours can be scheduled in English, French, German, Japanese, Chinese, Spanish, and, of course, Thai. Although several galleries in the United States have world-class East and South Asian collections, Bangkok's National Museum is the place to go to see the finest Southeast Asian collection in the world.

National Theatre of Thailand. The National Theatre is the producing wing of the Thai government's Department of Fine Arts. Located in Bangkok, the National Theatre works hand-in-hand with Witthayalai Nadasin (the School of Dramatic Arts; see page 223). Several times each year, the National Theatre produces performances of lakawn (Thai classical dance) and khon (Thai classical masked drama, based on the *Ramakien*). Performers include both graduates (professionals) and continuing students of the School of Dramatic Arts.

Panyawutho, Pra Boonsong (b. 1941). A Buddhist monk and environmental activist in South Central Thailand. Since the late 1970s, Boonsohng has promoted the fundamental relationship between Buddhist ethics and environmental responsibility. His particular agenda has been (1) the restoration of deforested hills through massive fruit tree planting projects, and (2) the creation of "pardon zones," or sanctuaries, where rivers run adjacent to monasteries, so that all water animals in those areas will be protected, and thereby allowed to breed and flourish. Boonsohng started with the Chin River where it flowed by his monastery (Wat Phranon); with governmental support, over one hundred temples throughout Thailand have followed his lead.

Pramoj, Kukrit (1911–1995). This twentieth-century Thai statesman and author was highly regarded as a leading authority on Thai culture and fine arts. Oxford-educated, Kukrit Pramoj (the surname is pronounced "prahmoht") was involved in Thai politics throughout his life, from the opening decades of the constitutional monarchy. He served as prime minister of Thailand from 1975 to 1976. An accomplished poet and author, his novel *The Red Bamboo* (1961) is listed among the top twenty works of modern Thai literature. As far as I am aware, *The Red Bamboo* is not available in English, but several of Pramoj's other works are (see Annotated Bibliography). In 1985 Kukrit was honored as "National Artist" in the field of literature by the National Culture Commission of Thailand.

Ramkahmheng (r. 1278–1318). The most famous king of the Sukhothai period (1238–1350), Ramkahmheng created the first written Thai script in 1283 and unified his kingdom under the teachings of Theravada Buddhism. Ramkahmheng strove to rule as a *dhammaraja,* or "a king who is guided by the wisdom of the Buddhist teachings."

Shinawatra, Thaksin (b. 1949). As Thailand's current prime minister (2001–present), Thaksin, with his political party *Thai Rahk Thai* ("Thais love Thais"), has initiated numerous programs and reforms designed to aid in Thailand's continuing recovery since the economic crisis of 1997–1998. Thus far, "Thaksinomics" have had a positive effect on the health of the Thai economy.

"Siam" Becomes "Thailand" (1939). Following the establishment of the constitutional monarchy in 1932, civilian bureaucrats, led by left-wing intellectual Pridi Panomyong, and a military alliance, headed by Phibul Songkram, competed for political control of Siam; Prime Minister Manopakawn more or less mediated the tension between them. Power balances shifted until 1938, when, following Manopakawn's retirement, Phibul's military-based alliance took control of Siam. Being a very strong nationalist, and one who felt that the independence, ethnicity, and language of the Thai people should be acknowledged, Phibul announced in 1939 that the nation's name—Siam—was now Thailand, from *Brahtayt Thai,* or "Land of the Free."

Student Revolution (1973).   During the early 1970s, Thailand was under military rule and martial law. As the Vietnam War continued, a growing number of Thai university students were being exposed to the communist teachings of internal grassroots insurgency movements that, although originating in the border regions of the north and northeast, had made themselves known among the university populations of Bangkok. In June 1973, government authorities discovered an underground student-run newspaper at Ramkahmheng University. Highly critical of the government, it was shut down. But the government overreacted and went on to force the university to expel those responsible and to terminate certain faculty members who were suspected of supporting them. This action resulted in massive student demonstrations throughout Bangkok. Tens of thousands marched from Thammasat University to the Democracy Monument. As is often the case in such tenuous circumstances, miscommunications and misunderstandings abounded among military forces, police, and students alike. Demonstrations erupted into riots over the next few months, and on October 14, more than four hundred people—mostly students—lost their lives in the ensuing chaos. October 14 is still commemorated each year as *Wan Maha Wippasok* ("the most tragic day").

Sudham, Pira (b. 1954).   Pira Sudham is one of Thailand's most well-known contemporary authors/novelists. His major works, *Siamese Drama* (1983, re-released as *Tales of Thailand*), *People of Eesarn* [Eesahn] (1987), *Monsoon Country* (1988), and *Force of Karma* (2002), are novels and short-story collections about the rural inhabitants of Northeastern Thailand (Eesahn), of which he is a native. Sudham's English-language writing gives poignant expression to the heart, spirit, joys, and hardships of this impoverished and often overlooked segment of Thai society. He was nominated for the 1990 Nobel Prize for literature. See Annotated Bibliography for more information on Sudham's work.

Sukhothai.   The first truly Thai kingdom in Southeast Asia, Sukhothai ("the dawn of happiness") was the Siamese capital from 1238 until 1350. Located in Central Thailand approximately 450 kilometers (280 miles) north of Bangkok, Sukhothai is one of the most important archaeological sites in Thailand. Old Sukhothai, also known as the Sukhothai Historical Park, is a site of 70 square kilometers (28 square miles) that contains numerous wats (temples), Buddha images, and other preserved architectural marvels of Thai, Singhalese, and Khmer origin.

Queen Suryothai (?–1549).   Revered as one of Thailand's greatest heroines, Queen Suryothai is remembered for sacrificing her life in battle for her husband, Maha Chakraphat, king of Ayutthaya. In 1549 the Burmese army of King Tabengshweti invaded Ayutthaya. Mounted on elephants, the two opposing kings came face to face in combat. Unknown to Chakraphat, Suryothai donned the clothing and armor of a soldier, mounted an elephant, and joined her husband on the battlefield. Suryothai drove her elephant between them and was herself slain by Tabengshweti. According to legend, this selfless act of devotion so moved and ashamed the Burmese king that he ceased fighting and withdrew his army. Suryothai's ashes are enshrined in a *chedi,* or reliquary, at Suan Luang Sobsawan Temple, located in the modern province of Ayutthaya.

Thompson, Jim (1906–1967?). Thompson is remembered as the American entrepreneur who introduced Thai silk to the world. During World War II, James H. W. Thompson was a U.S. military officer with the OSS (Office of Strategic Services, forerunner of the CIA) in Africa and Asia. After the war ended, Thompson found himself in Bangkok and decided to make Thailand his home. He turned his entrepreneurial attention to the reviving of the Thai silk industry (at that time little more than an isolated village craft). Through the efforts of Thompson and the company that he created, Thai silk gained an international reputation as one of the most exquisite and sought-after fabrics in the world. The Thai silk industry is still regarded as one of the top success stories of post-WWII Asia. In 1967 Jim Thompson vanished while on holiday in Malaysia. To this day, his disappearance remains a mystery.

Wat Arun. Literally "the Temple of the Dawn" (after Aruna, the Indian God of the Dawn), Wat Arun has a very strong Khmer influence; the stylistic elements of its lofty *prahngs* (towers) remind one of Angkor Wat in Cambodia. Wat Arun is located on the banks of the Chao Praya River, but it is unusual because it is on the Thonburi side of the river and not in Bangkok itself. Wat Arun is probably the most photographed and the most prolific image depicted in publications about Thailand.

Wat Pra Chetupohn (Wat Po). Located near the Grand Palace complex, Wat Po is the massive temple complex that houses the Reclining Buddha. This image depicts the Buddha at the moment of his death, just before his passage into Nirvana. It is 46 meters (nearly 152 feet) long, 15 meters (50 feet) high, and completely gold-plated. This immense sculpture is said to depict all 108 of the "auspicious marks," or physical characteristics, of the true Buddha. Not simply "a temple," Wat Po is composed of numerous buildings and structures, some of which date back to two hundred years prior to the Rattanakosin (Bangkok) period (1782–present). In total, there are at least one thousand Buddha images at Wat Po, many of them brought here from the ancient ruins of Sukhothai and Ayutthaya. Circumscribing the outer walls of the temple hall are 152 marble slab bas-reliefs that depict the *Ramakien*, the Thai version of the Indian epic the *Ramayana*. Each bas-relief panel is an equilateral square that measures 45 centimeters per side (about 18 inches), or approximately 2.25 square feet.

Wat Pra Gaow.   This is the Temple of the Emerald Buddha, located on the enclosed grounds of the Grand Palace complex in Bangkok. Built in 1782 at the founding of the Rattanakosin (Bangkok) period, Wat Pra Gaow is the home of the famous Emerald Buddha. Also known as Wat Pra Si Rattana, its interior walls are decorated with murals of the *Jataka* tales, stories of the life of the Buddha. Wat Pra Gaow is the only Buddhist temple in all of Thailand that does not have any resident monks. The Emerald Buddha is Thailand's most revered Buddhist icon and national treasure. The image is in a traditional seated/meditative position and is about 60–75 centimeters (24–30 inches) in height. The origins of the Emerald Buddha are sketchy at best. Old records indicate that in 1434, lightning struck and destroyed a chedi (Buddhist reliquary) in the Chiang Rai Province of Northern Thailand. A Buddha image made of stucco was discovered inside. But underneath the stucco was the Emerald Buddha, carved from a single block of jade. In 1468 the image was moved to Chiang Mai and installed at Wat Chedi Luang. King Tilok of Chiang Mai had no sons, but his daughter was married to the King of Laos. They had one son, Prince Chaichetta. After Tilok died in 1551, Chaichetta was invited to assume the kingship in Chiang Mai. When his own father died in 1552, he returned to Laos and took the Emerald Buddha with him. It remained in Laos for the next 226 years. During the Thonburi Interim (1767–1782), the son of King Thaksin captured the Laotian capital of Vientiane (in 1778) and brought the Emerald Buddha back to Thonburi (the son later became Ramathibodi, or Rama I). In 1784 the image was moved to Wat Pra Gaow in the new capital of Bangkok. As a ritual acknowledgment of the seasonal cycles, the Emerald Buddha has three gold mesh "robes," one for each of the three seasons (hot, rainy, and cool). The seasonal changing of the Emerald Buddha's robes is performed three times a year by H.R.H. King Pumipohn Adunyadayt.

Wittayalai Nadasin.   The oldest and most successful school of the classical performing arts in all of Southeast Asia, the school that evolved into Nadasin was established in 1934 by the Thai government's Department of Fine Arts. Located adjacent to the National Theatre of Thailand in Bangkok, Nadasin educates and trains future dancers and actors in the Thai classical performing arts. In a manner somewhat similar to the "high schools of the performing arts" in the United States, girls and boys as young as ten years old are auditioned for the various role "types" that are necessary for the classical dance and theater. In addition to daily classes in these highly disciplined performance techniques, students are enrolled in coursework that fulfills their traditional academic education.

Yupho, Danit (b. 1907).   A major figure in the development of twentieth-century Thai classical theater and dance training/ performance, Yupho was director-general of the government Department of Fine Arts from 1956 to 1968. Under his direction, the National Theatre of Thailand was opened.

Thai Language, Food, and Etiquette

THE THAI LANGUAGE

Not unlike the culture itself, the Thai language is something of a paradox—it is quite logical and yet very nonrational; it is easy to pick up and yet just as easy to lose; it can be blatantly direct and yet delightfully nuanced; it is a walk in the park grammatically but can seem like mile after mile of bad road if one doesn't have an "ear" for it. But learning to read, to write, and especially to speak the Thai language has been worth every moment I have devoted to it. What may have begun as an abstract classroom exercise in Berkeley, California, became in Bangkok, Thailand, an avenue into the very heart and soul of a people, a means of discovering a worldview and a perception of self and others that is completely different from my own cultural experience. In short, the Thai language (or *any* language, for that matter) is not merely a means of communication; rather, it is a living entity that flows forth on the breath of the people who speak it.

Spoken Thai

Ultimately derived from the ancient South Asian languages of Pali and Sanskrit, modern Thai consists of forty-four consonants. Some of those consonants share the same basic sounds; some appear much more frequently than others; a few are so rare that they appear in only a slight handful of words; and two of them, although formally taught, are obsolete altogether.

Several even change their sounds, depending on whether they appear at the beginning or at the end of a syllable.

The Thai language also contains over thirty vowel sounds—long and short vowels as well as a number of diphthongs, combined forms that move directly from one vowel sound to another. If one hastens to conclude that Thai has over six times as many vowels as English has, it should be remembered that English, too, has long vowels, short vowels, and numerous diphthongs. When all is said and done, the Thai vowel system contains only four or five sounds that do not occur in English.

In stark contrast to most Western languages, Thai nouns and verbs have no declensions or conjugations. Regardless of tense, person, or number, their forms remain the same, except that short prefixes are appended to denote simple past or future tenses. At this point one might want to declare joyfully that Thai must be one of the most user-friendly languages on the planet. But the Thai language has its own array of challenges, which are, to some, utterly daunting. Aside from its completely non-Western alphabet, the Thai language is "tonal"; the inflection or sound pattern that is given to a word is as much a part of its meaning as is its spelling. There are five tones in Thai: middle, rising, falling, high, and low. The alphabet is divided into three categories or classes (referred to as high, middle, and low), and each of these classes is governed by different tone rules. There are many Thai words whose consonant and vowel patterns are identical, but as they are spoken with different tones, their meanings are completely different. For example, the word *mah,* if spoken with a middle tone, means the verb "to come." But if the same word *mah* is spoken with a rising tone, it means the noun "dog." And finally, if the same word *mah* is spoken with a high tone, it means the noun "horse." In written Thai, the spelling and the tone markings make these differences quite clear, but in spoken Thai, the word must be identified through one's vocal inflection.

Because of tonal inflection, there is a good deal of word

play, or "pun," in the Thai literary tradition, as well as in everyday humor. Below is a traditional tone exercise taught to Thai school children. Although the consonant and vowel sounds of the words are completely identical, their respective tones identify them as separate words with separate meanings. Try to say the words with the tonal inflection that is indicated in the parentheses:

ไม้ใหม่ไหม้ไหม   *Mai* (high) *mai* (low) *mai* (falling) *mai* (rising)?

ไม่ไม้ใหม่ไม่ไหม้   *Mai* (falling) *mai* (high) *mai* (low) *mai* (falling) *mai* (falling).

These words translate as the question, "Does new (i.e., green) wood burn?" and the response, "No—new wood doesn't burn."

Developing an ear for tonality is very much like developing an ear for music. In my own experience, I have found that people who like to sing or who play a musical instrument catch on to tonal inflections quite easily. But because tonal inflection is so intrinsic to the spoken language, one truly has to hear it in order to learn it. Thai phrase books for travelers that provide English transliterations are not all that helpful, as it is virtually impossible to transliterate a tonal inflection. Nevertheless, a number of basic words and phrases are included in this section. The best way to make use of them is to find a Thai speaker, native or otherwise, who can pronounce them for you, so that you begin to gain a sense of tonality along with the vocabulary. He/she may teach you a good Thai word-play joke in the process!

Another very unique aspect of the Thai language is the use of "classifiers." These are special words that are used to denote types or categories of things, particularly when referring to a specific number of them. For example, the statement "I would like five shirts, please" would be *Pohm kaw seuah hah dtuwah nah krahp.* This sentence translates literally as "I would like shirts, five of *that particular category of things,* please." The word *dtuwah* is the classifier. Now, I could also say *Pohm kaw gao ee ha dtuwah na krahp,* which is the same, except that it is asking for five chairs, not five shirts. But both use the same classifier, *dtuwah.* Why? Because *dtuwah* is the classifier for "things with limbs" (including animals but not humans)"—shirts have arms, and chairs have legs! There are over eighty classifiers altogether, but one can get by in everyday conversations with perhaps twenty of them.

Written Thai

As noted earlier in this text, the first Thai alphabet was created in 1283 by Ramkahmheng, the famous king of the Sukhothai period. The following chart shows the forty-four consonants, followed by the major vowel sounds, of the Thai alphabet. In each sequence is written the consonant in Thai script, followed by an English transliteration of the sound (pronounced by uttering the consonant plus the vowel sound "aw"), and then a simple Thai word that begins with or contains the given consonant. The learning process for children is therefore not unlike that of the English alphabet, as one is taught that A is for "apple," B is for "bear," C is for "cat," and so on. As noted, the reader will see that several different consonants make the same sound (depending on their placement in a word). Also, the third and fifth consonants are so old that they are obsolete (not even available on modern Thai fonts). The two corresponding words now begin with the second and fourth consonants, respectively. Because there are multiple consonant letters with the same or similar sounds, the consonant sound plus the simple "learning word," for example, *Gaw–Gai,* together identify the actual name of the given consonant letter. Therefore, it is particularly important to know these words, especially if you are spelling a word orally for someone. For the correct order, read the lines across from left to right, not down each column:

ก. ไก่ *Gaw-Gai* (chicken)

Kaw-Kuat (bottle) obsolete, now sp. ขวด

Kaw-kohn (person) obsolete, now sp. คน

ง. งู *Ngaw-Ngoo* (snake)

ฉ. ฉิ่ง *Chaw-Ching* (finger cymbal)

ซ. โซ่ *Saw-Soh* (chain)

ญ. หญิง *Yaw-Ying* (woman)

ฏ. ปะฏัก *Dtaw-Badtak* (buffalo goad)

ฑ. มณโฑ *Taw-Mohntoh* (demon queen)

ณ. เณร *Naw-Nain* (novice monk)

ต. เต่า *Dtaw-Dtao* (turtle)

ท. ทหาร *Taw-Tahahn* (soldier)

น. หนู *Naw-Noo* (mouse)

ป. ปลา *Pbaw-Pblah* (fish)

ผ. ฝา *Faw-Fah* (lid, top)

ฟ. ฟัน *Faw-Fuhn* (teeth)

ม. ม้า *Maw-Mah* (horse)

ร. เรือ *Raw-Reua* (boat)

ว. แหวน *Waw-Waan* (ring)

ษ. ฤษี *Saw-Reusee* (hermit, seer)

ห. หีบ *Haw-Heep* (large box)

อ. อ่าง *Aw-Ahng* (large bowl)

ข. ไข่ *Kaw-Kai* (egg)

ค. ควาย *Kaw-Kwai* (water buffalo)

ฆ. ระฆัง *Kaw-Rakung* (bell)

จ. จาน *Jaw-Jahn* (plate)

ช. ช้าง *Chaw-Chahng* (elephant)

ฌ. เฌอ *Chaw-Cheu* (type of tree)

ฎ. ชฎา *Daw-Chadah* (Thai headdress)

ฐ. ฐาน *Taw-Tahn* (platform for Buddha)

ฒ. ผู้เฒ่า *Taw-Pootao* (an old man)

ด. เด็ก *Daw-Dek* (child)

ถ. ถุง *Taw-Toong* (small bag)

ธ. ธง *Taw-Tohng* (flag)

บ. ใบไม้ *Baw-Baimai* (leaf)

ผ. ผึ้ง *Paw-Peung* (bee)

พ. พาน *Paw-Pahn* (ceremonial bowl)

ภ. สำเภา *Paw-Sahmpow* (sailing ship)

ย. ยักษ์ *Yaw-Yahk* (giant demon)

ล. ลิง *Law-Ling* (Monkey)

ศ. ศาลา *Saw-Salah* (open-sided shelter)

ส. เสือ *Saw-Seuah* (tiger)

ฬ. จุฬา *Law-Joolah* (kite)

ฮ. นกฮูก *Haw-Nokhook* (owl)

The Thai vowels are a little more difficult to grasp, as their placement in the word varies with the given sound. For example, in the written word *mah* (high tone, "horse"), the vowel sound "a" is simply written after the consonant, as it would be in English. However, in the written word *maa* (falling tone, "mother"), the vowel sound "a" is written before the consonant. Shown below are both of these examples in Thai script, along with the appropriate tone marks as well:

Consonant *Maw-Mah*   ม   + vowel sound *a* า = ม๊า   *mah* ("horse")
(as in "father," held long)

Consonant *Maw-Mah*   ม   + vowel sound *a* แ = แม่   *maa* ("mother")
(as in "bad," held long)

Some of the major vowel sounds are shown below with English transliterations. The inserted Thai letter อ serves as a place holder, in that it represents where any given consonant letter(s) would be in relationship to the vowel:

a (as in "father") held long: อา   held short: อะ

a (as in "day") held long: เอ   held short: เอะ

a (as in "bad") held long: แอ   held short: แอะ

u (as in "food") held long: อุ   held short: อุ

e (as in "tree"): อี   i (as in "it"): อิ

eu (u as in "food" with teeth together) held long: อื   held short: อึ

o (as in "old"): โอ

ai (as in "cry"): ใอ or ไอ

eu-a (as "eu" above, followed by "a" as in "father"): เอือ

e-a (as in Italian "mia"): เอีย

oo-a (as in the sound "oo-ah"): อัว

Two other Thai letters (very rare) function as "consonant-vowels." They are ฤ (reu) and ฦ (leu).

Here are the traditional Thai numerals. They are still used in formal circumstances, but today one will usually see Western (i.e., Arabic) numerals in print (newspapers, advertising, etc.):

One ๑ *Neung*	**Six** ๖ *Hohk*	**Twenty** ๒๐ *Yeesip*
Two ๒ *Sawng*	**Seven** ๗ *Jeht*	**Fifty** ๕๐ *Hah sip*
Three ๓ *Sahm*	**Eight** ๘ *Paad*	**One hundred** ๑๐๐ *Neung roy* (r –aw-ee)
Four ๔ *See*	**Nine** ๙ *Gow*	**Five hundred** ๕๐๐ *Hah roy*
Five ๕ *Hah*	**Ten** ๑๐ *Sip*	**One thousand** ๑๐๐๐ *Neung pahn*

Some Common and Useful Expressions

The Thai language is very sensitive to relational circumstances, that is, with whom one is speaking at any given time. In the examples that follow, the reader will note the words *krahp* and *kah* at the end of each sentence or expression. *Krahp* (for male speakers) and *kah* (for female speakers) are untranslatable terms of respect that are placed at the end of virtually anything that one would say to a person with whom one is not acquainted on a familiar basis, or to an elder in one's own family. They are somewhat equivalent to saying "Sir" or "Ma'am." If you are at all in doubt as to with whom you are speaking, do not hesitate to use these words—in Thailand, there is no such thing as being too polite! *Once again, the reader is advised that because Thai is a tonal language, it is virtually impossible to transliterate the proper inflection. Your best bet is to find a native Thai speaker (or a knowledgeable nonnative speaker) who can pronounce these for you.*

Hello.	*Sahwaht dee krahp (kah).*
Goodbye.	*Waht dee krahp (kah).*
Thank you.	*Kawp khun krahp (kah).*
Excuse me.	*Kaw tohd nah krahp (kah).*
How are you?	*Sahbai dee reu krahp (kah)?*
I'm fine, thank you.	*Sahbai dee krahp (kah).*
Never mind/no problem.	*Mai pehn rai krahp (kah).*
Where is _____?	*_____ yoo tee nai krahp (kah)?*
What is your name?	*Khun cheu ahrai krahp (kah)?*
Do you/Can you speak English?	*Khun poot pahsah Ahngrit dai mai krahp (kah)?*
Where are you going?	*Khun jah bai nai krahp (kah)?*
Where have you been?	*Khun bai nai mah krahp (kah)?*
What time is it, please?	*Waylah tao rai* (or) *Gee mohng krahp (kah)?*
How much (cost) is this, please?	*Nee tao rai* (or) *Nee gee baht krahp (kah)?*
Is this food very spicy?	*Ahahn nee peht mahg reu blao krahp (kah)?*
How long have you been/lived here?	*Khun yoo teenee wayla nahn tao rai krahp (kah)?*
What/how is this called in Thai?	*Nee pahsah Thai reeahk wah ahrai krahp (kah)?*

That last one is essential for learning new Thai words wherever you happen to go! The Thai phrase above for "Hello," *Sahwaht dee krahp (kah)*, is used for face-to-face greetings.

But when answering a telephone at home, for example, a Thai will simply use the English word "Hello."

The following phrases use the personal pronouns "I" and/or "me." With *very* few exceptions, males use *pohm* and females use *deechahn*. When speaking to a peer or to someone with whom one is very familiar, the pronoun is sometimes simply understood and therefore dropped altogether. But when in doubt, use it; all in all, it is much better to be too polite than a little impolite!

My name is _____.	*Pohm (Deechahn) cheu _____ krahp (kah).*
I can speak a little Thai.	*Pohm (Deechahn) poot pahsah Thai dai nit noi krahp (kah).*
I would like/May I have _____, please.	*Pohm (Deechahn) kaw _____ dai mai krahp (kah).*
Can you take me to _____?	*Khun pah pohm (deechahn) bai _____ dai mai krahp (kah)?*

When in Thailand, speak Thai as much as you can. Don't be embarrassed to ask how to pronounce these phrases or anything else. Unlike many countries, Thais are truly flattered when you try to speak their language (and very pleased when you learn to do it well!). I have met many Thai people and have yet to meet one (in Thailand, at least) who reacted otherwise.

All in all, the best way to learn the Thai language well is simply to commit oneself to learning how to read, write, and speak it. Once the alphabet, vowels, and the tone rules are learned, they will become second nature, and the correct tonal inflection will be as automatic as singing a familiar tune. In our multimedia culture, there are indeed many clever ways to learn many things on one's own, but a spoken language (especially a tonal one) still requires a speaking teacher. For those who are interested in pursuing formal Thai language study, several U.S. universities offer full Thai language programs in their respective Departments of Southeast Asian Studies. Most are members of the Consortium for the Advanced Study of Thai (CAST). A list of the CAST members may be found in the reference section under Thai-Related Organizations. *Chohk dee* (good luck)!

THE FOOD OF THAILAND

The word *companionship* is derived from the Latin words *cum* ("with") and *panis* ("bread"). In light of this little etymological morsel, the most important observation one can make about Thai food is this: Thais love to eat together. In Thailand, eating is family; eating is doing business; eating is socialization. Without the presence of food, all of those relational arenas are diminished. And so perhaps it is partly because of this that over the course of the past twenty-five years, the cuisine of Thailand has gained a profile of world-class dimensions. Its ingredients are diverse and unique, its spices can be lethal, and its recipes are sought after by countless Western chefs and restaurateurs. Thai restaurants abound in the United States and Europe, and many English-language Thai cookbooks have been published in recent years. But even the best Thai cuisine in Chicago or Los Angeles cannot quite compare with that which one encounters in Thailand. The ingredients are fresher, the spices are more potent, and the companionship is more engrained into the very experience of dining. In addition, Thai restaurateurs in the United States have become accustomed to adapting their recipes to American tastes and expectations, particularly in terms of spiciness, a fundamental characteristic of all Southeast Asian cooking. In other words, "mild," "medium," and "hot" do not mean in Thailand what they mean in Chicago (unless you are a Thai customer!). But more about that later.

As in all East and Southeast Asian cultures, the basis of all Thai food is rice. It is so fundamental that there are very few instances in which Thais would be eating anything without it.

A common Thai question is *Gin kao reu yahng?* Translated colloquially, this means, "Have you eaten yet?" but its literal meaning is "Did you eat rice yet?" In other words, the presence of rice with a meal is simply assumed. It is the "glue" that holds the other components of the meal together.

Thailand's indigenous rice comes in several varieties, but two stand out as the most common. *Kao hawm mali,* or jasmine-scented rice, is Thailand's finest long-grain rice. Usually prepared in an electric rice steamer, jasmine rice is the staple of virtually every Thai household and restaurant (not to mention every Thai household and restaurant in the United States). It is exceptionally fragrant (hence the name), and if covered and refrigerated, it stays fresh over several days. Though most Thais would find this a decidedly strange thing to do, it is even delicious to eat by itself.

Surprisingly, jasmine rice does not have an ancient history. In 1945, a rice farmer of Chonburi Province (southeast of Bangkok) developed it through random hybrid experiments. Once the government "discovered" his creation, further tests and research projects were run between 1950 and 1967, through which it was concluded that the soil and climate of Northeastern Thailand produced the very best quality of jasmine rice. The rest, as they say, is history.

In the northern and northeastern regions of Thailand, one will also encounter *kao neow,* or glutinous rice, sometimes called "sticky rice." Shorter-grained and denser in consistency, kao neow is, in a word, sticky. When prepared and served, the individual grains adhere together into a large ball-shaped mass. Although kao neow adheres to itself, it doesn't stick to anything else. Therefore, it is usually eaten with the hands. One simply breaks off a piece and uses it to dip into a variety of sauces and the like. It is common for a Northeastern Thai farmer to take a good-sized ball of kao neow with him into the field—he simply places it in his pocket or shoulder bag and eats from it throughout the day. *Kao neow* is especially good with traditional country-style foods like barbecued chicken or spicy salads. And finally, as a traditional Thai dessert that is an absolute must for the visitor to Thailand, kao neow can be sweetened with coconut milk and served with fresh mango or ice cream. Rarely will one find a Thai restaurant in the West that serves this delicacy!

Categories and Types of Thai Cuisine

Aside from peppers, herbs, and seasonings, Thailand's primary culinary influences are Chinese and Indian. From China there came a seemingly endless array of noodle styles, stir-frying techniques, and the fiery hot flavors of the western Szechuan and southern Yunan regions. Both the Hindu and Muslim cultures of South Asia developed unique applications of the aromatic spice known as turmeric. Made from the ground root of an Indian plant of the same name, turmeric is the basic component of curry powders and sauces. Some of Thailand's most popular dishes are curries. (*Curry*, from the South Indian word *kaari*, means "sauce").

In regard to Chinese influences, most Westerners assume that Thais, like the Chinese, eat their food with "chopsticks." Indeed, the Thais do use chopsticks to eat most of their noodle-based dishes, but virtually everything else is eaten with spoons and forks. The spoon is the primary implement for carrying food to the mouth, and the fork is used essentially as a "rake" to gather the food into the spoon.

Listed below is an extended summary of the basic categories of traditional Thai foods as one would encounter them on a typical Thai menu (in Thai, of course), followed by descriptions of some of the essential elements that go into them.

The Basic Categories

- *Yahm* (salads): compilations of ground meats (usually chicken or pork) served with lettuce and/or cabbage; usually very spicy.
- *Dtohm* (soups): rice soup (usually a home meal in the

morning, very bland, comparable to Western oatmeal); for noontime/evening meals, chicken and/or shrimp soups, often with a coconut milk base; moderately spicy.

- *Gwih deao* (noodles): bean thread noodles, rice noodles, and egg noodles of various widths; each type is associated with specific dishes.
- *Gaang* (curry): usually red or green, and moderately spicy; also *gaang massuman,* a delicious thick brown curry that was most likely introduced to Thailand by Muslim visitors from India (the Thai word *massuman* is based on the English word *musselman,* an archaic colonial reference to Middle Eastern or Muslim peoples).
- *Neuah, moo, gai* (beef, pork, chicken): usually stir-fried in a wide variety of dishes.
- *Pahk* (fresh vegetables, such as string beans, broccoli, bell peppers, bamboo shoots, cabbage, and Asian varieties of lettuce): usually stir-fried in a wide variety of dishes. There are many vegetarian dishes in Thai cuisine; although strict vegetarianism is not particularly pervasive in Thailand, there are nevertheless many people who practice it for either religious (Buddhist) or health reasons.
- *Ahahn tahlay* (seafood): shrimp, crab, and fish, usually steamed, broiled, or stir-fried in a wide variety of dishes.
- *Pohnlamai* (fruit): fresh tropical fruits in Thailand are the best of the best (mango, jackfruit, bananas, rambutan, to name a few); for most Thai children, these fruits are traditional desserts, although now Western and Japanese manufactured confections are found everywhere.
- *Kreuahng dteum* (beverages): in a tropical climate such as Thailand, iced coffee and iced tea are quite popular. But unlike their American counterparts, Thai iced coffee and tea are very dark, rich, and sweetened with condensed milk. Both are served over ice in tall glasses with a layer of cream at the top. Thai iced coffee or tea constitute great desserts in themselves. Generally speaking, most Thais drink water along with their meals when they are eating at home. But in restaurants, soft drinks are quite popular as well, especially among young people in the fast-food venues. Although Thais do drink various flavors and types of

hot tea, it is not a beverage that would normally accompany a meal, as one would find in China, for example. On the other hand, it is quite common for Thais to drink conventional coffee or tea at breakfast. As for alcoholic beverages, Thais do enjoy a wide variety, particularly in the context of an evening's socialization. Both in Thailand and throughout the world, Thai beer, such as *Sing Ha* (called *beah sing* by Thais) is quite popular. Although most Thais prefer Western brands of liquor, there are a few domestically-manufactured ones that have, for good or for ill, gained a global reputation among those who have imbibed in them! But kreuahng dteum would not be complete without *ahahn gahp glaam,* or "foods to accompany drinks." Usually quite spicy, ahahn gahp glaam encompasses a variety of choices, ranging from spicy salads (*yahm*, described above) to various "finger foods," such as fresh cashews mixed with diced ginger, green onion, and hot chili peppers. If cocktails are a prelude to an entire meal in a restaurant, ahahn gahp glaam essentially fills the role of an appetizer.

The Essential Elements of Thai Cuisine

- *Nahm plah* (fish sauce): a very salty, fish-flavored liquid used to season the vast majority of Thai dishes; in the Thai kitchen, it is as basic to cooking as salt and black pepper.
- *Kreuahng tayt* (herbs): fresh aromatic herbs such as basil leaves, mint leaves, ginger root, cilantro leaves, garlic, lime kaffir leaves, and lemongrass make Thai food smell as good as it tastes.
- *Prik* (peppers): along with herbs, truly a signature element of Thai cuisine; in Thailand, there are dozens of varieties of peppers, from conventional bell peppers to the deceptively diminutive *prik kee noo* ("rat poop pepper") that packs a punch that can quite literally incapacitate the novice diner. In fact, it is used in some traditional rural dishes from the northeastern region that are so hot that many Central Thailand/Bangkok people cannot eat them. Surprisingly, these hot peppers are not indigenous to Thailand, nor even to India or China. They were discovered by Portuguese explor-

ers in the Andes mountains of South America. From that point, there are numerous possible paths to Thailand, none of them certain. They could have been brought directly to the Thai by the Portuguese, as these were the first Europeans to establish trade relations with Siam in the early sixteenth century. Or, the Portuguese could have introduced them directly into the Indian spice trade, thereby passing into Siam. But an even more circuitous route is more likely: the Portuguese probably took these peppers back to their home on the Iberian Peninsula, where Muslim/Moorish influence was quite prevalent in Spain. From there, the new spice sensation traveled back across North Africa, into the Near East, and then was finally introduced to both the Muslim and Hindu cultures of India. But however they arrived on the scene, there are three important things to know about *prik kee noo:* (1) adding them to a stir-fry dish makes it hot; adding them to a stir-fry dish and then breaking them open with the edge of a spatula makes it VERY hot; (2) a mouthful of jasmine rice cuts the spiciness; a mouthful of water simply makes it stronger; and (3) if you have or think you may have picked up or touched the exposed seeds or inner surface of a *prik kee noo,* DO NOT inadvertently scratch or rub your eyes. Death and/or blindness will not ensue, but rest assured that it will be at least a half an hour before you can open them again (the author writes from experience, not hearsay!).

And finally, a word about *ahahn tahnon* (street vendor foods): in Bangkok alone there are thousands of small "restaurants" that simply spring up on the streets at daybreak. They may consist of little more than a storefront grill or steam table on wheels and three or four small tables and chairs. Early morning fare includes such delights as *bahtongo* (deep-fried, barely sweetened donut-like pastries that are delicious with coffee); later in the day, vendors selling large bowls of noodles with meatballs, fried rice, and so on can be found almost everywhere. The street may not be clean, but this should not be a deterrent—the food is very inexpensive and usually very good.

As is evident from the categories listed above, Thai cuisine encompasses an overwhelming variety of components: meats, vegetables, rice varieties, fruits, seasonings, and spices, all of which should be surrounded with good companions and good conversation. After all, no matter how wonderful the food may be, dining alone is simply not the Thai way! If the reader has never eaten Thai food before, perhaps the best way to provide some definitive examples of actual traditional dishes is to offer a brief description of those dishes that have become my favorites over the years. My "dream Thai meal" looks like this:

- Cocktails with *ahahn gahp glaam:* for me, fresh roasted cashews, ginger slivers, *prik kee noo* chili peppers, and green onion
- *Tawd mahn:* deep-fried fish cakes, made from a fish paste seasoned with cilantro and lime, served with an onion/cucumber sauce
- *Lahb moo:* a very spicy room-temperature salad made from ground pork, cilantro, and lime
- *Dtom kah gai:* a coconut milk–based chicken soup seasoned with cilantro, lemongrass, and kaffir lime leaves
- *Gai grahprao metmahmuahng himapahn:* spicy basil chicken with cashews
- *Massuman gai:* a thick and moderately spicy curry with chicken and potatoes
- *Kao neow mamuahng:* sticky rice with coconut milk and mango slices
- *Gahfaa yen:* iced coffee, very sweet, with condensed milk

As Thai cuisine has become quite popular throughout the world over the past twenty years or so, there is a seemingly endless array of Thai cookbooks out there. If one is interested in learning how to cook Thai food at home, it is difficult to know where to begin and what cookbook is to be deemed reliably authentic, as opposed to being simply "trendy." If the reader counts him/herself among that adventurous culinary group, please refer to the annotated bibliography, in which I have included three highly recommended cookbooks. Not only are the recipes good, but they are presented along with all sorts of interesting reading—historical, cultural, and regional "appetizers" that are as fun to digest as the food.

Thai cuisine is a sensory experience of myriad dimensions. In response to its multiplicity of tastes, aromas, and visual presentations, one can only say *Mai mee ahrai ja kanaht nahn,* a colloquial expression that simply means "There is just nothing else quite like it!"

ETIQUETTE IN THAILAND

A visitor to a foreign country must always remember that he/she is not visiting a country filled with "foreigners"; on the contrary, it is the *visitor* who is the foreigner! Therefore, as a visiting foreigner, the greatest compliment one can give to a culture is to make every effort to conduct oneself in accordance with its customs and expectations, particularly in the context of social interaction.

As I tell my humanities students on occasion, the best place to begin the analysis of anything is by "reading" what one sees on the surface. The Thais would appreciate this, for a primary agenda of Thai social etiquette is the manner in which one presents oneself in the public realm. In recent decades, the tourist industry has come to promote Thailand as "The Land of Smiles." To be sure, the Thais are a very friendly people. But from the standpoint of social etiquette, the significance of the "smile" goes ever so much deeper than mere congeniality. The Thai smile is, in a word, a mask. It is a mask that is designed to conceal the self on those occasions when a display of genuine emotion would be inappropriate, unseemly, or simply rude. As it has been said, when a Thai is elated, he smiles; when a Thai is depressed, he smiles; when a Thai is embarrassed, he smiles; when a Thai is angry, he smiles. But when the mask is understood, it can reveal what dwells below the surface. And so whether one is dealing with a family member, a business associate, or a political counterpart, it is essential to develop a sensitivity to the subtle details and nuances of what is taking place. Being straightforward and "telling it like it is" may be considered a desirable character trait in the West, but in Thailand, as in many East and Southeast Asian cultures, it is more important to be able to achieve the same end more indirectly by "exhibiting what it isn't." It is not a question of intentional deception but of social propriety.

For a Thai, the most profound social blunder is to be placed in a position of embarrassment and disgrace, or to cause someone else to suffer the same indignity. The Thai expression is *seeyah nah,* which means "to lose face." Although the Thai smile may appear to be an impenetrable mask to the Western foreigner, more often than not, it is the smile of grace under pressure, the mask that "saves face."

More straightforward than the Thai smile, the traditional Thai greeting is a bowing movement called a *wai.* Outwardly, it is more or less equivalent to a handshake in the West. To perform a wai, the hands are raised to the front of the body, with open palms pressed together in a prayerlike position. The hands may be placed at any of several different levels, ranging from the chest/sternum to the forehead. As this is done, the head is bowed slightly forward. A girl or woman performing a wai might also bend slightly at the knees. The position of the hands is usually determined by the recipient of the wai. If one is greeting a parent, a teacher, or a Buddhist monk, the hands will be higher, at or near the forehead. If one is simply meeting a friend or peer, the hands will be placed lower, toward the chest. The wai may be offered by one person and then returned by the other, or both persons may offer it simultaneously. But if one of the two parties is younger or of a lesser standing (in a school or workplace, for example), he/she will always initiate the exchange. Under no circumstances would the older person offer a wai first, except in the case of greeting

The traditional wai posture of greeting and respect. (Courtesy of Baikaew Hoare)

a Buddhist monk or, if the situation presents itself, a member of the royal family. The wai is Hindu in origin. Although it serves the outward purpose of a handshake, its implicit meaning goes much deeper. A wai is a prayerful offering of respect to the divinity that dwells within each human being. Although traditional Buddhist doctrine does not specifically address this idea, the wai nevertheless serves as a gentle reminder that all human beings are worthy of respect.

Another fundamental aspect of Thai etiquette is the disposition of the head and the feet. The head is the highest and therefore the noblest part of the body. The head of another person should never be touched, except in the case of infants, small children, or perhaps peers within one's own immediate family. Conventions concerning feet are conversely similar. As the lowest part of the body (as well as the part of the body that walks on the ground), the feet should always be folded under the body when one is sitting down on the floor; they are never extended out in the direction of another person. The feet should never be used to move or slide other objects along on the floor, nor should they be utilized to point toward an object or indicate a direction, as a Westerner might be apt to do when his/her hands are full. And finally, like every East and Southeast Asian culture, one's shoes are always removed before entering a home, be it one's own residence or another's. The home is like a sacred space, and the dirt and dust from the street should be left at the doorstep. Although some urban Thais wear light house slippers inside their homes, the vast majority simply prefers to go barefoot.

Somewhat related to the disposition of one's head and feet is the question of one's overall posture. If one is engaged in an extended conversation with another person, one's head should never be higher than that of the person with whom one is speaking, especially if that person is an elder, a parent, a teacher, or the like. If, for example, a child's parents are seated in the living room of a Thai household, it would be very disrespectful for the child to stand before them (above them) while speaking to them. The child must seat him/herself at their level (or preferably lower) and then begin speaking. Traditionally, this acknowledgment of respect even extends to one's posture when simply passing by an elder. Suppose that my wife's mother is seated at a table or even on the floor and I am about to pass in front of her as I walk across the room. I show my respect by dipping my head slightly until I have passed by her.

Proper Thai behavior is also expressed through one's apparel. Generally speaking, Thais dress very conservatively in public: no short pants unless one is at home (usually only children wear shorts), no sleeveless shirts that expose the shoulders, and no skirts or dresses that are shorter than knee length. Western tourists in Thailand need to become more mindful of this, for when the climate is warm, they are quite used to walking about in public wearing very little clothing. For many Thais, this is considered to be offensive. It can create a good deal of embarrassment, not only in restaurants and stores, but also in Buddhist temples where modesty and decorum are mandatory. For this reason, virtually every Thai Buddhist temple that is anywhere near a tourist venue will have a sign posted by the entrance that explicitly states in English how one must be dressed if one wishes to enter.

We have already discussed the various types and components of Thai cuisine, but how should one behave while dining? For the most part, proper etiquette during a Thai meal is not all that different from what one would expect to find in the West. But there are a few distinctive expectations that stand out. As in many households throughout the world, all of the food to be served is placed on the table. Each person has his/her own plate and helps him/herself to what he/she wants to eat. But unlike many cultures, the Thais do not simply "load up" their plates. They take relatively small portions of one or two items (accompanied by rice, of course). Once those are consumed, they may take some more. The implicit meaning behind this is simply that one's plate should be empty by the conclusion of the meal—one should not take more than one can eat, as it is not polite to leave uneaten food on one's plate. Furthermore, while lively conversation is expected and encouraged, it is considered impolite to make excessive noise with utensils or dishes. Spoons and forks, for example, should be handled carefully, so as not to rattle or make harsh scrapping sounds against one's plate. Similarly, when stirring a cup of coffee, one should be careful not to allow the spoon to make harsh sounds against the inside of the cup.

In Thailand, proper etiquette is very much like going to a dance. Depending on the style of the dance, the music, and the nature of the occasion, there are certain ways to dress, to move, and to react in response to one's dancing partner. And so perhaps the best way to summarize the spirit of Thai etiquette is to say that one should always know where, and especially with whom, one is "dancing."

Thailand-Related Organizations

BUSINESS AND ECONOMIC

American Chamber of Commerce
18th Floor, Kian Gwan Building 2
140/1 Wireless Road
Lumphini, Pathumwan
Bangkok 10330
Thailand
http://www.amchamthailand.org

With over six hundred company members, the American Chamber of Commerce in Thailand serves the needs of U.S. business interests in Thailand while contributing to the economic development of Thailand.

Department of Internal Trade (DIT)
44/100 Sanam Bin Nam-Nonthaburi Road
Muang Nonthaburi 11000
Thailand
http://www.dit.go.th/english

The Department of Internal Trade was established to promote, develop, and regulate domestic (Thai) businesses, and to ensure that their commodities, goods, and services can compete on a par with those of foreign companies. The DIT is under the authority of the Ministry of Commerce.

Thai Trade Centers in the United States
401 N. Michigan Avenue, Suite 544
Chicago, IL 60611
(312) 467–0044 (or –0045)

611 N. Larchmont, Third Floor
Los Angeles, CA 90004
(323) 466–9645
200 S. Biscayne Boulevard, Suite 4420
Miami, FL 33131
(305) 379–5675

Thai Trade Centers in the United States help to promote, establish, and maintain mutually beneficial trade relationships between Thailand and U.S. companies. Their primary focus is to assist Americans in the legal, economic, and cultural dimensions of introducing their companies to Thailand and doing business with Thais.

CULTURAL AND EDUCATIONAL

The Asia Society
725 Park Avenue
New York, NY 10021
(212) 288–6400
http://www.asiasociety.org

The Asia Society is a nonprofit, independent organization that promotes cultural awareness and understanding between Americans and the diverse cultures of Asia and the Pacific. It sponsors a wide variety of educational activities, exhibitions, and presentations. Its Web site provides links to numerous nation-specific sites.

The Consortium for the Advanced Study of Thai (CAST)
(no address)

CAST educational institutions have Departments of Southeast Asian Studies that offer formal programs in Thai language study. CAST members include Arizona State University, the University of California at Berkeley, the University of California at Los Angeles, the University of Chicago, Cornell

University, the University of Hawaii at Manoa, the University of Michigan, Northern Illinois University, the University of Ohio, the University of Oregon, the University of Washington, the University of Wisconsin at Madison, and Yale University. CAST does not appear to have a specific Web site or home address. Inquiries about university Thai language study should therefore be directed to the individual institutions listed.

The East-West Center
1601 East-West Road
Honolulu, HI 96848
(808) 944–7111
http://www.eastwestcenter.org

Established by the U.S. Congress in 1961, the East-West Center is an internationally recognized nonprofit education and research organization that promotes understanding and strengthens relations between the United States and the countries of the Asian Pacific region. The East-West Center is the home of the Asian Studies Development Program (ASDP), which offers a wide variety of Summer Institutes in Hawaii, regional workshops in the United States, and international study tours for educators who seek to infuse Asian Studies into their academic programs.

Ministry of Education
319 Wang Chan Kasem
Thanon Ratchadamnoen Nok
Bangkok 10300
Thailand
http://www.moe.go.th/English

The Department of Fine Arts
http://www.moe.go.th/finearts

Supervised by the Ministry of Education, the Department of Fine Arts was established in 1934 for the purpose of preserving and teaching Thailand's visual and performing arts heritage, primarily through Silapakawn University and Wittayalai Nadasin (the College of Dramatic Arts). The department is also responsible for the Thai government's continuing archaeological research at ancient sites such as Ban Chiang, Sukhothai, and Ayutthaya.

The National Research Council of Thailand (NRCT)
196 Paholyothin Road
Chatuchak, Bangkok 10900
Thailand
http://www.nrct.net

The National Research Council is a government-sponsored organization that provides assistance and guidelines for those who are conducting government, academic, or independent research projects/field work in Thailand. All international researchers are required to apply to the NRCT for permission to conduct their work in Thailand.

The Peace Corps
(800) 424–8580
http://www.peacecorps.gov

Established by President John F. Kennedy in 1961, the Peace Corps is an agency of the U.S. government that trains volunteers with specialized skills in such areas as agriculture, engineering, medicine, and education to work in developing nations throughout the world. As a part of their training, volunteers also receive intensive language training. There are eleven regional offices in the United States. The Peace Corps has a long and successful history in Thailand, particularly in the northern and northeastern regions.

The Siam Society
131 Soi Asoke, Sukumvit Road
Bangkok 10110

Thailand
http://www.siam-society.org

Thailand's oldest and most respected cultural organization, the Siam Society was founded in 1904 and continues to be supported under royal patronage. The Siam Society promotes the study and preservation of Thai heritage, culture, history, art, and natural environment through study trips, lectures, exhibitions, and publications. Regular publications include the *Journal of the Siam Society* and the *Natural History Bulletin of the Siam Society.* Membership information is available online.

Thai Cultural and Fine Arts Institute
1960 Oak Knoll Drive
Lake Forest, IL 60045
http://www.thai-culture.org

As the Chicago area has a very large Thai population, this is one of the larger organizations in the United States that promotes Thai culture, language, and fine arts. It offers a wide variety of exhibitions and touring programs on Thai visual arts, dance, cooking, martial arts, and language.

The Thai Environmental Institute
16/151–154 Muang Thong Thani
Bond Street
Dambohn Bangpood
Ahmpur Pakkred
Nonthaburi 11120
Thailand
http://www.tei.or.th

Established in 1993, the Thai Environmental Institute is a nonprofit, nongovernmental organization that is focused on environmental issues and the conservation of Thailand's natural resources. It works closely with the private sector, academic institutions, and other international environmental organizations to formulate and encourage meaningful environmental progress in Thailand.

Wildlife Fund Thailand
251/88–90 Paholyothin Road
Bangkhen, Bangkok 10220
Thailand

Wildlife Fund Thailand is a nonprofit organization that promotes public awareness of natural resources and wildlife conservation. It organizes conservation education programs and conducts endangered species research/recovery projects.

GOVERNMENT AND TOURISM

Association of Southeast Asian Nations (ASEAN)
ASEAN Secretariat
70A Jalan Sisingamangaraja
Jakarta 12110
Indonesia
http://www.aseansec.org/home

Initially established in 1967 with five members (Thailand, Malaysia, Philippines, Indonesia, and Singapore), ASEAN now includes Brunei Darussalam (1984), Vietnam (1995), Laos and Myanmar (1997), and Cambodia (1999) for a total of ten member nations. ASEAN seeks to accelerate economic growth, social progress, and cultural development in the region, and to promote regional peace, cooperation, and stability in adherence to the principles of the United Nations Charter.

Permanent Mission of Thailand to the United Nations
351 E. 52nd Street
New York, NY 10022
(212) 754-2230

As a member of the United Nations, the Thai government maintains a staffed office, or "permanent mission," in New York City for its ambassador to the United Nations.

Royal Thai Embassy to the United States
1024 Wisconsin Avenue NW, Suite 401
Washington, DC 20007
(202) 944–3600
http://www.thaiembdc.org.

Royal Thai Consulates General in the United States
700 N. Rush Street
Chicago, IL 60611
(312) 664–3129

611 N. Larchmont Boulevard, Second Floor
Los Angeles, CA 90004
(323) 962–9574

351 E. 52nd Street
New York, NY
(212) 754–1770

The Royal Thai Consulates General are essentially subsidiary embassies that address the more immediate needs of regional populations. Along with the Thai Embassy, they provide information and services to both Americans and Thais living/visiting in the United States, such as immigration guidelines and advice, travel visas, and cultural/educational information for both tourists and general inquirers. Sub-branches of the three primary consulates-general are located in numerous cities across the United States. Their individual addresses can be accessed through a comprehensive directory on the Thai Embassy's Web site.

Royal Thai Government
Government House
Thanon Pissanulok
Dusit, Bangkok 10300
Thailand
http://www.thaigov.go.th

Government House is the formal home of the Thai government. The office of the prime minister is located here, as is the office of the National Security Council. It serves as the venue for official meetings of the cabinet and formal state ceremonies and is also the primary reception site for foreign leaders and dignitaries. The Web site provides links to the Thai government's twenty ministries (Education, Commerce, Defense, etc.) and to several government-sponsored public agencies.

Tourism Authority of Thailand

61 Broadway, Suite 2810
New York, NY
212-269-2597

611 N. Larchmont Blvd., First Floor
Los Angeles, CA 90004
323-461-9814
http://www.tourismthailand.org

The Tourism Authority of Thailand is a source of reliable information for both first-time and veteran travelers to Thailand. Its Web site provides statistical information, hotel and tour recommendations, cultural guidelines, and immigration laws, as well as links to youth hostels, tourist police, and current monetary exchange rates.

United States Embassy in Thailand
120/22 Wireless Road
Bangkok
Thailand
http://www.usa.or.th

The U.S. Embassy in Thailand provides services to both Thais and Americans living/visiting in Thailand, such as immigration guidelines and advice, and travel visas. The embassy's Web site is a good source of current information and press releases about U.S.-Thai government relations and activities, as well as cultural information about Thailand or travel guidelines and recommendations for visitors.

Annotated Bibliography

The books and periodicals noted here are organized in accordance with the chapters in this book as well as the section on language, food, and etiquette. Every effort has been made to include accurate and readable sources that should assist readers who want to know more about Thailand.

CUISINE

Loha-Unchit, Kasma. *It Rains Fishes: Legends, Traditions, and the Joys of Thai Cooking.* Petaluma, CA: Pomegranate Communications, 1995.

Thompson, David. *Thai Food.* Berkeley, CA: Ten Speed Press, 2002.

Yu, Su-Mei. *Cracking the Coconut: Classic Thai Home Cooking.* New York: Harper Collins, 2000.

Thai cooking is still something of a fad in the West, so dozens of Thai cookbooks are available. As I live in a Thai household, most all of our recipes are in our heads. Therefore, we don't have many Thai cookbooks around the house. But I have chosen these three books because they contain so much more than simply a categorized collection of recipes. These books also feature traditional stories, descriptions of Thailand's regions and ethnicities, philosophical reflections on the proper preparation of basic Thai ingredients, and explanations as to how history and geography have influenced the many styles and ingredients of Thai cuisine. After all, there is no such thing as simply "Thai food."

FINE ARTS

Brandon, James. *Theatre in Southeast Asia.* Cambridge, MA: Harvard University Press, 1967.

————. *The Cambridge Guide to Asian Theatre.* London: Cambridge University Press, 1993.

James Brandon is an internationally recognized authority on Asian performance arts. His chapters on the diverse theater traditions of Thailand are very informative and accessible. They cover both developmental history and contemporary practice.

Cadet, J. M. *The Ramakien.* Bangkok: Kodansha International, 1970.

This is one of the most interesting and entertaining treatments of the *Ramakien* that I have come across. Cadet presents the epic against the illustrative backdrop of the famous marble bas-relief panels that circumscribe the exterior walls of Wat Pra Chetupohn (Wat Po) in Bangkok. The introduction gives a comprehensive history of the *Ramakien,* the 152 marble panels of the wat, and the social role of the *Ramakien* in both traditional and contemporary Thai culture.

Rawson, Philip. *The Art of Southeast Asia.* London: Thames and Hudson, 1967, 1995.

Written by a noted Southeast Asian art historian, this is a very informative and well-illustrated text on the sculpture, architecture, and painting of the various cultures that comprise this unique region. Of particular interest are his treatments of Khmer sculpture and architecture, as well as the introduction and development of the Buddha image in Thailand. Generally speaking, as art references go, Thames and Hudson texts rank among the best. Covering virtually every style, culture, and historical period of art history, they are lavishly illustrated with both black-and-white and color plates and are small enough in size to carry around conveniently.

Warren, William. *The Legendary American: The Remarkable Career and Strange Disappearance of Jim Thompson.* Boston: Houghton Mifflin, 1970.

A detailed account of the colorful life, multiple careers, and mysterious disappearance of Jim Thompson, the American whose entrepreneurial skills, efforts, and overall love of the Thai people elevated Thai silk from an isolated and relatively unknown regional craft to one of the most sought after textile products in the world. The book covers Thompson's post–World War II travels in Thailand, his initial exposure to Thai silk weaving, and the development of his world-famous company, as well as various theories concerning his disappearance, which remains unsolved to this day. The text also contains some impressive photographs of the interior of the famous Jim Thompson House in Bangkok, now maintained as a museum.

Thai Culture Series
Published by the Fine Arts Department of the Thai government, this is a very well-done and prolific series of short and beautifully illustrated paperback texts. At this writing there are about twenty-five different volumes. Each one presents a different subject of Thai culture and fine arts, such as the development and evolution of Thai Buddha images and iconography, Thai classical theater and dance, classical Thai music, the royal palaces, and an overview of Sukhothai art. Were it not for the creation of the Royal Department of Fine Arts in 1934, much of Thailand's cultural heritage would have been lost and forgotten. The Thai Culture Series texts are available through Silapakawn University (usually transliterated as "Silpakorn") and the National Museum, both in Bangkok.

HISTORY AND CURRENT AFFAIRS

Bello, Walden, Shea Cunningham, and Li Kheng Poh. *A Siamese Tragedy: Development and Disintegration in*

Modern Thailand. London: Zed Books, 1998.

A hard-hitting look at the twentieth-century development and 1997–1998 downfall of the Thai economy. The text includes a particularly incisive analysis of the conditions that led to Thailand's economic crisis, as well as chapters on Bangkok's urban sprawl and the AIDS epidemic of the 1980s and 1990s. Although the authors pull no punches in their assessments of the overall socioeconomic challenges facing Thailand, it must also be understood that they were writing in the immediate aftermath of a crisis from which Thailand had yet to make its recovery.

Leonowens, Anna. *An English Governess in the Siamese Court: Being Recollections of Six Years in the Royal Palace at Bangkok.* 1870. Reprint, New York: Oxford University Press, 1988.

Although this text has a rather infamous reputation among both Thais and Thai-knowledgeable westerners, I include it here for the same reason I noted it in the main body of this text: although its factuality is certainly questionable in many respects, it nevertheless presents a viewpoint that westerners should know about—that of nineteenth-century Eurocentric "orientalism." If nothing else, it serves as a good reminder that at one time or another, we are all guilty of looking at the world through culturally biased eyes. The best way to begin to correct it is to acknowledge that we do it.

Syamananda, Rong. *A History of Thailand,* 6th ed. Bangkok: Thai Watana Panich, 1988.

A nice English-language Thai history by a Thai historian from Chulalongkawn University. Although this particular edition obviously does not address the 1990s and early 2000s, its treatment of the histories and monarchs of the Sukhothai, Ayutthaya, and Chakri periods is comprehensive and informative. Being a Thai, the author presents some perspectives and opinions that a Western author would not be likely to have. The text is interesting to read because, traditionally speaking, Thailand has not been known for chronicling or documenting its history in the linear manner—that is, "first this, then that"—that is indicative of the West.

Wyatt, David K. *Thailand: A Short History,* **1st ed.** New Haven, CT: Yale University Press, 1984; 2nd ed., 2004.

This straightforward and informative chronicle has served as the standard of Thai history for twenty years. Written by one of the leading Thai historians, it provides a thorough treatment of subjects ranging from the kingdom's diverse ethnic origins to contemporary social, economic, and political developments. A newly revised edition of Wyatt's history was released in 2004.

Time-Life Books. *Southeast Asia: A Past Regained.* Alexandria, VA: Time-Life Books, 1995.

As a volume of Time-Life's Lost Civilizations Series, this text is significant because it devotes an entire chapter (one-fourth of the book) to the work that has been accomplished at the major archaeological sites of Southeast Asia, particularly Ban Chiang in Northeastern Thailand and the so-called Spirit Cave in Northern Thailand. The chapter is a virtual biography of archaeologists Wilhelm Solheim II and Chester Gorman, whose discoveries and seminal work in the 1960s and 1970s at both of these sites revealed the existence of a prehistoric Southeast Asian Bronze culture that may well have predated the more high-profile cultures of India, China, and even Mesopotamia. Very descriptive text with dozens of color photographs of excavations and artifacts.

LANGUAGE

Campbell, Stuart, and Chuan Shaweevongs. *The Fundamentals of the Thai Language,* **5th ed.** Bangkok: Marketing Media Associates, 1968.

Although not even the best book can replace a live teacher in language education, this teaching text is a well-known standard in Thai-produced English language reference. Since I received my first copy from my Thai father-in-law years ago, it has probably gone through another two or three reprints. Its presentation of the alphabet and grammar is quite logical. Its appendices are top-notch, in that they include a very concise and well-written English-Thai dictionary, categorical listings of such things as family relationships, government officials, cooking terms, classifiers, and one of the best collections of Thai idiomatic expressions that I have ever seen.

Haas, Mary. *Thai-English Student's Dictionary.* Stanford, CA: Stanford University Press, 1964.

For American students of the Thai language, the Haas dictionary is, in my opinion, simply the best format out there. To be sure, there are other standard texts that should be acquired as one advances (e.g., McFarland, *Thai-English Dictionary*). But what makes Haas special is its practicality: the major entries include numerous examples, variations in spelling, and idiomatic usage. In other words, Haas does an excellent job in presenting the language not simply as it is written but as it is used on a day-to-day basis.

LITERATURE

Pramoj, Kukrit. *Four Reigns* (1953), translated by Tulachandra. Bangkok: DK Editions, 1998.

———. *Many Lives* (1954), translated by Meredith Borthwick. Bangkok: DK Editions, 1999.

Novelist, poet, actor, and politician Kukrit Pramoj (1911–1995) was Thailand's "renaissance man" in the twentieth century (see Significant People, Places, and Events in this text). *Four Reigns* is a novel about four minor courtiers and how their lives and fortunes change along with the evolution of the Thai sociopolitical landscape, from late nineteenth-century absolute monarchy through the Japanese occupation of Thailand during World War II. *Many Lives* begins with the capsizing of a river ferry on its way to Bangkok. Through an interwoven literary fabric of experiences and emotions, the lives of those who perished are traced from their births to the circumstances that brought them to the ferry boat at that particular time and place. Both novels are available through www.dcothai.com.

Sudham, Pira. *Siamese Drama.* Bangkok: Shire Books, 1983.

———. *People of Esarn.* Bangkok: Shire Books, 1987.

———. *Monsoon Country.* Bangkok: Shire Books, 1988.

———. *Force of Karma.* Bangkok: Shire Books, 2002.

Pira Sudham is one of Thailand's most well-known contemporary authors/novelists. His major works, listed here, are novels and short-story collections about the rural inhabitants of Northeastern Thailand (*Eesahn,* spelled *Esarn* by Sudham). A native of Eesahn himself, Sudham's English-language writing gives poignant expression to the unique ethnic identity, spirit, and hardships of this impoverished and often overlooked segment of Thai society. Pira Sudham was nominated for the 1990 Nobel Prize for literature. Further details about Pira Sudham's books, as well as direct ordering information, can be found at www.pirasudham.com.

NEWSPAPERS, JOURNALS, AND PERIODICALS

Bangkok Post

The Nation

These are two of the major English-language newspapers in Thailand. Both are daily publications that are also accessible online, at **www.bangkokpost.com** and **www.nationmultimedia .com**. They each cover the entire spectrum of news, that is, world/domestic news, politics, business, economy, sports, arts, and so on. An online site that has links to these and other English-language newspapers in Thailand is **www.thai landnews.net**.

East-West Center. *The Future of Population in Asia.* Honolulu: East-West Center, 2001.

One of many research publications released by the East-West Center in Hawaii, this is an excellent source for current statistical information about gender, sexuality, employment, marriage, and education in Thailand as well as other East/Southeast Asian nations. It can be acquired by contacting the East-West Center (see entry in "Thailand-Related Organizations.")

Education about Asia. Edited by Lucien Ellington. Ann Arbor, MI: Association for Asian Studies.

This informative and well-illustrated periodical/journal is published three times a year (spring, fall, and winter). It is geared toward educators in high schools and universities. Virtually every major article is a potential teaching topic for those who infuse Asian content into their coursework. Reviews of current books on Asian studies are also included in each issue. Subscription information (both individual and institutional rates) is available by writing: Subscription Department, Association for Asian Studies, 1021 East Huron Street, Ann Arbor, MI 48104.

Journal of the Siam Society
Natural History Bulletin of the Siam Society
Covering such topics as social/political history, fine arts, and archaeology, both of these scholarly journals are complimentary for members of the Siam Society. Membership

information is available online (see "Thailand-Related Organizations"). As an alternative to membership, several U.S. university libraries also carry current and back issues, particularly member institutions of CAST (Consortium for the Advanced Study of Thai); for a list of member institutions, see "Thailand-Related Organizations."

RELIGION

Rahula, Walpola. *What the Buddha Taught,* 2nd ed. New York: Grove Press, 1974.

Although somewhat technical in content, this classic text is a very readable introduction to the basic tenets and social/ethical teachings of the Buddha. Clearly and passionately written, it is a solid alternative to the Western fad-inspired, pop-religion/self-help "Buddhist" texts that presently clutter our bookstore shelves.

Eerdmans' Handbook to World Religions. Grand Rapids, MI: William B. Eerdmans Publishing, 1994.

The Eerdmans' Handbook offers a very user-friendly approach to the world's major religious traditions, with many pictures, maps and charts. The chapter on Buddhism presents a variety of separate features and short articles on the history, beliefs and various sects of the Buddhist tradition.

National Identity Board of Thailand. *Buddhism in Thai Life,* 3d ed. Bangkok: National Identity Board, Office of the Prime Minister, 1984.

This book is a part of the Thai Life Series that was published by the Thai government's National Identity Board. Although now out of print, it can still be found in many public libraries in the United States and is worth searching for in used bookstores. It resembles a thick magazine, and has chapters on Buddhist history in both India and Thailand, the relationship of Buddhism to the Thai monarch, Buddhist influence in Thai literature and visual arts, and the social roles of Buddhist temples and monks in Thai culture.

TRAVEL AND COMMENTARY

Parkes, Carl. ***Thailand Handbook*, 3d ed.** Emeryville, CA: Moon Travel Handbooks, 2000.

Travel guides come and go, but this award-winning volume is by far the most comprehensive guide that I have ever seen. Organized by geographic region, its coverage is exhaustive. Wherever you may want to go in Thailand, he (or at least someone he knows) has been there! In addition to a plethora of maps covering everything from regional province to local neighborhood, this guide also includes several interesting "insert sections" on such things as Buddhist iconography, environmental issues, cuisine, and even the origin and mystique of the Siamese cat. Highly recommended to anyone who is planning a trip to Thailand.

Segaller, Denis. ***Thai Ways.*** Bangkok: Post Publishing, 1981.

———. ***More Thai Ways.*** Bangkok: Post Publishing, 1982.

———. ***New Thoughts on Thai Ways.*** Bangkok: Magazine Distribution Service, 1989.

These little books are essentially collections of essays, the first collection initially appearing as a weekly newspaper column in the *Bangkok World.* They are very informative and entertaining reflections of a British documentary film-maker-turned-journalist who came to work in Thailand, married a Thai woman, became a Buddhist, and, in the process, made Thailand his permanent home. Written in an easy-going journalistic style, the essays cover a wide array of topics, including Thai customs, festivals, food, and traffic jams, as well as Segaller's time spent living in a Buddhist temple as a monk.

Index

About the Author

Timothy D. Hoare, Ph.D., is associate professor of humanities and religion at Johnson County Community College in Overland Park, Kansas. In 1992, he received his Ph.D. in religion and the arts from Graduate Theological Union in Berkeley, California. Also an ordained Presbyterian minister, Dr. Hoare received his M.Div. in 1988 from McCormick Theological Seminary in Chicago, Illinois. Dr. Hoare has published articles and given presentations on a variety of Asian themes, including the aesthetic and religious dimensions of the classical masked theater of Thailand and the psychology of the mask in theater and religion. His academic work with masks and theatrical movement is a product of a decade of professional experience as a performer and teacher of mime prior to his graduate work. Dr. Hoare's interests in Thai theater, dance, language, and culture (and also cuisine!) are by no means random: his wife, Baikaew, is from Thailand and has a formal background in Thai classical dance.